T0312060

# Good Ethics and Bad Choices

**Basic Bioethics**

Arthur Caplan, editor

A complete list of the books in the Basic Bioethics series appears at the back of this book.

# Good Ethics and Bad Choices

The Relevance of Behavioral Economics for Medical Ethics

Jennifer S. Blumenthal-Barby

The MIT Press
Cambridge, Massachusetts
London, England

This book was set in Stone by Westchester Publishing Services, Danbury, CT.

Library of Congress Cataloging-in-Publication Data

Names: Blumenthal-Barby, Jennifer S., author.
Title: Good ethics and bad choices : the relevance of behavioral economics for
    medical ethics / Jennifer S. Blumenthal-Barby.
Other titles: Basic bioethics.
Description: Cambridge, Massachusetts : The MIT Press, [2021] | Series: Basic
    bioethics | Includes bibliographical references and index.
Identifiers: LCCN 2020031704 | ISBN 9780262542487 (paperback)
Subjects: MESH: Decision-Making--ethics | Ethics, Medical | Personal Autonomy |
    Physician-Patient Relations--ethics | Economics, Behavioral
Classification: LCC R724 | NLM W 50 | DDC 174.2--dc23
LC record available at https://lccn.loc.gov/2020031704

# Contents

# Acknowledgments

There are many people to thank. One is Philip Laughlin, senior acquisitions editor for Cognitive Science, Philosophy, Linguistics, and Bioethics at MIT Press. Book writing is a marathon requiring perseverance and resilience at times. Phil provided the support, encouragement, and strategic advice to help me see this project through to its end. I especially appreciated his support and wisdom for first-time authors and timely updates throughout the process. I feel fortunate to have had the opportunity to work with a top-notch senior editor on my first book. If I ever have to work with another editor again, I will have ridiculously high expectations.

The Greenwall Faculty Scholars (GFS) community has been incredibly supportive of my work on the intersection of behavioral economics, medicine, and philosophy/ethics. I am especially indebted to Bernie Lo for his unwavering support over the years. I have benefited from learning from and working with the following scholars on behavioral economics and ethics issues: Neal Dickert, Gidon Felson, Scott Halpern, Doug Opel, Peter Reese, Jon Tilburt, and Doug White. For the past year, I have been part of a GFS book-writing group that includes Mara Buchbinder, Lori Freedman, and Efthimios Parasidis. They graciously read and commented on all chapters of the book at various points, kept me accountable, and made writing this book more fun.

Locally, here in Houston, there have been two decision scientists who have kept me engaged and who have been open to and inclusive of my work as an ethicist and philosopher over the past decade: Scott Cantor and Bob Volk. I am thankful to have had them as colleagues and I look forward to future collaborations. My colleagues in the Center for Medical Ethics and Health Policy here at Baylor College of Medicine have supported me in various ways, and I wish to acknowledge and thank them. In the introduction, I mention a group of decision-making researchers at the University of Michigan who first introduced me to decision science and behavioral economics. That group was based at the Center for Behavioral and Decision Sciences, directed by Peter Ubel. Peter's energetic introduction to these fields changed my research trajectory and enriched my philosophical work. Ten years later, Peter remarked that I should write a book on these topics—he convinced me that this book was worth writing and that I was the right person to write it. So, I thank him for that.

Finally, I am especially indebted to Abby Halm for research support during the writing of this book over the past couple of years. As Abby has advanced from a bright and shining undergraduate student to a medical student with a promising career ahead of her, her sharpness, effort, and enthusiastic support for this project has helped me push it through with smiles along the way.

Finally, if not an acknowledgment then a dedication. I dedicate this book to my parents, Mike and Jean, who have, most of all, always believed in me and shown me unconditional love. It's particularly special that my dad and I were each writing our own book and celebrating that achievement at the same time. I also dedicate this book to an incredible human being who came into my life during the planning and writing of this book: my three-year old son, Ian. While one might think that an infant/small child would compromise book writing, on the contrary. Ian, your presence made my days more joyful and more meaningful, and motivated me to produce an artifact that you might one day read and be proud of. I love you. I am also indebted to Martin Blumenthal-Barby for advice on academic book writing, and for keeping me intellectually interested and engaged in aspects of the world and culture outside of this book.

# Introduction

I first became interested in, and perplexed by, decision-making when I was a graduate student. I was working as a bioethics intern at the Cleveland Clinic. Day after day, I would wake up at 4:30 a.m. and make the dark and cold commute to the clinic. During those bus rides I had a lot of time to think about the haunting cases I had encountered in the hospital.

One case in particular preoccupied my thoughts. It involved an otherwise healthy 70-year-old man who had been in a head-on motor vehicle accident and was paralyzed from the neck down. I was shadowing the ethics consultation team, and they were called to see the man who "couldn't make up his mind." Although communication was difficult because of the ventilator and the paralysis, he could nod "yes" and "no," and he seemed quite able to understand what was being asked of him. The problem was that sometimes he indicated that "yes" he wanted to continue to live, and other times he indicated that "no" he did not. With each day came a different answer, and it was emotionally challenging for everyone—his family, the care team, and the patient himself, who would often weep during these attempts to have his preferences clarified.

I'm not sure what bothered me so much about this case, but perhaps it was that it couldn't be easily resolved by the principles and theories I had spent so much time learning about in my philosophy graduate seminars. Autonomy seemed particularly relevant, but I was perplexed by what respect for autonomy meant in a case like this. I was perplexed enough that I decided to write my dissertation on ambivalence in decision-making and its relationship to autonomy.

That was the first time that my theoretical thoughts about decision-making became challenged by practice. The second was when I was just finishing graduate school, about to move from Michigan to Texas to start my new job, and I met a group of decision-making researchers at the University of Michigan. I had never encountered data about decision-making before (remember, I was getting a PhD in philosophy!), and I was blown away. This group introduced me to the world of behavioral economics and decision psychology, and I started to get a strong and uncomfortable sense of how much I needed to rethink some of the basic assumptions and ideas that I had relied on in my theoretical work on patient autonomy—and in my work in ethics and philosophy more generally.

That is essentially what this book is about. It focuses on how some of the work coming out of the science of judgment and decision-making challenges fundamental assumptions in medicine and medical ethics about patient decision-making and autonomy.

This book takes the reader through my journey of learning about some of the empirical findings regarding human decision-making and considering what they mean for our core assumptions, theories, and arguments in medical ethics. In doing so, it brings together work from decision science, clinical medicine, and philosophy and ethics.

## The Core Ideas and Arguments

The field of behavioral economics has exploded in its relevance and interest in recent years, kicked off with the popular book *Nudge: Improving Decisions about Health, Wealth, and Happiness*, by Richard Thaler and Cass Sunstein (2008), followed by others such as *Predictably Irrational*, by Dan Ariely (2008), and *Thinking, Fast and Slow*, by Daniel Kahneman (2011). The relevance of such books has guided the establishment of "nudge units" in the US and UK governments to help consider how behavioral economics can be used to improve policy. *Nudging* refers to the use of insights from behavioral economics and decision psychology to influence choice via "shallow" cognitive processes such as decisional heuristics and emotions rather through traditional modes of reasoning and argument.

This book operates on a different level; it does not aim to think about the relevance of behavioral economics for governments and policy, but rather for medical ethics. More specifically, for the ethics of patient decision-making and patient–clinician interaction. In some ways, much of bioethics has been surprisingly out of touch with these ideas—a gap that this book hopes to fill.

Research in behavioral economics has taught us that humans are boundedly rational (they can only absorb and deal with so much information) and that one way people deal with bounded rationality is to rely on decisional shortcuts (heuristics). Chapter 1 of this book explores some of these effects on patient decision-making through a discussion of empirical studies and examples.

The book then takes a normative turn and argues that these findings challenge fundamental assumptions in medicine and medical ethics about patient decision-making and autonomy, as well as raise concerns about negative effects on patient decision-making and protecting and promoting patients' interests. This is the focus of chapter 2.

At the same time, a better understanding of these effects can be used to improve patient choice and to shape patient decision-making for the better. This suggestion of engaging in nudging or intentional choice architecture of patient decision-making raises several ethical issues, which this book considers.

At the forefront, there is a demand for a basic set of arguments to support and defend nudging in patient decision-making. Chapter 3 provides one, showing that the use of choice architecture is supported by several arguments. The central ideas advanced are that nudging can improve patients' decisions and prevent harm. Moreover, doing so need not interfere with patient autonomy and may even promote or enhance it on several different theoretical accounts of autonomy.

Once past the initial arguments that crack the door open in defense of the use of behavioral insights (nudges) to shape patients' decision-making, a host of further questions emerges—ranging from concerns about whether this amounts to manipulation, to what extent and at what point in the decision-making process these techniques can be used, when and how their use would be wrong, and whether transparency about the use of these techniques is required, to name a few. Chapter 4 concerns itself with a more detailed ethical analysis.

Chapter 5 brings abstract ideas to life. Whereas philosophers and ethicists tend to create fanciful hypothetical examples to make their points or apply their analyses, this chapter is a case study of real nudging "in the weeds." It is a snapshot of how I observed nudges to operate in clinical settings, either intentionally or unintentionally. The examples were collected from my research in the following settings: psychiatry, pediatric critical care, fetal surgery, and oncology (prostate cancer).

My favorite philosopher, Harry Frankfurt, states in the preface to his *The Importance of What We Care About* (1998): "It would, no doubt, be appropriate for me to provide a succinct but comprehensive articulation of the general philosophical themes or ambitions. ... Unfortunately, however, this is not to say that I understand what I have been up to well enough to be able to give a perspicuous and straightforward account of it." While I admire his humility and relate to his hesitance to boil down a complex analysis, I do in fact have a prevailing theoretical commitment to communicate with this book: there is no single, simple account of the ethics of nudging. Much depends on nuances and contextual factors of cases. I am, however, offering a qualified defense of nudging. Part of that defense involves embracing a constrained welfarism whereby a nudge is justified in part—but not sufficiently—by the extent that it makes patients better off. This book does *not* offer a theory of rationality. That is, I do not advance my defense by arguing that people are irrational, as many scholars who apply and defend behavioral economics do. I do, however, advance it in part by arguing that patients, when left to their own devices, do not act or decide as autonomously as bioethicists typically assume. This book also does *not* offer a theory of nudging in the sense of a robust defense of what counts as a nudge and why. While I do embrace a working definition of nudging, this book is much more concerned with providing an account of the ethical considerations related to the use of insights from behavioral economics and the psychology of judgment and decision-making to shape patient choice.

**Intended Audience and Reading Tips**

This book should be of interest, I hope, to a wide variety of audiences, including experts in the domains of medical ethics and the ethics of nudging, and experts from the interdisciplinary field that the nudging literature addresses: medical experts, psychologists, behavioral economists, philosophers, and ethicists. In addition, it is relevant to medical practitioners (physicians, nurses, caretakers) who want to reflect on the opportunities and challenges provided by new behavioral insights. It might also be of interest to leaders of health care institutions who have the responsibility to think about how they and the care providers that work for them design the choice architecture that inevitably influences patients' decisions.

Although as a whole this book is of interest to a broad audience, some sections will be of greater interest to certain readers. For example, chapter 1 may be of particular interest to those less familiar with behavioral economics and empirical decision science in the medical context. Chapters 2 and 3 are core chapters that advance the main claims of the book. Chapter 4 may be of special interest to those concerned with more detailed and specific philosophical complexities in the ethics of nudging. Chapter 5 is wholly concerned with case studies of nudging in various clinical settings.

Several of the chapters include summary tables at the end. These might be particularly useful for students and for readers short on time who are looking for the core arguments advanced in the book. Chapter 1 includes a useful table of various decisional heuristics and biases identified by behavioral economists, along with definitions. Chapter 2 includes a table outlining the various ways that these heuristics and biases threaten dimensions of patient autonomy, decision quality, and well-being. Chapter 3 includes three tables. One outlines when to avoid or limit nudging in patient decision-making, a second outlines when to prefer rational persuasion and argument to nudging, and a third outlines key arguments (along with objections and replies) for nudging in medical practice.

# 1  Decision Psychology and Medical Decision-Making: How Patients Decide

Research in the psychology of judgment and decision-making has taught us that humans are boundedly rational, meaning they can only absorb and deal with limited amounts of information in the finite amount of time they have to make decisions. One way that people deal with bounded rationality is through the use of heuristic strategies or "decisional shortcuts." Heuristics represent part of what Daniel Kahneman calls "System 1" decision-making. System 1 decision-making is quick and intuitive, subject to framing effects, and uses shortcuts (heuristics) and emotions, resulting in predictable biases and potentially nonoptimal decisions. This is in contrast to what Kahneman calls "System 2" decision-making, which is slower and more logical, potentially resulting in more optimal decisions.[1]

Reliance on decisional heuristics is a normal part of decision-making and not necessarily bad, but in some situations, reliance on shortcuts can become problematic—for example, if doing so leads to predictable biases whereby a person over- or underestimates probabilities, ignores probabilities, over- or underestimates the value of some consequence, or does not engage in thinking about the consequences of all the options. Medical decisions are often complicated, high stakes, and novel—leaving patients particularly susceptible to the use and effects of decisional heuristics. Moreover, in the medical context, we typically aim for patients' personal values, rather than heuristics and biases, to play a significant role in decision-making.

In what follows, I describe some of these decisional heuristics and biases and how they impact patient decision-making. The heuristics and biases discussed in this chapter are ones that have been found to affect medical decision-making in a systematic review of the topic.[2] Importantly, my intention is not to communicate the idea that patients are the only ones who are susceptible to decisional heuristics and biases. Most of the examples that follow involve patient decision-making because this book is concerned with the ethical implications of these findings. After all, while physicians certainly make important decisions about prognosis and about what treatments to offer patients, patients make the final decisions about which options to pursue or how to manage their health conditions. But decisional heuristics and biases are present in all of us, including physicians. In fact, in a systematic review that my colleague and I conducted, we found that although decisional biases and heuristics have been studied more often in patients than in health providers, providers were equally susceptible.[3] This is not surprising given that these are psychological phenomena of *human* decision-making.

### Heuristics and Biases in Decision-Making

I organize the discussion of these heuristics and biases according to a helpful schema developed by Buster Benson—namely, heuristics and biases that occur when a person has too much information, when a person does not have enough meaning or information, when there is a need to decide or act quickly, and when the heuristics and biases are related to what a person remembers (see table 1.1 at the end of the chapter).[4]

### Heuristics and Biases Related to Too Much Information

Humans are not very good at dealing with large amounts of information. When we face information overload, we filter the material in predictable ways. For example, we pay more attention to things that are vivid and are repeated in our memory. This leads to several biases.

A well-known bias is the *availability bias*, which occurs when people rely on vivid cases or events to assess risk and make decisions, rather than relying on actual probabilities. For example, consider a study in which women explained their decision to either seek or delay evaluation when they noticed symptoms of breast cancer. Those who delayed treatment cited stories of pain and distress in women they knew who had undergone treatment. Those who sought evaluation cited stories of women who underwent suffering and loss because they did not seek treatment.[5] In another study, researchers interviewed patients about their decision to get an ICD (implantable cardiovascular defibrillator) or not. The researchers found that availability bias played a central role in decision-making. As one patient who declined reasoned, "My brother-in-law had an incident. He has a defibrillator ... and they had to change the leads on him ... and he nearly died in that procedure."[6] A third example involves patients making a hypothetical decision about bypass surgery or balloon angioplasty. Patients who read more stories where the bypass worked to cure chest pain (3 of 4 stories vs. 2 of 4 stories) were more likely to choose bypass (44% vs. 30%), even though both groups received the same actual facts and figures about the success of the procedure.[7]

Another response to information overload is called the *focusing effect*. This refers to a tendency to place too much importance on one factor in decision-making, resulting in a miscalculation of expected value. For example, a patient might decide not to have colorectal cancer screening because of its inconvenience or "grossness" despite wanting to live as long as possible.[8] Similarly, research has shown that participants presented with a hypothetical choice between two surgeries to cure colon cancer chose a surgery with a lower success rate (80% vs. 84%) but with fewer complications (0% vs. 4%), despite the fact that 92% of the participants indicated that they would prefer living with each of the complications to dying.[9]

Information overload is one cause of omission and commission biases. If you are a clinician, you have probably seen both of these biases in your patients' or potentially your own decision-making. *Omission bias* occurs when we judge a harmful action as worse than an equally harmful inaction.[10] This bias has gained much attention in medicine with regard to forgoing vaccinations. People find it easier to tolerate the idea of a person's getting sick from something that happens to them by chance (i.e., contracting the illness they were vaccinated against) than from something that was done to them (i.e., getting the vaccination)—even if the risk of getting sick from the latter is significantly smaller.[11] In contrast to the omission bias is the *commission bias*, the tendency to choose action over inaction, even when the action is harmful. This bias is often seen in cancer patients' decision-making, as there seems to be a general desire to aggressively treat cancer even when doing so increases the chance of death.[12] In one study, 65% of participants who were told to consider that they hypothetically had a cancer that had a 5% chance of death said they would choose active surgery with an associated 10% risk of death over watchful waiting.[13]

A supermarket often has sales with a specified limit on the number of sale items a customer can purchase. That limit sets an "anchor" and produces an *anchoring effect*. Put the number at 12 (e.g., cans of soup), and people will buy 7 on average. Do not put an anchor at all, and people will only buy 3 on average.[14] Anchoring can produce a sort of "priming effect."[15] In one study, researchers found that emergency room patients' preferences for hospitalization versus discharge (for low-risk chest pain) depended on the original anchor given (either the highest risk associated with discharge first or the lowest first).[16]

This raises an important topic in decision psychology and behavioral economics decision-making: the way information is presented matters. The *framing effect* is an umbrella term that describes how presenting the same information in a different way has the tendency to change one's judgments and decisions. For example, one study found that asking patients to cross out symptoms they did not have versus circling symptoms they did have significantly altered the number of symptoms they reported (21.34 vs. 11.83 symptoms).[17] As another example, consider brand-name versus generic medications. Even though the actual drug that comes in a generic versus a brand-name bottle is *exactly* the same, research suggests that individuals would prefer to take the drugs carrying the brand name.[18] In another study of framing effects, researchers demonstrated that presenting treatment benefits in absolute terms (e.g., reduces risk from .05 to .025) rather than relative terms (e.g., reduces risk by 50%) affects individuals' choice (17.4% opting for it vs. 56.8%, respectively).[19]

Another example of a framing effect is what is sometimes called the *contrast effect*. This refers to the change in evaluation of one option when presented on its own versus when it is compared to others. For example, a patient presented with two treatment options, A and B, might be indecisive between the two. But when presented with a third option, C, the patient may then have a preference for B because it feels like a "middle-of-the-road" option.[20] We might call this the Starbucks effect—a grande-sized drink (16 oz.) seems like a "just right" option compared to the tall (12 oz.) and the venti (20 oz.), but evaluated on its own, prior to the invention of the larger sizes, it might have seemed quite large.

The final set of biases I want to discuss in this category have to do with how people respond to threatening information, which threatens what they already believe or threatens their mental or physical health. The first is the *confirmation bias*, the tendency to search for information that further confirms or supports one's initial judgment or decision while disregarding information that contradicts it. Consider the example of a patient who is diagnosed as being in a vegetative or minimally conscious state. The family members of this patient believe that the patient is more fully conscious and as a result see signs of consciousness that the clinical team does not see. Confirmation bias has been found in physicians as well.[21] A similar bias is the *ostrich effect*, the tendency of an individual to "bury his head in the sand" when he receives bad news.[22] This bias is of particular concern to patient care and safety, given that patients cannot arrive at an informed choice if they ignore the pertinence of a health issue even after having its risks explained. One study found that after reading an article about a link between coffee intake and cystic fibrosis, participants who drank two or more cups of coffee a day reported a lower belief in the link compared to those who were not coffee drinkers.[23] Another study found that varying results of a cholesterol test significantly impacted both participants' perceptions of the seriousness of high cholesterol and their belief in the accuracy of the test. Participants receiving borderline-high results reported high cholesterol to be a less serious threat and perceived the test administered to be less accurate than did those who received a desirable test result.[24] As we see in the next chapter, all this raises concerns for our ideals of informed decision-making as well as for patient well-being.

### Heuristics and Biases Related to Lack of Meaning

Sometimes decision-makers do not have a lot of information, or they are confronted with information that is confusing or lacks meaning. In these cases, they employ gap-filling heuristics through which they attempt to make meaning, which leads to several predictable cognitive biases. One interesting bias, the *gambler's fallacy*, lies in thinking that events should balance over time. This fallacy can lead to the idea that one can "catch a break" after a string of bad events. Consider, for example, a patient who for the past three years has come down with the flu each year. She may think that this year she will catch a break, and she chooses not to get a flu shot. One study found the gambler's fallacy to be present in participants' predictions of the likelihood that a family would have a boy or girl as their next child.[25] In reality, whenever a woman is pregnant, there is roughly a 50/50 chance that she will have a boy or a girl. This is true for each time she is pregnant, so even if she already has three girls, there is still a 50% chance that the next baby will be a girl. This study showed that people believed that the more babies of one sex a woman has, the less likely it is that her next child will be that sex.

People yearn to learn information about their futures, but another common cognitive mistake that can negatively impact their ability to do so is the tendency to ignore the sample size when evaluating a future probability. This is referred to as *insensitivity to sample size*, the common failure to understand that larger samples will approach a mean, whereas smaller samples will show more variation. To illustrate this bias, consider an office building that has 16 female employees. If, nationally, 1 in 8 women develop breast cancer in their lifetime, it may be tempting to assume that 2 out of the 16 women in the office will develop breast cancer. However, this would be an inaccurate assumption given that "1 in 8 women" is taken from a very large sample. If you aggregated all offices across the country, for example, some would have more than 1 in 8 women develop breast cancer, and some fewer. The 1/8 statistic might, however, be seen in a very large group of women that represented a microcosm of the nation in terms of diversity, health status, and so on.

One way to make meaning when confronted with confusing or missing information is to defer to an authority figure. This can sometimes be rational, but it can also manifest as a bias.[26] The *authority bias* is the tendency for individuals to trust and defer to authority figures because of their status rather than their expertise. For example, an individual may believe *whatever* a physician says or do whatever they recommend just because they are wearing a white coat. A related phenomenon studied by behavioral economists is the *messenger effect*—the person delivering the message has a powerful influence on the individual's subsequent decisions simply because the messenger is similar to the recipient or is an authority figure such as a physician, etc. To the extent that recommendations shape choice because of an effect attributable to the person making the recommendation (such as his or her attractiveness, authority, or power) rather than the content of the recommendation itself (such as the reasons appealed to), the effect is a bias. The authority bias is powerful in patients' decision-making.

Another way we make meaning and respond to uncertainty or lack of information is to look at what others are doing. If there is a sure way to convince someone to do something, it is to tell him that everyone else is doing it. This relates to what behavioral economists refer to as the *bandwagon effect* and the *power of social norms*.[27] Fad diets, social media, and dressing in suits for interviews are examples of the power that social norms have on our day-to-day lives. Social norms affect medical decision-making as well. Consider one study that found that the highest factor associated with a college-aged woman's intentions to get the HPV vaccine was the perception that getting vaccinated was a social norm—that her classmates were also doing it.[28] In another study, women were asked to imagine that they had breast cancer and were deciding whether to get adjuvant chemotherapy after surgery. Women's choices depended on what other women chose. Significantly more women chose to add the treatment (53.9% vs. 34%) when they were told that 60% (vs. 15%) of women chose to get the additional chemotherapy.[29]

The final two heuristics and biases that I will discuss in this category are intimately related. *Affective forecasting errors* refer to the tendency to project one's current emotional state onto one's future self in order to make meaning of the future. This leads to decisions that, while perhaps good in the "now," may be misaligned with one's actual future self. For example, we might make plans when we are stress-free and happy, only to find that when the event comes we are tired from work and want nothing more than to rest, or we might turn down invitations for a future activity because we do not have the energy to go right now.

This phenomenon relates to the *impact bias*, which is the tendency to overestimate the intensity and duration of future states. Perhaps we think that we will never get over a relationship breakup or job loss. This bias has important implications in the context of medical decision-making since patients are often asked to project and imagine future health states. In one example, hemodialysis patients and healthy patients were asked to estimate the mood of a patient on hemodialysis, ranging from –2.0 (very unpleasant) to 2.0 (very pleasant). The healthy patients imagined it to be 0.38 (mean), whereas the dialysis patients reported it to be 0.70. Healthy controls reported their mood in a typical week as 0.67.[30] The lesson is that patients adapt, but healthy people fail to realize that fact and as a result overestimate how negative life on dialysis would be. This might cause people to decline dialysis and die because of an incorrect prediction about future value.

A similar study found that current colostomy patients were willing to give up far fewer months of life (19 out of 120 months) to live without a colostomy than healthy controls were (44 months).[31] Interestingly, the self-reported quality-of-life measures did not differ significantly between the two groups, suggesting that healthy controls had difficulty predicting what their future emotions would be in their hypothetical need of a colostomy.

Impact bias can result in erroneous judgments about the duration and intensity of positive events as well. One study found that renal failure patients waiting for a kidney estimated that their quality of life after receiving a kidney would improve significantly more than the quality-of-life score reported by posttransplant patients (90.4 out of 100, vs. 78.1).[32]

### Heuristics and Biases Related to the Need to Act Quickly

Biases can also emerge when there is a perceived or actual need to decide or act quickly. These situations introduce a host of predictable behaviors such as favoring simple options and pieces of information over complex, nuanced, and ambiguous information or options. Furthermore, there is an inclination to shy away from irreversible decisions and mistakes and go with the preset flow. The pressure of limited time, whether perceived or actual, causes us to continue to do or confirm those things that we have already put time and energy into, or that are immediately in front of us, rather than to explore other options.

*Ambiguity aversion* is a bias described by the preference for known risks over unknown risks. The classic example of ambiguity aversion is demonstrated by the Ellsberg paradox. In a version of this paradox, the reader is asked to imagine an urn with 50 black balls and 50 red balls, and another urn with 100 balls in which an unknown number are red versus black. As it turns out, most people would prefer to pick from the first urn because they do not like the ambiguity presented by the second urn. In reality, the probability of pulling a red or black ball from each urn is exactly the same (50%).[33] In medical decision-making, ambiguity aversion could result in a patient's choosing a procedure with a very low success rate over a clinical trial that could have a higher success rate but does not yet have data to confirm. Medicine is often rife with uncertainty, yet this bias implies that patients might have a tendency to avoid uncertainty with concerning costs.

One way to act quickly and easily is to go along with the preset flow or default. This tendency is called the *status quo* or *default bias*. Defaults can be very powerful in influencing individuals' decision-making because they relieve people of having to make an active choice, which can often be cognitively or emotionally taxing. We are affected by defaults on a daily basis. For example, we often receive promotional emails from companies because we forget to uncheck the box that opts us out. Defaults affect major decisions like organ donation as well. Countries with the highest rates of donation are those with opt-out programs: all citizens are designated as donors unless they take initiative to remove themselves from the list. Conversely, those with the lowest rates of donation are ones where an individual has to actively sign up to be a donor. These findings have been duplicated in a lab experiment that found that even when the choice was hypothetical, a significantly higher percentage of participants consented to being donors in the opt-out condition (82%) than in the opt-in condition (42%). Of respondents who were given no default and forced to make a choice, 79% consented.[34] A final example of the default bias involves its impact on end-of-life decision-making. Studies have found that when hypothetically constructing a living will, participants who are asked to choose which treatments they would want (the default option is no treatment) are less aggressive than those who are asked to remove treatments they would not want (the default option is all treatments).[35] These findings are significant because they show how even high-stakes and preference-sensitive decisions can be driven by simple changes in defaults.

Another quick heuristic is the *decoy effect*, which occurs when individuals exhibit a change in preference between two options when the addition of a third option makes one of the original two seem significantly better. In one fascinating study, participants were asked about their willingness to receive a liver from a genetically modified pig. When the choice was between a liver from a pig and one from a human, participants were mostly unwilling to receive the pig liver. With the presence of a third option, however, the liver of a genetically modified dog, participants were significantly more willing to accept the liver from the genetically modified pig.[36] A similar study was done regarding prescription drug decision-making. When physicians were choosing between Tylenol and Cardec for sinusitis, 70% prescribed Tylenol and 30% Cardec (the correct answer), but when Rhinosyn (which is objectively worse than Cardec) was added as an option, 57% prescribed Cardec (and 43% prescribed Tylenol). This trend held across prescribing for three different conditions.[37]

While ambiguity aversion, default bias, and the decoy effect are well-studied phenomena in behavioral economics, perhaps the most famous bias of all is *loss aversion*, the finding that people weigh losses heavier than they do gains of equal or greater magnitude. One study found that 66% of women received a mammogram when presented with the risks of neglecting mammograms, whereas only 51% of women received a mammogram when presented with mammograms' benefits.[38] Another study found that when told that 1 out of 100 angioplasties result in complications (loss-framed message), 49% of participants refused to get one. However, when told that 99 out of 100 angioplasties have no complications (gain-framed message), only 15% of participants refused.[39] This bias has extremely important implications for medical decision-making and informed consent, since physicians present information about outcomes on a daily basis; whether those are framed in terms of loss or gain can significantly impact choice—for example, whether a patient consents to or refuses a surgery.

Another concept from behavioral economics that has significant import for medical decision-making is *escalation of commitment*. This describes the tendency to put increasing amounts of resources into something once you have already invested time, money, or energy into it. A prime example may involve intensive care unit (ICU) decision-making in which physicians or family members decide to continue to treat a patient who is dying and no longer benefiting from treatments.[40] Similarly, the *sunk cost bias* is the tendency to continue a suboptimal course of action just because resources have already been invested in it. Consider the nonmedical example of a family who has paid $40 for baseball tickets for a game 60 miles away. They decide to drive to the game through a storm just because they've already paid $40. Whether the family goes to the baseball game or not, they are not going to get back their $40. Their past investment should not determine their future-oriented choice about what to do given current decisional factors—there is now a storm that makes driving dangerous.[41] In medical settings, the sunk cost bias could cause patients or physicians to continue with treatments that are not working rather than trying approaches that might have better outcomes. For example, one study found that in a computer simulation, participants' commitment to chiropractor services over treatments with better success significantly depended on the effort and money they had already invested in chiropractic treatment.[42]

The final three biases in this category fit together in a way that will become apparent through explanation of each.[43] One is *illusion of control*, which is the tendency to believe that we have more control over the outcome of a particular event than we do. Consider, for example, a terminally ill patient who believes that by living a healthy lifestyle she can reverse the fate of her illness. Studies have demonstrated this illusion in patient thinking. One study describes the thought process of surrogate decision-makers for patients in the ICU. A common belief was that their loved one had unique strengths unknown to the physicians and would thus pull through. For example, one person said, "I don't think they [physicians] know her. … It's hard for them to know how well she can respond, unless you've actually been with her through other illnesses." Similarly, another person said, "I feel that my brother's a fighter and I know him more than what the doctor do [sic]."[44]

Similarly, the *optimism bias* describes our general tendency to think that we are better than average. This bias operates in many domains (e.g., beliefs about our intellectual abilities, chances of marital success, etc.) but has significant implications for medicine and medical decision-making. One study found that female university students reported themselves as being 38% less likely than their classmates to have a heart attack before the age of 40, 37% less likely to contract a venereal disease, and 32% less likely to develop lung cancer.[45] These findings could be quite alarming if the beliefs caused the women to be less careful about maintaining a healthy lifestyle. Another study of heart-failure patients at Duke University Medical Center found that although the predicted median survival is 10 years, 63% of patients overestimated their life expectancy.[46] Finally, a study of family members of patients in the ICU compared their prognostic estimates to those of physicians and found that 43% had more optimistic estimates.[47]

A similar bias, the *overconfidence effect*, is the tendency to have greater confidence in one's own judgments compared to objective assessments. For example, one study examined discrepancies in physician and patient mortality estimates related to stem cell transplantation. It found that when mortality rates were low, physician and patient estimates were similar to the actual mortality rate. As mortality increased, however, physicians adjusted their estimates, but patients estimated mortality rates much lower than the actual reported mortality rates.[48]

### Heuristics and Biases Related to What to Remember

The final set of heuristics and biases I will discuss relates to the fact that when we receive information or experience events, we try to remember the most important parts, but this can lead to biases, including recency bias, primacy bias, and the peak-end effect.

*Recency* and *primacy biases* are part of the phenomenon of *order effects*, which tells us that the order in which information is presented affects individuals' subsequent judgments and decisions. For example, one study found that women were more or less inclined to get genetic testing for breast cancer depending on whether they were presented with the positive or negative information about testing first (primacy bias).[49] In a similar study, researchers found that women who heard either first or last about the benefits of Tamoxifen, a drug to prevent breast cancer recurrence, were more interested in taking the drug than women who heard about the risks first or last (primacy and recency biases).[50]

In addition to remembering and being more influenced by information or options that we hear first or last, we are also inclined to remember the peak, or most intense, moment and the end of events or experiences. Known as the *peak-end effect*, it can color medical experiences. One study asked women (with epidural and without) to assess their pain every 20 minutes during labor. After delivery, they were asked to recall their pain. Two days postdelivery, the nonepidural group reported a mean pain recall of 87.6 (out of 100) while the epidural group reported a mean pain recall of 69.5— even though the two groups reported similar pain ratings during labor prior to the moment that the epidural was administered. The women's postdelivery pain reporting was driven by the peak moment in delivery, which differed based on why they had an epidural at that moment or not, rather than on the overall experience.[51] Another study found that simply leaving a colonoscopy probe in the rectum for three minutes after the procedure, which is uncomfortable but not painful, decreases patients' pain ratings and causes them to rate the experience as overall less unpleasant. This is because the end moment that they remember and to which they anchor their evaluation is a nonpainful one. Patients who received this "extended procedure" even demonstrated slightly higher rates of returning for a follow-up procedure (median 5.3 years later; 53% vs. 47%, not significant).[52]

One might think that knowledge of these biases can help decision-makers resist their pull and negative effects. Unfortunately, the existence of a meta-bias, a *bias blind spot*, poses a challenge to recognizing these and other biases at play in our decision-making. The problem is not necessarily that people are unaware of decisional biases generally. Rather, while we seem to have a somewhat easy time recognizing biases in others' decision-making, we often have an especially hard time recognizing them in our own. One study found that Stanford psychology students considered themselves less susceptible to a list of cognitive biases compared to the average American (5.31 vs. 6.75 on a scale of 1–9) and to their classmates (5.05 vs. 5.85).[53]

## Theoretical and Normative Issues in Heuristics and Biases Research

Having described various decisional heuristics and biases, it is worth acknowledging and discussing several of the underlying theoretical and normative issues and debates that have been raised with respect to the heuristics and biases research program. These include conceptual and explanatory issues, the normative status of heuristics and biases, and issues regarding the replication crisis in psychology and the reliability of heuristics and biases research.

### Conceptual and Explanatory Issues in Heuristics and Biases Research

The Benson framework that I have used to organize the examples discussed in this chapter is merely an organizational and not an explanatory framework. Reasonable people might disagree about the way Benson organizes the four categories of heuristics and biases, or about where he places various biases within the categories. My intention in using this framework is merely to provide a useful mechanism for organizing the discussion of heuristics and biases so that they are more understandable to the reader. But this speaks to a larger theoretical challenge in the heuristics and biases research program, which is whether there *is* an explanatory framework for these phenomena. Research studies on heuristics and biases are fascinating, but as some critics have pointed out, they rarely offer mechanistic information. For example, as Gerd Gigerenzer has emphasized, the most commonly cited framework to explain the phenomena discussed in this chapter is the System 1 versus System 2 framework introduced at the beginning of the chapter.[54] But this system is itself a heuristic. It does not offer any kind of unifying explanation—there is not a System 1 part of the brain distinct from a System 2 part.

These critics might contend that although behavioral economists study all the biases and heuristics discussed in this chapter, it is unclear what, beyond that fact, groups them together absent some underlying mechanism. Is it that they violate rationality, lead to errors, or involve shallow cognitive processes of the sort described as System 1 thinking? Some heuristics and biases meet some, but not other, of these conditions.[55] For example, while the gambler's fallacy may lead to errors, people might commit this fallacy when engaging in complex System 2 thinking. Similarly, while an authority bias may lead us to make errors, deference to experts is not clearly irrational, nor does it necessarily involve System 1 thinking. Thus, it is conceptually unclear why all of these very different phenomena are lumped together by psychologists.

I think that all of these criticisms are fair, but for my purposes, what links the phenomena under discussion is that they can negatively affect patients' choices in ways that I explain in the next chapter. There are important questions for psychologists and philosophers of science to examine, but my motivations here are practical and my concerns are normative. Namely, there are a set of phenomena that behavioral economists and decision psychologists have called heuristics and biases, they have been shown to impact medical decision-making in ways described in this chapter, and this has normative import in terms of how we think about patient autonomy and well-being—all points to be argued in this book.

### Normative Issues in Heuristics and Biases Research

One of the biggest criticisms of the heuristics and biases research program is that its researchers imply, or sometimes explicitly state, that reliance on decision-making heuristics is bad, irrational, or always involves error. The term "bias" itself has a negative connotation. As Gerd Gigerenzer has pointed out, however, sometimes System 1 and its shortcuts are efficient and correct where System 2 fails—so System 1 is not always irrational or in error. He gives the example of a framing effect whereby a patient chooses surgery in a survival frame (e.g., 80% survival) but not in a mortality frame (e.g., 20% mortality).[56] He argues that a patient might infer that the physician is making an implicit recommendation by presenting the odds of survival, and so the patient is being socially intelligent or socially rational rather than in error when she is more likely to consent to surgery in the survival frame.

Beyond this general point, it seems clear that some of the heuristics and biases discussed in the chapter are more normatively defensible than others. Compare the gambler's fallacy versus the omission bias. While the gambler's fallacy is clearly an error, someone might argue that the omission "bias" simply reflects a different normative worldview. For example, certain theories of ethics hold an action-inaction distinction whereby harmful acts of omission are more morally defensible than harmful acts of commission.[57] Similarly, deference to experts, as seen in authority bias and messenger effects, could be seen as defensible, especially in the medical context. Similar points could be made regarding bandwagon effects/social norms: following norms could arguably be a form of robust social intelligence. Arguments could also be made in defense of ostrich effects, overconfidence effects, and optimism bias. While some might see these phenomena as various forms of denial or errors of belief, it is empirically difficult to tease out what people really believe versus what they merely express, say, to appear positive. Moreover, there may be some situations where these mental states offer more benefit than harm for patients and are ethically defensible.[58]

All of this is to say that (1) it is true that the heuristics and biases discussed here are not always erroneous, irrational, or normatively indefensible, and that much depends on context, and (2) we can draw some rough distinctions between heuristics and biases that may be normatively defensible, debatable, or based on different worldviews from ones that more clearly are not. For example, heuristics and biases that fall into the normatively debatable category might include omission bias, authority bias, messenger effect, bandwagon effect/social norm effect, optimism bias, overconfidence effect, ostrich effect, illusion of control—and possibly commission bias, impact bias, affective forecasting error (depending on views of temporal ethics and future versus current selves), sunk cost bias, and peak-end effect. Heuristics and biases that are more clearly erroneous or normatively indefensible might include availability bias, gambler's fallacy, insensitivity to sample size, confirmation bias, focusing effect, anchoring, framing effects such as loss aversion, and order effects such as recency and primacy biases.

The point of this book is not to make general claims about irrationality or error in human decision-making. Rather, it is to explore how, in the context of medical decision-making, many of the effects that behavioral economists and decision psychologists have dubbed "heuristics and biases" might impair patients' decision-making in systematic and problematic ways that can be addressed if acknowledged. Although this chapter reviews a large set of heuristics and biases, a smaller subset features predominantly throughout the rest of the book. These appear particularly central to the clinical cases that I have observed and use as examples throughout the book. They include availability bias, omission/commission biases, bandwagon/social norms, authority/messenger effects, and framing effects.

### The Replication Crisis and the Reliability of Heuristics and Biases Research

A third major issue involves questions about the reliability of the heuristics and biases research program in light of the replication crisis facing empirical psychology. "Replication crisis" refers to findings indicating that many scientific studies and their effects are impossible or difficult to reproduce. For example, a report by the Open Science Collaboration estimated the reproducibility of 100 psychology studies from three of the top-ranking psychology journals and found that only 36% had significant findings, compared to 97% of the original studies.[59] A 2018 study attempted to replicate 21 behavioral science studies from the journals *Science* and *Nature* and found that only 13 could be replicated successfully.[60] Relatedly, some have argued that there is a bias in publishing studies that confirms the presence of a cognitive bias as opposed to those that do not, making these phenomena seem more pervasive than they actually are.[61]

In response to this concern, as Kahneman has argued, given that there are *so many* findings and examples, even if there were a reporting bias in the literature—or even if certain heuristics were shown not to exist or to be as robust as once thought—it is unrealistic to deny that there is a set of concerning phenomena about the peculiar ways that humans make decisions.[62] Also, replication crises for certain heuristics and biases might not be as devastating as they initially appear. Take, for example, a recent critique calling into question the robustness of one of the most well-known biases, loss aversion bias. A review paper found that whereas *sometimes* loss frame proved to be most powerful, sometimes gain frame was, and sometimes losses and gains had similar psychological impacts.[63] The robustness of the effects depended much on context, the review concluded. While this is an important insight, it is still the case that there *was* a framing effect—the sort that might matter for patient decision-making. We just need to understand which frame is more influential in the particular context in question. So, while the manifestation of certain heuristics and biases may be complicated and nuanced, they are by no means nonexistent or irrelevant.

## Conclusion

My goal in reviewing these numerous decisional heuristics and biases and illustrating their impact on patients' decision-making is to set the ground for the normative arguments that will follow. My aim is to give readers a set of empirical findings that they can draw on as they consider the theoretical and practical issues discussed in the remainder of the book.

**Table 1.1**
Definitions of heuristics and biases.

Heuristics and biases related to too much information

| | |
|---|---|
| Availability bias | The tendency to turn to vivid examples rather than actual likelihoods when evaluating the frequency with which something occurs. |
| Focusing effect | The tendency to place too much importance on one factor of a decision, resulting in a miscalculation of the expected value of an option. |
| Omission bias | Judging a harmful action as worse than an equally harmful inaction. |
| Commission bias | Choosing action over inaction, even when the action is harmful. |
| Anchoring | When the first piece of information presented influences or anchors subsequent judgments and decisions. |
| Framing effect | A shift in judgments and decisions based on the same information being presented in a different way. |
| Contrast effect | A change in evaluation of an option when it is presented on its own versus compared to other options. |
| Confirmation bias | The tendency to search for information that confirms, rather than disconfirms, one's initial judgment or decision. |
| Ostrich effect | The tendency to "bury one's head in the sand" when receiving bad news. |
| Bias blind spot | The failure to recognize biases in one's own judgments and decisions while being able to recognize them in others. |

**Table 1.1 (continued)**

Heuristics and biases related to lack of meaning

| | |
|---|---|
| **Gambler's fallacy** | The assumption that events will balance over time. |
| **Insensitivity to sample size** | The common tendency to ignore the sample size when evaluating a probability. While smaller samples will show more variability in their mean value, larger samples will approach the true mean. |
| **Authority bias** | When figures of authority influence one's decisions because of their perceived status rather than their credibility. |
| **Messenger effect** | When the person delivering a message greatly influences the observer's subsequent decisions because of some attribute(s) of the messenger (e.g., the messenger is similar to the observer or is an authority figure). |
| **Bandwagon effect/power of social norms** | When an individual's decisions are shaped by what those around them are doing. |
| **Affective forecasting errors** | The tendency to project one's current emotional state into the future when making decisions for the future. |
| **Impact bias** | The tendency to overestimate the intensity and duration of future feelings when making decisions based on projected future states. |

Heuristics and biases related to the need to act quickly

| | |
|---|---|
| **Ambiguity aversion** | Preferring known risks to unknown risks. |
| **Status quo/default bias** | The tendency to stick to a "default" option rather than making an active choice. |
| **Decoy effect** | When the addition of a third option significantly improves one's evaluation of one of the two original options. |
| **Loss aversion bias** | The tendency to weigh losses as heavier than gains of equal or greater magnitude. |
| **Sunk cost bias** | When one stays the course of a suboptimal path if they have already put significant time or energy into it. |
| **Illusion control** | The belief that one has more control of an outcome than she actually does. |
| **Optimism bias** | When individuals tend to think that they are better than the average statistic. |
| **Overconfidence effect** | Placing greater confidence in one's own judgments than in objective estimates. |

**Table 1.1 (continued)**

Heuristics and biases related to what to remember

| | |
|---|---|
| **Order effect** | When the order in which information is presented affects one's judgments and decisions. Specifically, information presented at the beginning and end tends to have greater impact on one's decisions than information presented in the middle. |
| **Recency effect** | When later information has a greater impact on one's decisions than earlier information. |
| **Primacy effect** | When earlier information has a greater impact on one's decisions than later information. |
| **Peak-end effect** | The tendency to best remember the peak (most intense) and the end of an experience while evaluating it. |

This table was originally published in my and my colleague's systematic review of heuristics and biases in medical decision-making. See Blumenthal-Barby and Krieger, "Cognitive Biases and Heuristics in Medical Decision Making."

## 2 Bad Decisions? What Behavioral Economics Means for Patient Autonomy, Decision Quality, and Well-Being

The predominant ethos in medicine and medical ethics is to assume that patients are capable of making autonomous decisions that promote their own personal goals and values so long as they are properly informed of the options and their risks/benefits. Behavioral economics and the examples of decisional heuristics and biases discussed in the previous chapter significantly challenge this assumption. Behavioral economics shows that patients' decisions can fail to be autonomous or to improve their well-being in ways beyond the usual ones that clinicians and bioethicists worry about (e.g., poorly informed consent, coercion, weakness of will). Specifically, in this chapter, I will argue that behavioral economics demonstrates that patients' decision-making is often at risk for being (1) nonautonomous or autonomy impaired, (2) of poor quality, and (3) harmful to patients and their interests.

### Are Patients Generally Autonomous? Lessons from Behavioral Economics

Autonomy is a complex philosophical notion that can mean many different things, but for our purposes I will focus on the definition of the principle of autonomy outlined by Tom Beauchamp and James Childress in *Principles of Medical Ethics*.[1] They tell us that there are two necessary conditions for autonomy: liberty (independence from controlling influences) and agency (capacity for intentional action). Autonomous action is analyzed in terms of three components: (1) intentionality, (2) understanding (of the options, their risks and benefits, and the foreseeable consequences), and (3) independence of controlling influence.[2] Some views require a fourth component: that a patient reflect on her preferences, and that her final decisions accord with her deeply held values or considered judgments.

Most readers will already begin to sense tensions between some of these requirements and the realities of decision-making presented in chapter 1, but let me provide depth to the argument by examining each of the components of autonomy in light of insights from the psychology of decision-making and behavioral economics.[3]

### Behavioral Economics and Challenges for Intentional Choice

The first requirement of autonomous action is intentionality. Autonomous actions or decisions are not simply a matter of mere happenstance or habit in the way that nonvoluntary ones are. Forming an intention to do something generally involves making plans.[4] A person who acted with intention can look back at a decision or action and agree that she behaved as planned. Things may not have turned out as planned, but that is another matter.[5] Intentionality is a fundamental aspect of mainstream notions of autonomy.

If we take into account the various heuristics and biases in decision-making discussed in chapter 1, we see that patients often do *not* act intentionally or according to plan. Instead, they are influenced by habit, random environmental cues, framing effects, and so on. Heuristics and biases may interfere with intentionality in at least two ways. First, they may cause a *bypass* of planning that results in a patient looking back and feeling as if she never really intentionally chose what she ended up doing. Take for example a patient who falls prey to the default bias and fills out an advance directive with life-sustaining treatment checked as the default, or a person who lives in a country where organ donation is set as the default. In both cases, there is a mechanism to opt out, but due to the default bias, the person avoids deliberating about the pros and cons and goes along with the default. This results in a bypass of planning, which may cause the patient to look back on her decision and feel as if being on a ventilator at the end of her life or organ donation is not what she planned. Or consider a patient who chooses one medication over another just because she heard about the benefits before the risks (a framing effect—specifically, an order effect) or because she heard about it from one person rather than another (a messenger effect). Each might look back at her decision and, upon learning of these effects, feel that she did not act intentionally.

A second way in which the heuristics and biases discussed in chapter 1 might threaten intentionality is by *countering* or negatively impacting what the patient has decided on and intends to do. Consider a pregnant patient who had decided against amniocentesis for genetic testing but who sees a young boy with a genetic abnormality in her obstetrician's office, which triggers the availability bias (associating probability of an event with ease of example) and causes her to request the test.[6] Or imagine that, via the bandwagon effect, she hears about many women she works with who received the test, and so elects to have it. In a different example, imagine that a patient recently diagnosed with low-risk prostate cancer considered the odds, determined that surgery is not worth the risk, and intends to not pursue it. However, the intensity of the commission bias ("do something!") thwarts his intention and causes him to elect surgery.[7]

Finally, consider Carl Schneider's more general point made in his extensive study of patient decision-making: "Even patients sufficiently well-educated and reflective to write memoirs frequently describe no decisional process at all. Instead they invoke intuition, instinct, and impulse."[8] Behavioral economics and empirical investigation show us that much of decision-making turns out to be less intentional than we might think.

## Behavioral Economics and Challenges for Understanding and Appreciation of Choices

In medical ethics, a second important component of autonomous decision-making involves a patient's understanding and appreciation of key aspects of her decision. As bioethicists Ruth Faden and Tom Beauchamp have said, this requires that a patient tend to, process, grasp, and internalize the meaning of the information related to her options, the foreseeable consequences, and the possible outcomes.[9] There is always a question of how much (in terms of scope and depth) understanding is required for a patient to make an informed and autonomous decision. In *Principles of Medical Ethics*, Beauchamp and Childress argue for a "substantial amount," but at the very least, patients should understand and appreciate the key facts or "get the gist."[10]

But behavioral economics shows that patients may often lack sufficient understanding and appreciation. For example, a patient may believe that her future quality of life will be poor when in fact it will likely not be (i.e., the patient makes an affective forecasting error due to the impact bias). Or a patient focuses only on some aspects of the risks, benefits, or side effects but not others (due to a focusing effect)—and in doing so, fails to understand or appreciate what the different options entail. Or a patient may have an optimism bias that leads her to believe that the odds of some desired outcome are better than they actually are.

Some have objected to the idea that acting autonomously requires having accurate or true beliefs about important aspects of a medical decision. As Moti Gorin writes,

> If actions based on false propositions cannot be autonomous, then the majority of health-care related actions in history (e.g., those taken prior to the acceptance of the germ theory of disease) do not count as autonomous. Put simply, understanding does not require truth, for if it did we could not understand false propositions. Therefore, even if biases and heuristics threaten people's ability to apprehend true propositions, this would not show that they necessarily threaten people's autonomy.[11]

This reflects a larger debate in theoretical philosophy about whether understanding (and true belief) is required for autonomous action. James Stacey Taylor uses the example of Martin Fobisher to argue that it is not. Fobisher was the English explorer who thought he was making trips to collect gold but was really collecting fool's gold. Taylor writes that Fobisher was certainly autonomous in the sense of being "extremely self-governed" in those excursions despite the fact that he did not understand what he was bringing back.[12] A related point can be seen in the case of a patient who decides to pursue a miraculous faith healing. Some might take the view that even though the person's decision is in tension with what the scientific or medical communities believe about her situation, we need not say that she is nonautonomous, though we might say she lacks understanding and appreciation of the medical facts in some important way.

Delving too far into this issue would take us far afield into theoretical debates about the nature of personal autonomy, but suffice it to say that most predominant accounts of autonomy in medical ethics build in understanding (true, correct beliefs) of the facts as we know them as a basic and important component of the principle of autonomy.[13] For example, beyond Faden, Beauchamp, and Childress, Robert Veatch, Paul Appelbaum, and Al Mele have also argued for the importance of understanding for autonomous action. Paul Appelbaum and Tom Grisso define understanding of relevant information as a key component of a patient's "competence to consent to treatment," whereby the patient exercises his or her autonomy. They write,

> The delirious patient who pulls out an intravenous line has not made an autonomous decision. ... It lacks several of the indicia of autonomous choice, including

the abilities to comprehend the current circumstances, to reason about the available options, and to select a course of action. Choices made in the absence of these abilities, or when they are substantially impaired, cannot be said to be autonomous; they are, in the language we used earlier, not meaningful decisions.[14]

Or, as Robert Veatch writes succinctly, "Informed consent is a critical element of a theory that gives weight to autonomy."[15] I take this to concern not just the process of "informing" the patient, but also the actual result of the patient "being" informed (i.e., adequately understanding the relevant information). And finally, Al Mele has argued similarly, writing in philosophical terms that "a sufficient condition of S's being informationally cut off from autonomous action in some domain in which S has intrinsic pro-attitudes is that S has no control over the success of his efforts to achieve his ends in that domain, owing to his informational condition."[16] Veatch gives the example of a king who is trying to make decisions that would improve his kingdom but is subject to false beliefs and misinformation. Because of this "unfortunate informational condition," the king is unable to achieve his political ends—he is "informationally cut off from ruling autonomously."[17] To the extent that, as I have shown in several examples, heuristics and biases impair understanding, thereby creating a similar unfortunate informational condition, they impair autonomous decision-making.

### Behavioral Economics and Challenges for Voluntary Choice

A third component of autonomous decision-making involves the idea that truly autonomous decisions or actions are driven or controlled by *me* and not blocked or controlled by an external or substantially controlling, unwanted influence. This aspect of autonomy is closely tied to the concept of liberty. If, for example, a person is in prison, she has lost the liberty to do as or go where she pleases. Similarly, if a person holds a gun to my head or threatens me with significant punishment if I do not do as they wish, then my actions are substantially controlled by that person. Even if I choose to comply with their request, it was not really *my* decision. I *could* have done otherwise, but not in any meaningful sense.

How does this component of autonomy fare under the data presented in chapter 1? On the one hand, heuristics, biases, and other System 1 processes seem irrelevant because they are all phenomena that are inside the person rather than external. But that thinking may be too simple. Even though these factors are inside a person, there is a way in which they could be considered external. Consider, for example, a patient who hears voices due to psychosis. Those voices are technically from within the person, but the person *feels* as if they are external—the person does not identify with them. It is ultimately an empirical question whether a patient might feel this way about some of the System 1 aspects of their decision-making discussed in chapter 1, but it is certainly imaginable. Refer to the example discussed in the section on intentionality, where a patient decides against surgery for cancer but is driven toward it by a commission bias. We might imagine that the patient feels as though this drive or pressure to "do something" is substantially controlling and alien to him—not something that he welcomes or identifies with. Some have also suggested that heuristics and biases pose a threat or make one more vulnerable to external control.[18] This, too, is an empirical question whose answer is relevant for the normative question of whether and how they impact the exercise of autonomy. I will not speculate on an answer here, but this notion strikes me as less plausible than the hypothesis that certain heuristics and biases may feel alienating, controlling, or unwanted to the agent who is experiencing them.

There is a second way in which decision-making biases and heuristics could be considered as external or unwanted controlling influences, thereby threatening autonomy, and that is if another person is intentionally triggering or using heuristics or biases to influence the patient's decision-making. We might then worry about the issue of substantial noncontrol and whether the patient is easily able to resist such pressures and go her own way. This is discussed at length in chapter 3, where I examine the ethics of "nudging," or shaping patient decision-making.

In sum, there may be ways in which organically occurring heuristics and biases pose concerns for the autonomy requirement of freedom from external control or substantially controlling influences, although admittedly they are not likely the major mechanism by which the phenomena discussed in chapter 1 pose a threat to autonomy. Intentionality, understanding, and considered judgment (discussed below) are probably the predominant mechanisms.

### Behavioral Economics and Challenges for Considered Judgment and Reasons-Responsiveness in Decision-Making

Some views of autonomous decision-making say that an important component of autonomy is the idea of considered judgment. The patient's decision or action should be the result of some amount of higher-order reflection or thoughtful deliberation. This idea hearkens back to the influence of Immanuel Kant on contemporary medical ethics. According to Kant, autonomy is a property of the will that all human beings have and can exercise. Autonomy relates intimately to our capacity to reason.[19] For Kant, the exercise of the will is inherently an exercise of one's rational capacities; nonrational factors such as desires, inclinations, or emotions are either irrelevant to or interfere with the exercise of autonomy.[20]

Clearly many of the findings related in chapter 1 pose a concern for this component of autonomy, given that they emphasize how little decision-making is driven by formal deliberation—let alone deliberation that follows basic norms of rationality.[21] It is worth noting that Kant was primarily concerned with moral judgment and decision-making, but contemporary philosophers and bioethicists have expanded Kant's ideas about autonomy to more general domains of decision-making. Autonomy as it is understood and applied by many contemporary bioethicists is very much about reflection and responsiveness to reasons. Even the formal criteria for "decision-making capacity" (a technical term that refers to a patient's ability to make her medical decisions) involve appeal to reason (along with understanding, appreciation, and ability to express a clear and consistent choice).[22]

### Behavioral Economics and Challenges for Choices-Values Concordance

Related to the idea of autonomous decisions involving considered judgment is the idea that considered judgment leads to a decision that actually reflects the patient's values (their "second-order" desires). This idea has been central to the defense of patients' rights to be informed of their options and of the risks/benefits of each, and to make their own decisions. Objections to paternalism and defenses of the importance of autonomy center around the idea that patients have varying preferences, goals, and values, and that they should have them listened to and respected.[23] Through the notion of autonomy, patients are granted the respect and freedom to make choices that reflect their own preferences, goals, and values, which might differ from those of the medical team or other patients. But the realities presented in chapter 1 pose a threat to the idea that patients' decisions mostly reflect their deeply held values and considered judgments.[24]

This threat is posed in at least two ways. First, patients may have deeply held values or considered judgments that their actual decisions do not match because of various decisional biases (e.g., the focusing effect, in which a person focuses on the immediate future rather than the long term; the bandwagon effect, or the tendency to follow social norms; the sunk cost bias, whereby a person continues something just because she has invested in it; or an affective forecasting error, in which a person errs in forecasting how she will feel in some future health state). Second, we might think that the many heuristics and biases discussed in chapter 1 mean that patients *lack* the sort of deeply held values and preferences that bioethics typically presumes and works to protect.[25] We need only think about the numerous framing effects discussed by behavioral economists to begin to see the point. If our preferences (even very important ones regarding our end-of-life decisions)[26] depend so heavily on both who presents the information and options and how they present it,[27] what are we to make of the very ideas of "preference-sensitive" decisions or "personal" values and goals? And if autonomy is fundamentally about patients exercising the freedom to make decisions in accordance with their own personal values and goals, then how often do patients actually do this? The answer is perhaps not as often as we tend to assume.

### Thick and Thin Notions of Autonomy and Matters of Degree

I have analyzed how various components of autonomy can be negatively impacted by decisional biases and heuristics. We could, however, adopt a thicker or thinner account of autonomy. Thicker accounts would require *all* of these components to be satisfied and thinner accounts only some. But what is particularly striking is that even if we adopt a very thin or minimalist view of autonomy, behavioral economics still raises serious questions about the extent to which even basic conditions of autonomous decision-making (e.g., freedom from substantial external or unwanted influence; basic understanding and appreciation of key information) are met in many scenarios.

It is worth mentioning that autonomy is a matter of degree. Just as patients can have more or less capacity to make a particular medical decision (depending, for example, on their degree of cognitive impairment), patients can be more or less autonomous with respect to a particular decision or course of action. This is because each of the various components of autonomy, with the possible exception of intentionality, is itself a matter of degree. Hence, heuristics and biases may not render a patient nonautonomous but rather impair their autonomy to some degree. Another way to put it is that patients' decision-making is perhaps *less* autonomous than we typically assume, and it may be impaired by a wider variety of factors than bioethicists and clinicians typically concern themselves with.

## A Possible Way Out? A Different View of Autonomy?

There is a philosophical view of autonomy that is quite different from the one presented thus far and that may help us avoid the conclusion that because medical decision-making is so heavily driven by System 1, patients are not as autonomous as we typically assume. We might call this a "meta-view" of autonomy. The idea is that as long as a person endorses (or would endorse, were her attention drawn to it) her decision-making process or decision-making style, then she is acting autonomously, regardless of the details of that style. This idea originates from philosopher Harry Frankfurt's "second-order" theory of action.[28] According to this view, what matters is a person's attitude toward her desires and the factors that cause her to decide or act one way or another. She can either accept those desires and factors or resist them. When she resists them, they block her from acting freely (think, for example, of the smoker who wants to quit but has strong desires preventing her from doing so, versus the smoker who has no desire to quit and does not mind such cravings).

To translate to our context, the proposal would be that a patient might not mind that her decision-making process is driven by various identifiable heuristics and biases. She might make decisions unreflectively, emotionally, or without sufficient understanding—but as long as she endorses these "decisional styles" or processes, then she is deciding autonomously. We see this view expressed by the philosopher Richard Double, who resists the idea that decision-making and action need to be particularly cognitive or reflective. He writes,

> There are autonomy exemplars that count against requiring reflectiveness. Rugged individualists may be preoccupied with evaluating their first order desires, but they need not. The man-of-action, so the paradigm goes, shoots first and asks questions later. The true free spirit may not ask questions at all. And what about the millions of persons to whom reflecting on their lower-order psychological states is not only an infrequent occurrence, but is an anathema to their individual management styles? For many persons, life is to be lived, not worried over.[29]

Double proposes that as long as unreflectiveness is part of a person's "individual management style" (how she believes she should go about making choices), then she is autonomous with respect to her desire.[30] Perhaps, then, in this view, heuristics and biases could also become part of a person's individual management style.

This view has some merit, but it also has some counterintuitive implications and challenges. One counterintuitive implication is that a person could adopt a management style of, say, flipping a coin whenever there is a decision to be made. According to this meta-view of autonomy, as long as coin-flipping is the person's decided style, they are making autonomous decisions. The character Dwight in Benjamin Kunkel's novel *Indecision* does exactly that: "People were always calling me and asking me to do things, and since only pretty rarely was I really sure I wanted to, my system was to flip a coin. ... I was proud of the system."[31] "But Dwight's method seems very far from ordinary understandings of autonomy.[32]

There is another, perhaps stronger, challenge to the idea that the meta-view of autonomy is going to save us from having to conclude that people are not very autonomous given the findings in chapter 1. That is, it is not as if people are making decisions full of heuristics and biases because they have endorsed this as their management style. First, they are probably not even aware that their decision-making is driven by so many of these types of factors. Second, if they were aware, it is unlikely that they would embrace it as their management style. Third, even if they did, the very process by which they came to endorse it might itself be distorted by psychological blunders—making it not an informed or autonomous endorsement. Philosopher John Christman makes this point when he develops criteria for an autonomous decision or action. Christman's view is a sort of meta-autonomy view in that a person can be considered to be acting autonomously so long as she accepts the factors (desires, processes) that drive her decision. But Christman argues that this lack of resistance must not be "under the influence of factors that inhibit self-reflection" and that the self-reflection must be "minimally rational," meaning "it does not involve self-deception or mistakes in logical inference."[33]

In sum, one implication of the fact that decision-making is driven by numerous cognitive biases, heuristics, and other System 1 processes is that patients' decisions are much less autonomous than we typically assume them to be and are potentially impaired by factors that are often quite commonplace.

## Rethinking the Value of Autonomy?

Given the various ways in which our decisions regularly fall short of "autonomous" as bioethicists typically conceptualize it, it is reasonable to ask whether we ought to rethink the value or importance of autonomy in medicine and bioethics. I think that we ought to rethink some of the assumptions we make about autonomy (e.g., that patients are choosing autonomously so long as they are competent, properly informed, and not coerced; that respecting autonomy mostly involves informing and then not interfering with patient decision-making; that autonomy is the most important principle in medical ethics; that the main value in letting patients choose for themselves lies in increasing the likelihood that they choose in ways that promote their interests and values). However, there is certainly value in the concept and in the guiding principle. After all, the principle of autonomy has steered us away from various ethically problematic practices in medicine, including not informing patients about a cancer diagnosis, performing procedures and research on a patient without their consent, and deciding on treatment options without involving the patient in the process. Moreover, for many patients there is some value in the feeling and process of "choosing for oneself," which the idea and principle of autonomy promote. All of that having been said, I am also persuaded by a comment I heard recently from a bioethics colleague at a conference. He remarked that bioethicists are so obsessed with the concept of autonomy that they will perform great mental gymnastics to make various views fit into the concept, developing various expansions, modifications, and subtypes (e.g., relational autonomy) when they would just as well embrace a broader principle such as respect for persons.

## Are Patients at Risk for Poor-Quality Decisions?
## Lessons from Behavioral Economics

Thus far, I have spent a lot of time considering the implications of behavioral economics findings for patient autonomy, but whether patient decision-making is more or less good or bad goes well beyond considerations of whether it is autonomous. The notion of *decision quality* is a much broader concept for which behavioral economics poses challenges as well. Decision scientists who work on medical decision-making have developed a robust theoretical framework for decision quality.[34] Tools and policies that aim to improve patient decision-making (i.e., to improve decision quality) are often measured and assessed according to this framework, which has been adopted by the International Patient Decision Aid Standards (IPDAS) Collaboration. The two major components are quality of the decision-making *process* and quality of the choice (decision *outcome*). Each of these components includes more specific components. Components of the quality of the process involve (1) recognizing that a decision needs to be made, (2) feeling informed about options and the risks and the benefits, (3) using values clarity (feeling clear about what matters most), (4) having a discussion of goals/concerns/preferences with the health care provider, and (5) being involved in making the decision. Components examining the quality of the choice made (the decision outcome) require that (1) the choice is informed (accurate understanding of options and outcomes, realistic expectations), and (2) the choice agrees with what matters most to the patient.[35] Developers of this framework leave room for other components of decision quality as well, such as high decision satisfaction/low decision regret, patient satisfaction with the decision-making process, and treatment choice made (with the idea that some choices would be objectively bad, perhaps—more on this in the section on harmful choices and welfare/well-being).

How do the components of decision quality fare under the realities of patient decision-making as described in chapter 1? Rather than marching through the list of components one by one, I will draw out several that I think we need to be particularly concerned about.

### Behavioral Economics and Challenges for Decision Quality: Choice Recognition

One element of decision quality set by the IPDAS Collaboration requires that the patient recognize that a choice needs to be made. Chapter 1 shows that patients' decision-making often bypasses the deliberative approach through which a person recognizes that a decision must be made. Instead, without even realizing it, patients go along with whatever the preset course of action is (default bias), what others are doing (bandwagon effect/ social norms), or what their doctor tells them to do (messenger effects). Often, patients do not see themselves as needing to make, or as making, a "decision" in the traditional sense. Consider, for example, the research my colleagues and I conducted on patient decision-making about left ventricular assist device (LVAD) placement. The majority of patients felt there was "no choice to make."[36] And this is in the context of a decision that is considered to involve significant trade-offs, and as such is thought to be highly preference-sensitive. Another example is the study of patients who "decided" to donate their kidney to a loved one; the reality was that the majority made an immediate commitment to donate without deliberation.[37] Essentially, behavioral economics shows that people do not notice or perceive the act of choosing as much as normative models might assume.

## Behavioral Economics and Challenges for Decision Quality: Informed Choice

Another important aspect of decision quality set by the IPDAS Collaboration is that the choice that is made is an informed one. Recall that this means that the patient has an accurate understanding of the options and outcomes, including realistic expectations. I have already argued that the phenomena outlined in chapter 1 call into question how often this component is actually satisfied. For this analysis see the above section on understanding and appreciation.

## Behavioral Economics and Challenges for Decision Quality: Values Clarity

Decision scientists measure decision quality in part by values clarity, which is defined as feeling clear about what matters most. The first thing to note about this component is the distinction between *feeling* clear about what matters most and actually *being* clear about what matters most. The focus is on feeling clear, of which the standard measure used by psychologists and decision scientists is the values clarity subscale of the decisional conflict scale. The questions in this validated survey ask whether the patient is clear about which benefits matter most to her, is clear about which risks matter most to her, and is clear about whether the benefits or the risks and side effects are more important to her. Although the measure asks about *feelings* of clarity, the central normative question is whether it is *actually* clear to the patient what matters most to her. While it is unlikely that the biases, heuristics, and quick processes described in chapter 1 will make patients *feel* less clear about what matters most to them, they may in fact result in patients failing to *be* clear about what matters most to them. This argument is expanded significantly in the section below on well-being and harm (specifically on preference-satisfaction accounts of well-being), but even intuitively it seems plausible that the more a patient's decision is driven by quirks of decision psychology (and is reflexive and intuitive rather than reflective), the less likely it is that she will be clear about her values.

### Behavioral Economics and Challenges for Decision Quality: Decisional Regret

One of the other components frequently measured to assess decision quality in medical decision-making is decisional satisfaction or regret. There is in fact a validated measure for this.[38] In theory, it seems plausible that decisions that are driven by heuristics and biases and made via intuition and impulse may result in more decisional regret. Consider other (nonmedical) aspects of life. If a person is deciding whom to marry and she chooses quickly, without much thought, or chooses as a result of some superficial characteristic or psychological quirk rather than reflection on which person is most compatible with her given her goals and values, the relationship may be less likely to work out and she may be more likely to regret that choice.[39] It is important to note that the framework is referring to *decisional* regret (i.e., regret about the decision or action) in contrast to regret about the *circumstances* the patient finds herself in. The assumption is that decisional regret is a bad thing and potentially avoidable, whereas circumstantial regret is often unavoidable and even desirable.[40]

Some might object that there is some evidence that people actually have *less* regret about choices made nonreflectively than about those made reflectively. Tim Wilson and colleagues conducted a study called Introspection Can Reduce Post-Choice Satisfaction in which one group of participants was asked to "just choose" a poster, whereas another was asked to think about reasons for their choice.[41] Three weeks later, the group that was asked to think about reasons was less satisfied with their choice (measured by asking them how much they liked the poster they chose, whether it was hanging on their wall, etc.). The researchers hypothesized that when people are asked to think about reasons, they focus on the attributes that are easiest to verbalize or that "sound plausible" rather than the things that really matter to them. Thus, they end up choosing in accordance with what there is "most reason" to choose—but those are not really their reasons or desires. Wilson et al. offer a quotation by Goethe: "He who deliberates lengthily will not always choose the best." The researchers use their findings to make the point that there are possibly harmful effects of thinking about the reasons for one's feelings, and that self-reflection is not a uniformly beneficial activity. Others have argued that when individuals spend significant amounts of time deliberating between options, they become more attached to or invested in the alternative choices (the ones they do not end up choosing) and thus experience more regret in their choice.[42] Similarly, proponents of the deliberation without attention hypothesis or the unconscious thought theory argue that while simple choices (e.g., between different sets of oven mitts) may produce better results after conscious thought, choices in complex matters where there are multiple considerations (e.g., between different houses or different cars) are better left to unconscious thought.[43]

Certainly more research is needed on the different styles of decision-making and their relationships to decisional regret generally, and particularly in medical decision-making. It is worth noting, however, that while the studies mentioned above are fascinating and insightful, they are in the domain of consumer choice and not medical decision-making. Making a decision about a poster, oven mitt, car, or house is often different from making a decision about what treatment to choose. Decisions about posters (or even cars) are aesthetic or financial and, in some respect, less serious than certain medical decisions, especially ones that are higher stakes, with the potential to significantly impact one's quality or length of life.

It seems that what occurred in the poster study, for example, is that people at first made a decision based on beauty or aesthetic taste (which *is* the normative way to make that type of decision) and were then led astray by being asked to rationalize their decision. But in moderate- to high-stakes medical decision-making, the normative model (since it is not a decision of taste or aesthetics) is to think about the options, weigh the pros and cons of each, and consider how each will affect one's life. This includes considering how it will impact physical experiences, activities, finances, relationships with family and friends, etc. It thus seems plausible that relying too heavily on gut reactions (which are full of heuristics and biases) might lead patients to decisions they regret. I do concede, however, that more empirical research is needed to determine if this is the case, especially since empirical evidence in consumer choice theory shows the opposite.

The idea of the "impossibility of regret"—a provocative philosophical thesis put forward by philosopher R. Jay Wallace—provides another objection to the idea that decisional heuristics and biases put people at increased risk of making decisions they regret. Wallace argues that there is a sense in which regret about many decisions is "impossible" or unlikely because of what he calls "the attitude of affirmation" that we develop about many decisions.[44] Basically, people have a tendency to look back on decisions and feel that they would make the same decision again because of the good things that have come from it, *even if* they can also look at the decision and say that from an "evaluative" or more objective perspective it was a "bad" decision. To demonstrate, Wallace gives the example of someone who becomes pregnant as a teenager, has the child, and is now an adult "looking back." Wallace holds that it is impossible for the person to regret the decision she made to have a child so young because of the attachment she now has to the child, despite the fact that she recognizes that this was, objectively, a "bad" or unjustified decision.[45]

I think this is to some extent a matter of semantics about what it means to regret something.[46] But certainly it is normatively significant if one looks back on a decision and sees it as bad from an evaluative perspective (which Wallace is willing to grant)—regardless of whether we want to call that "regret." Second, in medical decision-making as opposed to, say, decision-making about careers or relationships, attachments are less likely to result (and in Wallace's theory, it is the resulting attachments that make it "impossible" to regret decisions). I discuss the relationship between regret and decisional biases more in the next section on "harmful" decisions (specifically, as it relates to desire-based accounts of well-being), but for now suffice it to say that regret is far from impossible in medical decision-making and that the decision processes described in chapter 1 cause at least conceptual concern about decisional regret.

### Behavioral Economics and Challenges for Decision Quality: Choice-Values Concordance

A final component of good decision-making that is often measured by decision scientists involves concordance between the choice that the patient ultimately makes and her underlying values. The findings from behavioral economics discussed in chapter 1 cause concern for concordance between patients' choices and their values. An important question here is what is meant by "values," or more generally how we ought to conceptualize the concordance aspect of decision quality. Among decision scientists, this criterion is conceptualized in varied ways, including whether the patient's chosen option is concordant with her goals or preferences—that is, "what matters most" or "attributes of the choice that matter most." All these terms do not mean the same thing, but we need only note that one could mean something more or less demanding when speaking of choice-values concordance. On the less demanding end, we could look for whether the choice is concordant with attributes of the treatment that the patient says matter most or with the patient's expressed goals. For example, if a heart-failure patient completes a values clarification exercise in which she indicates that "bodily integrity" is the attribute that is most important to her, but then she elects to receive an LVAD, that would raise a concern about choice-values concordance. Or if a heart-failure patient indicates that her number-one goal is to see the birth of her grandchild in six months, but she elects not to receive an LVAD, a similar concern would arise about choice-values concordance. On the more demanding end, we could ask whether the patient's choice concurs with her "deeper" values. This links to a philosophical literature that asks whether the things that a person says are important to her are really important to her, or most important to her, or a reflection of her second-order desires (not just expressed desires, but desires that she endorses, identifies with, or is wholehearted about).[47] For example, to refer to the above cases, are the desires for bodily integrity and to see the birth of a grandchild desires that the patient really wants to be motivated by, or are they desires that the patient just finds herself having without much reflection? We can set this question aside, along with the more demanding view of "values," for there is reason enough to be concerned about choice-values concordance even if we opt for a less demanding view.

Even if we take a very thin view of a value—meaning something like a preference or a goal—some of the phenomena outlined in chapter 1 threaten choice-value concordance. Imagine if the decision of a person who is deciding about an LVAD is driven by escalation of commitment (she has already come this far in terms of medical management of her heart failure, so she might as well take the next step) or bandwagon effect (it seems as if most other advanced heart-failure patients opt for the LVAD). As a result, she elects to receive an LVAD, even though what she said was most important to her was bodily integrity. Predictable decisional heuristics and biases would probably result in choice-values discordance. Often in medicine, patients make decisions that clinicians find puzzling, in the sense that the decisions do not seem to match the patient's goals or the attributes of the choice that the patient has identified as being important to her. The LVAD example comes from a real case encountered during my research in which the patient's cardiologist was scratching his head at the fact that the patient had chosen an LVAD when it clearly contradicted her stated value of bodily integrity (among others). Understanding some of the behavioral economics factors that were potentially at play in the patient's decision helped to explain the discordance. The phenomena outlined in chapter 1 are potential causes of choice-values discordance. I will dig deeper into how decisional biases can interfere with decisions that are in line with preferences, values, and goals in the next section, on harmful decisions, specifically in the subsection on preference-satisfaction accounts of welfare.

## How Behavioral Economics Raises Concerns about Patient Harm and Well-Being

Thus far I have argued that behavioral economics demonstrates that patients' decision-making often risks being nonautonomous or autonomy impaired and of poor quality. I now argue that the field also demonstrates that patients' decision-making risks doing harm to both their health and their interests. This is significant because of the fundamental concepts of nonmaleficence and beneficence in medical ethics, which involve protecting patients from harm and promoting their interests. There are, however, several different ways to conceptualize harm and welfare.

### Can Heuristics and Biases Lead to Health-Related Harms?

By "harmful decisions" in medical decision-making, we often mean decisions that result in death, disability, pain, suffering, unnecessary hospitalizations or procedures, and other negative outcomes.[48] Do the psychological tendencies discussed in chapter 1 make it more likely that patients might suffer these harms? Of course, it is easy to think of particular cases where they would. Imagine that a patient decides not to undergo a needed surgery because her neighbor's grandmother died during that same surgery (availability bias). Or imagine that a patient refuses life-sustaining treatment because she incorrectly predicts the impact of an illness due to an affective forecasting error/impact bias—for example, as one study found, she inaccurately predicts that living with kidney failure and undergoing dialysis would be horrible.[49] Or imagine that a patient's demands for unnecessary tests, procedures, and further interventions do her more harm than good and cost a significant amount of money—demands that are driven by a sunk cost bias, an aversion to ambiguity, or a commission bias.

The astute reader might object that this shows only that we can think of particular cases in which such tendencies result in health-related harm, which is different from saying that they systematically result in harmful decisions. In response, I think that in certain contexts in medicine, heuristics and biases more systematically result in health-related harm. One of these is the intensive care setting, where the sunk cost bias, to name one example, will almost always result in harm—in the sense of pain, suffering, unnecessary tests, procedures, etc. I comment more at the end of this chapter about the frequency of bad decisions due to decisional heuristics and biases; I also discussed it in chapter 1.

### How Heuristics and Biases Can Lead to Frustrated Goals, Desires, Preferences, and Values

Harmful decisions can also be defined as those that get a person less of what she wants—that is, decisions that frustrate the satisfaction of a patient's own goals, desires, preferences, and values. This idea relies on desire-satisfaction accounts of well-being or welfare, which involve more than just health-related goods and harms. The philosophical notion of *subjective well-being* is central to this idea—meaning that one patient's goal might be to live as long as possible even if doing so involves significant pain, while another's might be to retain the ability to work, to have sex, or to ride a motorcycle. For yet another, maybe what she most wants is to do whatever makes her family members happy or best preserves her relationships.

Do decisional heuristics and biases make patients less likely to fulfill their goals and desires? In other words, do they make patients worse off according to their own perspectives? I argue that they can, but a few clarifying comments are in order. First, let me draw a distinction between medical decisions and health-related behaviors. If this were a book about health-related behaviors more generally, rather than medical decision-making specifically, this would be an easy argument to make. The phenomenon of hyperbolic discounting alone is responsible for subverting many health-related long-term goals such as exercising, eating right, and not smoking in favor of more immediate short-term gains such as eating tasty but fatty food.[50] Since this book focuses on medical decision-making by patients, the more precise question is: do the decisional processes discussed in chapter 1 mean that it is less likely that patients will make medical decisions that align with their desires, goals, and preferences, thus raising concerns about harmful decisions? Again, I argue that the answer is yes, but with clarification.

The second clarifying comment is to draw a distinction between a failure to maximize the satisfaction of goals, values, preferences, or desires versus harming important ones. This ambiguity needs to be worked out before we can answer the question of whether decisional biases result in this sort of harm. To see the distinction, imagine two different cases of men with prostate cancer deciding whether to undergo immediate treatment (surgery) or to maintain active surveillance of their condition. Smith's cancer is localized and at low risk for spreading. Living a long life is very important to Smith, but he also has a desire to maintain an active sex life with his partner. Smith is driven by an aversion to ambiguity or a commission bias and as a result decides to have the surgery just to "get the cancer out," which increases Smith's risk of sexual dysfunction.[51] One could argue that Smith has made a "harmful" decision because he has not maximized the fulfillment of his desires and goals; active surveillance would have allowed him to satisfy his desire to live a long life *and* to continue to be able to have sex as he previously had. Jones's cancer is more advanced, and he is at high risk for it spreading if it is not removed. Like Smith, living a long life is very important to him, as is sexual intercourse without dysfunction. But Jones decides *not* to have the surgery because of the ostrich effect (he buries his head in the sand and ignores the risk of the cancer spreading). One could argue that Jones has also made a "harmful" decision because his decision is in tension with his proclaimed goal to live a long time. But Jones is a bit different from Smith. The concern is not just that he is failing to maximize the satisfaction of his preferences; he is also putting himself at great risk of losing something that he has identified as being very important (namely, a long life). Smith could have perhaps made a "better" decision were it not for the influence of a decisional bias, but Jones is making a *very bad* decision because of one. I take it that the case of Jones is more concerning and the sort that we should focus our analysis on. That is, physicians are concerned about "harmful" decisions, particularly when patients have told us that something is very important to them but are making a decision that puts the thing at risk.

Now, to ward off criticism that the example of Smith and Jones really just demonstrates the importance of life per se, we could change the example. Imagine two men with equally low-risk prostate cancer who both want to live long, but Butler says that penetrative sexual intercourse is somewhat important, and Childers says it is very important, a central concern. Childers decides to have surgery because of ambiguity aversion and a commission bias; Butler does not. Even though Childers is not risking death, in opting for surgery he risks losing something that he has identified as of central importance to him. I believe that most physicians would be concerned that Childers is making a harmful decision—namely, a decision that jeopardizes the satisfaction of a goal that he has indicated is very important to him.

Having clarified these preliminary issues, let me return to the central question, more precisely formed: do the heuristics and biases discussed in chapter 1 potentially cause patients to make medical decisions that counter, frustrate, or threaten their most important goals or values, thus causing them harm? Another way to state the question is to ask whether the decisions possibly cause "severe harm," defined as harm to a patient's most important goals or values.[52] There are at least two ways in which they do.

First, because many of the decision-making processes described in chapter 1 are quick, are intuitive, and involve numerous decisional shortcuts, they may *cause people [to not take] the time to identify, protect, and promote what is important to them.* Only after the fact may patients find that they have lost something and realize how valuable it was. For example, a man with low-risk prostate cancer may make a quick and reflexive decision to undergo immediate treatment (surgery) to have his prostate removed, or he may make the decision because of a specific bias such as ambiguity aversion or authority bias (his urologist favors surgery). After the fact, he may come to realize that the ability to have dysfunction-free sexual intercourse was really important to him, and had he taken the time to deliberate and clarify what mattered to him, he would have realized that sex was important and chosen active surveillance, sparing him sexual dysfunction. Or a patient may realize after making a medical decision that retaining the ability to work was really important to her, and that the option she chose came with fairly regular hospitalizations, which will interfere with her working full-time. In both cases, the patient's interests are harmed, and that harm was driven by a decisional heuristic or bias.

A second way in which the decision-making processes described in chapter 1 can cause patients to make decisions that counter, frustrate, or threaten their goals or values is that certain decisional biases and heuristics may cause patients to focus on a particular irrelevant thing and *crowd out or dilute what is most important to them*. In other words, decisional biases and heuristics might make it so that patients' preferences, values, and goals are not central to their decision-making. What drives their decision-making may be temporary fixes or distractors. There are two subtypes of this phenomenon. In the first, the patient is so focused on something irrelevant that she is only vaguely aware of her goals or preferences or values and so decides in a way that frustrates them. In the second, the irrelevant aspects of the decision exert such power that even if the patient is aware of and tries to promote her values or considered judgments, she is weak of will and ends up deciding in accordance with the irrelevant thing rather than her values. Consider two versions of the following example that exemplify these subtypes. A patient with rectal cancer is deciding whether to have part of his rectum removed. The procedure would reduce the risk of the cancer returning but would require him to have a colostomy bag. In subtype one, the patient is so focused on the "disgustingness" of the colostomy bag (a focusing effect) that he cannot imagine how he would ever adapt (impact bias/affective forecasting error). As a result, the patient does not even think about which option best aligns with his values and considered judgments (say, to survive long enough for his grandchild to remember him). In subtype two, the patient does think about the importance of being around for his grandchild and leaving a legacy, but he is so influenced by the "disgustingness" of the colostomy bag (due to a focusing effect) that he decides against the surgery, endangering something that he has identified as being truly important to him.[53]

### Objections and Replies

One objection to the argument that heuristics and biases harm people by making them less likely to reach a decision that satisfies their goals and desires ("what is important to them") is that by definition those things must not have been so important since they were so pliable. In other words, patients are not making bad or harmful decisions in the sense of losing or deciding against what is most important to them. If something like a framing effect can trigger a bias that changes or shapes a patient's decision, then the underlying preferences or values that were supposed to inform the decision must not have been that important. A more radical way to state the point is that behavioral economics and the findings described in chapter 1 show that often people do not have established, preexisting preferences, values, and goals that might be compromised by decision processes that are quick, are intuitive, or involve biases and heuristics. Rather, preferences are "constructed" during the decision-making process, often by very irrelevant factors. Preferences and values are not as precious as we thought they were.

In response, I believe that this line of argument moves too quickly. Philosophers (dating back to Socrates) have discussed the notion of weakness of will, which occurs when a person's actions and decisions depart from what she most wants to do, what is most important to her, or what she thinks is best. While some philosophers (e.g., Socrates) believed that this departure means that the person did not actually value (or want) those things in the first place (essentially denying the phenomenon of weakness of will), this is a minority response.[54] Most philosophers (dating back to Aristotle) believe that it makes good sense that someone may believe something to be important but not act in accordance with its importance.[55] I believe that we can view our examples as cases of weakness of will—or at least as quite similar to the phenomenon. In the case of the colostomy decision, the patient does value spending time with his grandchildren, but achieving that, or increasing the odds that it will happen, requires doing something (getting a colostomy bag) that is difficult because of psychological factors (focusing on how disgusting the bag is, inaccurately predicting that he would never adapt, failure to take the time to think about what is important but rather doing whatever the surgeon says). The fact that these psychological tendencies or weaknesses pull the patient away from doing something in line with his goal of staying alive longer for his grandchild does not mean that he does not actually value the goal. It just means that he finds it hard to focus on or carry out his goal because of the psychological factors—a version of weakness of will. It is true that weakness of will is typically conceptualized as being caused by overriding urges or desires, but weakness of will can occur because of other psychological phenomena (heuristics and biases). In short, I am suggesting a more complex and interesting notion of weakness of will [as] established by findings in behavioral economics.

I can imagine that someone might want to push the point further, however, and argue that it is one thing for a person to give in to various psychological factors that exert a strong pull that would result in their trumping considerations related to goals and values (i.e., a traditional notion of weakness of will). It is another matter, however, to take the view that even when goals and values are shaped by trivial framing factors (e.g., whether odds are framed as odds of survival or mortality, whether a box was prechecked as a default on a form, or whether risks or benefits were presented first, etc.), they are still important to the person (so that it is a harm to the person if she does not satisfy them). Imagine that a patient who is filling out an advance directive chooses life-sustaining treatment (LST) only because it was checked as the default on the form. It is hard to be convinced that her "goal" or "preference" or "value" has something to do with life-prolonging or life-sustaining treatment since it was so easy to select that preference based simply on how the form was designed. Essentially, someone might push the point that if a preference is so easily shaped by framing, it is not a true preference that might be thwarted (or harmed) by heuristics and biases. To consider an analogy outside medicine, it is one thing to end a marriage because of a competing value that the current relationship does not achieve (e.g., having a high-quality relationship) or because of a strong psychological or emotional pull (e.g., toward another person). Few would argue that either case indicates that the person never really loved her spouse in the first place or that she did not view marriage as important. If, however, she ended her marriage because her spouse left the light switch on (something trivial), then we might be tempted to say that the person never really valued marriage in the first place as she claimed to. And one could not protest that the light switch incident caused harm by causing her to lose something important to her; all it did was demonstrate that the marriage was not truly important to her after all.

I have a brief reply to the "no true preferences and thus no harm" skeptic, and then a concession. My reply is that again this argument moves too quickly. Just because a preference was shaped by various trivial factors does not mean that the preference lacks importance to the person. Consider, for example, how easy it is to influence whether a person saves for retirement. Studies have shown that, because of the default bias, if companies enroll workers in retirement plans automatically but offer them the choice to opt out, more employees save for retirement compared to those who work for companies that ask employees to sign up themselves (91% vs. 42%).[56] However, if you ask people whether saving for retirement is important to them, they will likely say that it is. To return to a medical example, if you asked the patients in the advance directives and default settings study about the importance of quality of life and avoiding unnecessary pain and suffering at the end of life, most would probably insist it that is important to them, regardless of what they wrote in the advance directive. These assertions strike me as true.

My main point is that we should avoid making generalizations. The fact that we can sometimes easily or trivially shape or manipulate people's expressed preferences, goals, and values does not mean that people do not actually have any preferences, values, or goals. But admittedly (and here is the concession), behavioral economics raises deep and difficult questions about what people's preferences, values, or goals really are and how to identify them. Even if we resist the notion that behavioral economics shows that people lack preferences, values, or goals, it certainly does show us that things are complicated. Decision-makers might express one thing in the heat of the moment and another in the cold of the moment, in one mood or a different one, when things are framed one way or another; they may say one thing in the present moment but another at a future one. This issue will be especially relevant in the next chapter when we examine arguments about nudging or shaping people's decisions in order to "improve" them. Here, the point is simply that the phenomena outlined in chapter 1 cause concern because they can result in harmful decisions. More specifically, they can interfere with people identifying and obtaining their goals, satisfying their preferences, or making decisions that accord with their underlying values.

### How Heuristics and Biases Might Lead to the Frustration of Informed Desires

There is a third thing that we could mean by "harmful decisions" when we analyze whether heuristics and biases put patients at risk for harm. Harmful decisions could be defined as those that result in people getting less of what they would want if they were properly informed, rational, and strong of will. In other words, harmful decisions are ones that frustrate the satisfaction of their informed goals and preferences. The philosophical literature refers to these as *informed-desire accounts of welfare or well-being* (in contrast to accounts that focus on the satisfaction of actual desires, however ill conceived they might be). It is fairly straightforward to make the argument that the behavioral economics phenomena explored in chapter 1 cause concern about the thwarting of informed desires, because many of the heuristics and biases discussed can put decision-makers in the position of being less than fully rational, informed, and strong of will. It is easy to see how these quirks of decision-making could interfere with decisions a person might make if she were in a better cognitive state.

There are, however, a host of philosophical complexities inherent in the idea of informed-desire accounts of welfare. For example, what does "fully informed" mean? Does it mean that the person knows all the key information? And what does "know" mean in this context? Does it refer to a cognitive state, or is it important that the person has had some sort of relevant experience so that we can say she knows in a deep sense what it is like to have one set of desires satisfied over another? Additional difficulties with informed-desire accounts of welfare include the question of how we can know what someone would want if they were fully informed, since that is a purely hypothetical question. We can conjecture, but not much beyond that. The idea of what someone would want if fully informed can begin to feel like an abstract philosophical idea when we try to apply it in practice. These issues are considered more in chapter 3 when I examine the idea of using nudging or choice architecture to steer people toward better decisions, because a popular way to define "better" decisions is as those a person would make *if* she were fully informed, rational, and strong of will. For now, however, my point is that the phenomena discussed in chapter 1 often take a person out of the place of making the decisions she would make if she were fully informed (i.e., they cause concern for patient welfare based on informed-desire accounts).

### Objective Accounts of Well-Being and Harm

Fourth, and finally, we could define harmful decisions as those that *get people less of, or make people less likely to achieve* [items on] *a list of objective goods*. The idea here is that certain things are objectively good for people regardless of whether they desire them. Philosophers disagree about what is on this list of objective goods, but the various lists tend to all be derived from *perfectionist theories of well-being*, which focus on elucidating the ultimate goals or teloses of (most) human beings. For example, philosopher Martha Nussbaum has argued for the following list of objective goods, which she derives heavily from the work of Amartya Sen: bodily health, bodily integration, imagination, thought, emotions, practical reason, affiliation with animals, play, and control over one's environment.[57] Another list, developed by philosopher George Sher, includes understanding the world, the formation and execution of reason-based plans, relationships that involve companionship and mutual respect, developing one's abilities, becoming morally better, becoming more aware of beauty, developing decency or good taste, and privacy.[58] Roger Crisp and other hedonists put happiness on the list.[59]

These lists of objective goods contain items that are well beyond those typically involved in medical decisions. Individual medical practitioners do not usually work to make sure that their patients lead a life that is well-lived, in the sense of developing their moral or aesthetic abilities. It is the case, however, that health is often considered an objective good and named explicitly on such lists. It is also the case that health is an important precondition to being able to achieve many of the other objective goods. For example, it is more difficult to develop an understanding of the world, build relationships, engage in play or imagination, or do good for others when unwell (or dead). And, as argued earlier, in the section on well-being and harm, decisional heuristics and biases can lead to health-related harms. So, in an indirect way, the phenomena discussed in chapter 1 pose a threat to objective well-being because they pose a threat to health.

## Important Distinctions in the Philosophy of Harm

Thus far I have argued that findings from the field of behavioral economics show that patients are at risk of making medical decisions that are harmful to them, and I have been careful to explicate what we could mean by "harm" in terms of different philosophical theories of well-being. One of my arguments has been that decisional heuristics and biases can put patients at risk for decisions that result in death, disability, or pain. This raises a philosophical concern about whether I mean to imply that these outcomes are inherently harmful. Such a view would be problematic for several reasons. First, many medical decisions involve pain, but we would not say they are harmful decisions (e.g., the decision to receive surgery for an appendicitis involves pain, but it is certainly not harmful). Second, death is not always harmful (sometimes it is welcomed). Third, some have argued that disability is only, or mostly, harmful because we live in an ableist society. If we lived in a society that was "ableism-free" and people with disabilities were treated as equals, not subject to stigma, and had ideal accommodations, then disability would not necessarily be a harm.[60]

In order to address these concerns and further make my point about harm, it will be helpful to draw on some important harm-related concepts and distinctions from the philosophical literature. The first is the difference between extrinsic harm and intrinsic harm. A decision is extrinsically harmful if it leads to some bad effect. For example, smoking is extrinsically harmful if it leads to lung cancer. Lung cancer is extrinsically harmful if it leads to pain or a shortened life. On the other hand, something is intrinsically harmful if "its mere occurrence constitutes a harm to the person to whom it is occurring."[61] Pain is a potential example of intrinsic harm—being in pain is in and of itself harmful to the person who is in it. A second important distinction is pro tanto harm versus overall harm. Some event or decision might have a harmful feature (i.e., be a pro tanto harm) without being harmful overall (e.g., a surgery). A third relevant notion is the idea of comparative versus noncomparative harm. Some philosophers have argued for a comparative view of harm, whereby "a harmful event is an event that makes things go worse for someone, on the whole, than they would have gone if the event had not happened."[62] The worse the event makes things, the more harmful it is. Other philosophers have allowed for noncomparative harms as well, whereby an event harms someone just so long as it causes pain, mental or physical discomfort, disease, disability, or death—regardless of how it compares to a universe where the event did not happen.[63] It is easier to label something as a harm in a noncomparative view than it is in a comparative view because comparative views have a more demanding threshold for something to count as a harm. Finally, some philosophers have objected to the idea that an event is necessarily harmful if it causes pain, disease, or death because these states might be wanted or desirable or fine.[64]

With these concepts on the table, let me clarify my argument. First, my argument does not rely on a *particular* account of harm. Instead, I believe that the phenomena discussed in chapter 1 pose concerns for various accounts or notions of harm. In what follows, I will give concrete examples of how various biases and heuristics in decision-making may lead patients to various harms, including *increased risk of* **unwanted** *death (along with the deprivation harms that result from death, such as less time with family or less time to accomplish goals) and* **unwanted** *physical, psychological, and financial burdens and pains.* Second, the "unwanted" part of my thesis is normatively important. I am not claiming that death or disability are intrinsically harmful; if a patient has a preference for these states, I would not necessarily consider them so. In the real examples of harmful decisions that are the result of decisional heuristics and biases (see table 2.1), however, patients do *not* have a preference for these states—in fact, they consider them bad—and their decisions have made them worse off from a comparative view (the more stringent of the two accounts of harm).[65]

I list the examples in table 2.1 because they illustrate my central argument about potential for harm. That is, they span the various theoretical accounts or types of harm. Decisional heuristics and biases may result in states that most would agree are at least pro tanto harmful and probably overall harmful, and that patients have no preferences for. In many cases, they meet the threshold for comparative harm (meaning they made things worse for the person than they otherwise would have been).[66]

### Harm from Heuristics and Biases versus Harm from Systems

From the argument that decisional heuristics and biases may cause harm to patients comes a question about where harms from decisional issues separate from harms from systemic issues. One might object that many of the above-mentioned case examples are also, and perhaps more, the result of factors such as surgeons who are too eager, a profit-based health care system that favors intervention, branded drugs, insurance issues, and the like. In response, two points can be made. First, although there are certainly some cases where these factors are part of the cause, most of the examples provided above (and many more) have little to nothing to do with these structural factors—for example, delaying getting to the hospital after an appendix ruptures due to thinking it is just gas (availability bias), choosing a less effective heart surgery due to availability bias, failing to get vaccinated due to an omission bias, and more. Second, even for cases where systemic factors are at play, the decision-making phenomena in question are still partial causes of the resulting harms. On a counterfactual theory of causation, to say that A caused B is to say, "If A had not occurred, B would not have occurred," *and* there is a chain of stepwise influence from A to B.[67] This is significant because it shows that *were it not for* the bias or heuristic in question, the harm would not have occurred, even if other factors were also at play. For example, in the case of the patient with cancer who decided not to pay for a drug that would keep her white cell levels stable and infections at bay because it had not been originally "endowed"

Table 2.1

Harmful medical decisions resulting from heuristics and biases.

| | |
|---|---|
| **Focusing effect**<br>**Optimism bias** | A woman does not get recommended colorectal or breast cancer screening because of focusing effects (on drinking the "gross stuff" or having the "breast squished") or the optimism bias (believes she is less at risk than similar others), and an early cancer diagnosis is missed.[68] |
| **Omission bias**<br>**Gambler's fallacy** | A patient does not get a recommended vaccination due to an omission bias[69] (worse to "cause" a harm such as a side effect than to have something bad, such as a disease, happen) or the gambler's fallacy (he is on a roll with good health, or he is due for a break with bad health) and gets a disease that is painful, involves burdensome treatment, and may even result in loss of limbs or death. |
| **Commission bias**<br>**Sunk cost bias**<br>**Illusion of control** | A patient continues to pursue a cancer treatment or an intervention in the ICU that is unlikely to be effective due to the commission bias (better to do something even if makes one worse off)[70] or the sunk cost bias (I have already come this far) or an illusion of control (if I just want it enough). |
| **Commission bias** | A patient has a surgery for slow-growing prostate cancer that does not improve his mortality risk but does increase his risk of incontinence and sexual dysfunction (impacting his romantic relationship) due to a commission bias (the need to do something, even if it results in more harm). |
| **Framing effect** | A patient decides to request a name brand medication—when a generic is just as effective but much less expensive—due to a framing effect (against something labeled as "cheaper" or "generic"), thus putting him in financial trouble.[71] |
| **Ostrich effect** | A patient decides not to take or adhere to medication for high cholesterol because she minimizes or misremembers her test results due to the ostrich effect (sticking her head in the sand, proverbially speaking, in denial). |
| **Bandwagon effect** | A patient decides not to take a drug that lowers her risk of breast cancer recurring and spreading because she believes that most other women do not take it.[72] |
| **Base rate fallacy** | A patient picks a surgeon who is not as good as others due to the base rate fallacy. |

**Table 2.1 (continued)**

| | |
|---|---|
| Anchoring bias | A patient decides to leave the emergency room before being seen because she has anchored and adjusted her risk relative to the patients around her who seem sicker. |
| Framing effect | A patient underreports her symptoms because a form asks her to circle symptoms that she has rather than cross off ones she does not have (a framing effect), and her doctor fails to recognize her medical needs.[73] |
| Impact bias/affective forecasting error | A patient decides to forego dialysis or not get a colostomy because he imagines it to be worse than it likely will be (impact bias/affective forecasting error) and dies as a result. |
| Affective forecasting error Optimism bias | A patient decides to get an implanted cardiac device such as an LVAD but overestimates how good her quality of life will be afterward due to an affective forecasting error and optimism bias. |
| Ambiguity aversion bias | A patient decides on a procedure with a low success rate instead of a clinical trial that may have a higher success rate due to ambiguity aversion bias. |
| Default/status quo bias | A patient decides not to donate her organs due to a default or status quo bias (it is easier to do nothing, and "opting in" to donate requires action).[74] |
| Order effects/primacy bias | An at-risk patient decides not to get genetic screening for breast cancer because of order effects and primacy bias (she was informed about the risks of testing prior to the benefits, and as a result weighed them more heavily) and misses an opportunity to lower her risk by taking a preventive drug.[75] |
| Default bias | A patient decides that she wants LST even in circumstances of terminal or irreversible illness because she received an advance directive that presented LST as the default (default bias). She suffers longer than needed. |
| Framing effect | A patient refuses an available organ transplant from a genetically modified animal (pig) when she needs one, but had her choice been framed as a human organ versus pig organ versus dog organ (rather than human organ versus pig organ), she would have consented to the transplant and lived longer.[76] |

**Table 2.1 (continued)**

| | |
|---|---|
| **Endowment effect** | A cancer patient decides not to pay for a drug that would keep her white cell levels stable and infections at bay after chemotherapy because the drug had not been originally "endowed" to her as part of her insurance benefits (endowment effect).[77] Had it been, she would have paid to keep the drug, lived longer, and not suffered from infections and related hospitalizations. |
| **Loss aversion/framing effect** | A patient refuses a needed angioplasty because she was told that 1 in 100 have complications rather than that 99 in 100 have no complications.[78] |

to her as part of her insurance benefits, it is true that the insurance setup was part of the cause of her foregoing the drug, sustaining infections, and being rehospitalized. Had it not been for the insurance refusing to include the drug as part of the benefits package, she would not have suffered. But it is also true that had it not been for the endowment effect, she would not have suffered.

That having been said, it is certainly true that decisional heuristics are not the only cause or even the main cause of patients making decisions that are less than fully autonomous, of poor quality (in process and/or outcome), and harmful to them and their interests. Many other factors come into play, including systemic issues such as those mentioned above, but also poor communication, issues with health literacy and education, issues of justice and access, and so on.[79] Fixing biases or harnessing their power to improve decision-making, rather than hamper it, will not solve all the problems related to patient welfare and autonomy; that is not the claim being made here.

### Acknowledging Other-Oriented Interests

There is perhaps one final point to acknowledge following my argument that behavioral economics yields valuable insights into how decisional heuristics and biases can lead to decisions that are harmful to patients and their interests. And that is that patients can and do make decisions that appear to go against them and their interests for reasons that have nothing to do with problematic heuristics or biases. Indeed, in his widely cited essay "Rational Fools," Amartya Sen argued that if one is keen to develop a theory of rationality then the theory needs to accommodate the fact that choice is often the result of considering the interests of "groups" (units between the individual self and the entire population).[80] Consideration of other-oriented interests often results from commitment or sympathy. Nothing in my argument thus far involves the assumption that choices that yield lower personal welfare are always irrational, bad, or morally problematic. The main point is simply that when they result in lower personal welfare or harm *because of* heuristics and biases, clinicians and ethicists ought to be concerned.

### Clarifying and Concluding Remarks

In this chapter I have made three arguments: that behavioral economics (especially research on cognitive biases and heuristics) shows that patients' decision-making is at risk for being (1) nonautonomous or autonomy impaired, (2) poor quality (as defined and measured by decision scientists), and (3) harmful to patients and their interests (using many different philosophical accounts of well-being and harm). In short, the research shows that patients are making bad decisions far more often, and in far more ways, than has been appreciated in medicine and medical ethics.

It is important to clarify two things. First, I am not claiming that decision-making heuristics are *always* bad. Often we must use them, as we simply do not have time to employ lengthy deliberative processes for every decision we make, and sometimes they work quite well and without harm. In fact, the ideas of nudging and choice architecture, which I will define in the next chapter, propose making use of, or co-opting, known biases in decision-making to improve decisions. Thus, this is not a book against decisional heuristics and biases. Instead, it is a book about understanding and managing them better in medical decision-making. Second, this chapter should in no way be viewed as insulting or be read as an argument that patients or people are "dumb." Gerald Dworkin has made a similar point in debates about (hard) paternalism (e.g., requiring that those who ride motorcycles wear helmets). Some antipaternalists have argued that positions such as helmet requirements are "insulting," but Dworkin pushes back on this. He clarifies that the central claim being made in these debates is that "the group underestimates the degree of risk that is involved in riding without helmets, or that while they properly estimate the risk they underestimate the loss involved

**Table 2.2**
Behavioral economics' implications for the normative status of decisions ("bad decisions").

| Domain | Potential components | Behavioral economics poses concern |
|---|---|---|
| **Autonomy** | Intentionality | Y |
| | Understanding | Y |
| | Appreciation | Y |
| | Freedom from external control | N |
| | Freedom from substantially controlling influence | Y |
| | Considered judgment and reasons-responsiveness | Y |
| | Choice-values concordance | Y |
| **Decision quality** | Recognition of choice | Y |
| | Feeling informed | N |
| | Values clarity | Y |
| | Discussion with provider | N |
| | Involvement in decision-making process | Y |
| | Actual informed choice (accurate, realistic) | Y |
| | Choice-values concordance | Y |
| | Low decisional regret/high decision satisfaction | Y |
| **Well-being** | Health-related harms | Y |
| | Frustration of goals, preferences, desires (subjective harm) | Y |
| | Frustration of informed desires | Y |
| | Harm to objective well-being | Y |
| | Comparative and noncomparative harm | Y |
| | Overall and pro tanto harm | Y |
| | Intrinsic and extrinsic harm | Y |

in death or serious injury or overestimate the joys of riding helmetless." Dworkin asks why this claim (if correct) is an insult. He writes, "It amounts to saying they are making a mistake. But we say that to people all the time without insulting them."[81] Similarly, nothing articulated in this chapter should be seen as an insult. It is merely an articulation of how the heuristics and biases overviewed in chapter 1 might operate to impair the exercise of autonomy, affect decision quality, and result in decisions that are harmful to patients and their interests (i.e., that lead to "bad" decisions).

A third and final point to clarify is that the reader may notice that very little to nothing in this chapter involves a discussion of rationality/irrationality. I have argued that the research described in the previous chapter shows that people are less autonomous than we typically think, for more reasons than we typically concern ourselves with, and are at risk for poor-quality decisions that might cause harm to them and their interests (see table 2.2). I have not, however, argued that it shows that people are irrational. While this argument could certainly be made (and has been made), I do not need to make it.[82] The arguments about nudging and choice architecture that I make in the next chapter get off the ground without claims about irrationality. And such space is notoriously messy philosophically, so I largely avoid it.[83] Although I avoid directly making this line of argument, however, it is certainly compatible with arguments I do make.

In the next chapter I turn my attention to the implications of the arguments made in this chapter. I will argue that the risks (to autonomy, decision quality, well-being) created by unchecked decisional heuristics, biases, and similar phenomena permit (or perhaps even require) a certain form of paternalism. More specifically, they permit (and perhaps even require) shaping, nudging, and engaging in choice architecture of patients' decision-making.

# 3   The Ethics of Using Nudging and Choice Architecture to Improve Decision-Making: Four Arguments for Nudging

In chapter 2 I argued that due to various decision-making heuristics and biases, patients make decisions that are autonomy impaired, poor quality, and harmful to patients and their interests in ways and frequencies that have been underappreciated by bioethicists. In this chapter I argue that, in light of this, physicians and others ought to work to design choice architectures to bolster good decision-making. This amounts to the suggestion that physicians ought to "nudge" or shape patients' decision-making. The aim of this chapter is to provide a moral and philosophical rationale for nudging in medicine.

## Basic Terminology

"Nudging," "choice architecture," and so on are fairly technical terms, so before presenting the arguments, I will begin by reviewing some relevant conceptual terminology. *Nudging* refers to using insights from behavioral economics and decision psychology (outlined in chapter 1) to shape people's decisions. Richard Thaler and Cass Sunstein, the originators of this idea, define a nudge as "any aspect of the choice architecture that alters people's behavior in a predictable way without forbidding any options or significantly changing their economic incentives." They add that "to count as a mere nudge, the intervention must be easy and cheap to avoid."[1] More on the notion of choice architecture in a moment. Yashar Saghai offers a more precise definition: "A nudges B when A makes it more likely that B will φ, primarily triggered by B's shallow cognitive processes, while A's influence preserves B's choice-set and is substantially noncontrolling (i.e., preserves B's freedom of choice)."[2] By "shallow cognitive processes" Saghai means all the phenomena discussed in chapter 1 (e.g., biases, heuristics, emotions, fast or intuitive decision-making—sometimes called System 1 processes) and is contrasting them with more deliberative (System 2) processes. What Saghai means by "substantially noncontrolling" is that the person could "easily" not do what she is being nudged toward ($\varphi$) if she did not want to.[3] I will largely adopt Saghai's definition in this book.

Nudges can take various forms. Cognitive heuristics and biases that are understood and leveraged to shape and influence decision-making become prime examples of nudges. Thus, much of chapter 1 can be read as examples of potential nudges. The UK government has published a useful report with many examples of how nudges can be used to influence behavior. The report, organized around a mnemonic called MINDSPACE (messenger, incentives, norms, defaults, saliency, priming, affect, commitment, ego), outlines several strategies that count as nudges, including examples of framing, priming, the use of default rules, messenger effects, social norms, and pre-commitment devices.[4]

*Choice architecture* refers to the environment in which people make choices.[5] It can include the order in which options are presented, the way the odds or outcomes are framed (e.g., mortality or survival, frequency or percentage, more or less vivid detail), what, if anything, is presented as the default, who presents the choice, the physical location, even the odor of the room. All these aspects of the choice environment can impact the decision-maker's ultimate choice. Choice architects are the people that design or orchestrate (intentionally or unintentionally) the choice environment; in medical decision-making, physicians are very important choice architects. Nudgers are those who construct choice architecture in a way that preserves a person's choice set and is substantially noncontrolling, but that also makes it more likely the person will do or choose some particular option, primarily triggered by shallow cognitive processes.

*Soft paternalism* refers to taking away some amount of liberty either to prevent persons from harming themselves or to make them better off when they are acting nonvoluntarily.[6] Sometimes people use the term to refer to intervening in individual choice in any way that is softer or gentler than "harder" forms of paternalism[7] (e.g., compare a small fine to a large fine or imprisonment), but what soft paternalism technically means in the philosophical literature is restricting liberty in order to prevent someone from acting nonautonomously either out of ignorance or involuntarily. In other words, it is not about the means (soft or hard) but about the circumstances of intervention (whether the person is acting voluntarily or not). A classic example of soft paternalism is John Stuart Mill's bridge-crossing example: if someone were about to cross a bridge that you knew was broken and you did not have time to warn them, you could justifiably tackle them and prevent them from crossing the bridge out of ignorance.[8] Another common example of soft paternalism is preventing a drug addict from consuming drugs on the grounds that in doing so she is being prevented from an (arguably) involuntary action that may cause her significant harm. As I argue later in this chapter, using nudges to prevent bad decisions could be characterized as an instance of soft paternalism: often people are not acting autonomously (or are significantly autonomy impaired) because of various biases, heuristics, and decision processes. Nudging and thoughtful choice architecture can intervene in the trajectory of autonomy-impaired and potentially harmful decisions.

*Hard paternalism* refers to restricting a person's liberty even though the person is acting voluntarily and knowingly. For example, a person may want to ride a motorcycle without a helmet, knowing full well the risk of doing so, but the hard paternalist forbids her from it by making a law that requires helmets. In medicine, an example of hard paternalism would be forbidding a competent, adult, Jehovah's Witness from refusing a blood transfusion.

*Libertarian paternalism* is, with nudging and choice architecture, a concept developed by Thaler and Sunstein. Because Thaler and Sunstein view nudges through choice architecture as gentle ways to shape people's decisions and behavior in ways that make them better off without taking away freedom, they coined the term "libertarian paternalism." They write,

> The libertarian aspect of our strategies lies in the straightforward insistence that, in general, people should be free to do what they like—and to opt out of undesirable arrangements if they want to. To borrow a phrase from the late Milton Friedman, people should be "free to choose." ... When we use the term libertarian ... we simply mean liberty-preserving ... choices are not blocked, fenced off, or significantly burdened.[9]

The paternalistic aspect of the theory has to do with the fact that its aim is to make people better off. We will explore what this means in more depth later in the chapter, but Thaler and Sunstein stipulate that they mean "better off" as defined by the individual making the decision.[10]

With this basic conceptual apparatus in place, I now turn to the arguments. I present four arguments for why choice architects (often physicians) ought to use decision-shaping or nudging techniques in medical practice.

### Preface to the Arguments: Nudging Is Unavoidable, Neutrality Is Impossible

Before the arguments for nudging are presented, an important point needs to be recognized up front: to some extent, nudging is unavoidable. This is not an argument for nudging per se, but it is a normatively relevant fact that must be kept in mind as we proceed with the analysis. As Thaler and Sunstein point out in their book *Nudge*, choice architects have to provide starting points of one kind or another, and they have to frame things one way or another, which inevitably affect choices and outcomes. They conclude, "In this respect, the antinudge position is unhelpful—a literal nonstarter."[11]

As physician-ethicist Scott Halpern has pointed out, in many medical choices, a default option exists one way or the other; he gives the example of whether cardiopulmonary resuscitation will be provided to a patient who experiences a cardiac arrest.[12] Charles Douglas and Emily Proudfoot make a similar point in a study comparing a nudge approach to an "open or neutral" approach to decision-making about open surgical excision versus percutaneous biopsy of a "probably benign" breast lesion. The nudge was to imply to patients that the physicians believed that the excision was not necessary because the risk of cancer was so low (a "risk-tolerant nudge"). The other approach was to provide patients with the factual information, which involved letting them know that "if we want to be 100% certain we should excise it" (the "open choice" group). Of patients in the nudge group, only 2% chose excision, compared to 42% in the open choice group. But, as the authors write, "It was very quickly apparent that patients in *both* groups were being influenced by nuances in communication, such that neither group could be considered the 'un-nudged' control group."[13] Along those same lines, Thom Brooks points out, "Choices are always made within a context. It is clear that the presentation of the context may influence the choices made within that context. Nudges are not merely inescapable, but we might say that we are condemned to nudge." He concludes, "We should not ask whether or not to nudge, but instead how best to nudge."[14]

The first point in response to these statements about the unavoidability of nudging is to draw a distinction between *intentional* and *unintentional shaping of choice*. True, it may be impossible to avoid affecting people's choices, but it is possible to avoid intentionally shaping choice. And if nudging only refers to the intentional shaping of choice by nonrational means, then nudging is avoidable. George Sher has drawn a helpful distinction between *strong neutralism* and *weak neutralism*. Neutralism is the thesis that we (e.g., the state or the medical establishment) should avoid promoting particular conceptions of the good (e.g., by utilizing various forms of influence or supporting certain social structures). But there are two versions of neutralism: strong and weak. According to the strong version, by "avoid promoting" we mean avoid affecting at all. According to the weak version, by "avoid promoting" we mean "avoid intentionally affecting." So one way to put it is that strong neutralism may be an untenable idea given the evidence from behavioral economics that small nuances in the choice environment affect choice, but weak neutralism may hold. That is, *intentional* nudging may be avoidable (and normatively desirable), even if it is true that choice will inevitably be shaped to some extent by nonrational factors related to how the choice architect (unintentionally) sets up the choice environment. The problem with this response, however, is that once behavioral science helps us gain insight into how choice is affected, intentionality is forced, in a sense.[15] It becomes increasingly difficult for us to maintain that we did not know how various factors in the choice architecture would impact patient choice. In other words, we find ourselves in the position of knowing that if we present the benefits first, or the odds of survival, we increase the likelihood of consent. If we present the risks first, or the odds of mortality, we increase the likelihood of refusal. Given that we then have to make a decision about *how* to set things up, we are forced to engage in nudging or shaping choice one way or the other. In this sense, there is truth to Thaler and Sunstein's insistence that the "anti-nudge position is a non-starter."

But this takes us to a second important point about the unavoidability of nudging: that more or less nudging can take place. Thus, while it is true that complete elimination of influence is impossible, it is also true that we can attempt to lessen the amount of nudging in a particular case. Thaler and Sunstein, then, may move a bit too quickly in their claims about the "unavoidability of nudging." For example, imagine that a physician is engaging in end-of-life planning with a patient. The physician sets up the choice of whether to proceed with life-sustaining treatment (LST) or not in the case of a terminal or irreversible illness such as advanced dementia. The physician needs to inform the patient of the pros and the cons of LST, and she needs to do that in some order. She also needs to give the patient some numbers, and she needs to decide whether or not to provide those numbers as frequencies or percentages and as survival odds or mortality odds. All those decisions may impact patient choice. The physician does not, however, need to tell the patient what "most other patients choose" (making use of the power of social norms and the bandwagon effect), and she does not need to show the patient a video of another patient with advanced dementia (inducing an availability bias that will increase the likelihood of deciding to forego LST). These are extras added to the choice architecture to nudge the decision-maker in a particular direction. Thus, an important premise that I will make use of throughout the remainder of the book is that nudging can happen more or less.

Before moving on, let me address two potential moves to defend the possibility of neutrality and refute claims about the unavoidability of nudging. One is what Scott Gelfand has called the "meta-nudge," which posits that physicians could inform the patient about how a specific aspect of choice architecture is likely to affect her choices, and if they do that then the power of the nudge will be eliminated or significantly reduced.[16] The other move is the argument to "frame things both ways," which says that physicians can eliminate nudging by framing things in multiple ways (e.g., as odds of survival and mortality, as the risks first and then the benefits first, in terms of both frequencies and percentages, etc.). Both of these responses are highly theoretical and not practically grounded. First, regarding the meta-nudge suggestion, there is little evidence to support the idea that it will be effective. In fact, some evidence supports the opposite. In one study, researchers nudged patients by changing default settings in an advance directive they filled out, then informed the patients of the nudge, and then asked the patients to fill out the advance directive again. They found that informing patients of the nudge (the meta-nudge approach) neither eliminated nor reduced the effect of the nudge.[17] Regarding the suggestion to frame things both ways, this very quickly gets out of hand when one imagines all the factors that might influence choices that need to be framed in multiple ways. Patients are likely to become overwhelmed and confused by this presentation, and physicians do not have time to engage in such excessive exercises (imagine the time it would take to calculate and deliver all the different permutations of framing of options and information). Nudging, on the other hand, has the potential to improve and simplify patient decision-making, and, as I argue here, can be ethically defensible.

### Argument 1: The Argument from Decisional Improvement and the Rule of Easy Rescue

In the last chapter I argue that underlying heuristics and biases can distort patients' decision-making processes, resulting in decisions that do not match patients' goals or that harm them in some way. If we can understand the mechanisms by which patients make decisions, we can use that knowledge to help lead patients toward decisions that are better in line with their goals and values. In other words, the use of nudging and choice architecture is ethically defensible because it help can improve patients' decisions (the *decisional improvement argument*).

The mere fact that we *can* improve decisions does not by itself generate the normative claim that we *ought* to, or that we have a moral obligation to do so. We need an additional premise. One such premise is the *principle of easy rescue*: if we see someone erring, or know that they are about to err, then we should prevent them from doing so, especially when doing so is easy. The philosopher T. M. Scanlon puts it in the following terms: if we can prevent something very bad from happening to someone by making small to moderate sacrifices, then it would be wrong not to do so.[18] Peter Singer explains it by way of a powerful example:

> If it is in our power to prevent something bad from happening, without thereby sacrificing anything of comparable moral importance, we ought, morally, to do it. ... An application of this principle would be as follows: if I am walking past a shallow pond and see a child drowning in it, I ought to wade in and pull the child out. This will mean getting my clothes muddy, but this is insignificant, while the death of the child would presumably be a very bad thing.[19]

To transfer the idea to our context, if a patient is about to make a bad decision (as explained in chapter 2) and we have the potential to easily prevent it by thoughtful choice architecture or nudging, then we ought to do so. A very poignant illustration of how the principle of easy rescue can be applied to medical decision-making can be seen in a quotation from a physician my colleagues and I interviewed as part of a study on approaches to informed consent for tracheostomy placement in children with devastating neurological injuries.[20] Regarding the regret she had for not being more directive and nudging the parents away from tracheostomy in these cases, the physician said, "It weighs heavily on me ... because in the end, under the guise of good will to respect their wishes [by trying to be neutral], I allowed them to walk off a cliff. And in a way, I may have ruined their lives." She went on to explain that she believed that the parents were not making a truly informed, high-quality decision, because they did not have an accurate appreciation for what the life of the child or the family would most likely "really be like" long-term if they proceeded with the tracheostomy. This lack of appreciation was likely due to a mix of behavioral economics phenomena: affective forecasting errors, an optimism bias, and an availability bias focused on the "best" cases. The physician recognized that she could have fairly easily rescued the parents from this plight by shaping the conversation differently, but she failed to do so and felt as if she had committed a blameworthy moral omission in the failure.

### The Outcome versus Process Objection to the Decisional-Improvement Argument

There are several objections to the decisional-improvement argument, which supports using insights from behavioral economics to shape medical decision-making. One objection is that we need to press harder on the meaning of "improved," "good," or "high-quality" decisions. Recall that from chapter 2, a high-quality decision consists of both process and outcome aspects. Thus, someone might object that while the use of choice architecture and nudging may improve the outcome aspect of decisions, it does not improve the process elements. Nudging via the use of decision psychology will not, in many cases, lead people to be more knowledgeable, or reflective, or intentional.

There are two responses to this objection. One is to admit that this may be true, but to emphasize the value of improving decisional outcomes, which are, after all, a very important part of a good decision. In essence, this response is a narrowing of the scope of the decisional-improvement argument. Decisional outcomes are a very important aspect of a good decision. Some might even argue that outcome aspects are the most important and that the reason that we care about process aspects at all is because they make it more likely that a patient will make a good decision from an outcome perspective.[21] In other words, if a patient feels informed, is clear on her values, and takes a more active role in engaging in shared decision-making (process aspects, discussed in chapter 2), it is more likely that she will make a decision that is concordant with her underlying goals and values, one that she will not regret (outcome aspects). If by engaging in nudging and choice architecture we can decrease a patient's decisional regret and increase her welfare or well-being (i.e., improve decisional outcomes), then we ought to do so, all else being equal.

A second response is to argue that, in certain cases, the use of nudging and choice architecture can actually improve process aspects of people's decisions. In other words, use of behavioral science techniques can help a patient feel more informed, better appreciate the consequences of her choices, feel more clear about her values, and engage in more considered and intentional decision-making. Consider the example of a patient who is shown a vivid video of a cardiopulmonary resuscitation (CPR) to make salient the harms of attempted resuscitation.[22] It is true that the patient's decision about her do-not-resuscitate (DNR) status might be significantly influenced by the case highlighted in the video, but she may also end up with a better idea of what CPR would involve (enhancing her understanding), and it may cause her to think more deeply about what quality of life and aggressive medical interventions mean to her. This would be an instance of choice architecture or nudging that improves certain aspects of the decision-making *process*. Contrast this with a nudge where the physician gives the patient a form with DNR checked as the default, and the patient goes along with the default and chooses DNR without so much as a second thought. Certain types of choice architecture (e.g., the "attention-bypassing" types) such as framing effects and defaults are therefore less likely to improve the process aspects of decisions. Even so, these forms of choice architecture may still be ethically defensible if they improve various outcome elements of the decision without incurring other moral costs, which are discussed more throughout this chapter. The main point here is that behavioral economic interventions can possibly improve both the process and outcome aspects of decisions.

## Concerns about Defining "Improved" Decisional Outcomes

A second possible question raised by some who object to the decisional-improvement argument in favor of nudging and choice architecture is how to determine what end to nudge people toward. Choice architects claim to be able to nudge people toward decisions that make them better off or improve their decisional outcomes—but it is unclear how we should define and predict what will make a person better off. With these ambiguities, the claim that choice architects can make patients better off perhaps seems dubious.[23] This point relates to issues discussed at length in chapter 2 under the definition of "bad" decisions, defined in part as decisions that harm or undermine people's welfare. In chapter 2 we discussed the many challenges associated with defining well-being and welfare. For example, in wanting to protect and promote patient well-being, are we aiming for an outcome that maximizes some objective good? If so, what are the objective goods and how do we trade them off? Suppose we agree that good health and rich relationships are among the things that are objectively good for people. There may, however, be medical decisions that force a trade-off between the two. How does the choice architect know which to prioritize? Should she nudge a patient toward a decision that improves his physical health or his relationship with his spouse? If, on the other hand, we adopt a more subjective account of welfare with the idea that the choice architect is supposed to nudge patients toward outcomes that match their own individual desires, preferences, values, and goals, then which ones do we aim to maximize? Is it the goals and the preferences that patients in fact express ("expressed preferences"), the ones that are implied by their actions or life narrative ("revealed preferences"), or the ones that they *would* likely express if they were fully informed ("informed preferences")?[24] How do we know that their preferences are not just adaptive (e.g., to some impoverished and limited set of options or pressures) as opposed to ones that are true or authentic or worthy of respect?[25] Further, does the choice architect aim to nudge patients toward preferences expressed when things are framed as X or as Y (e.g., as chances of survival or as chances of mortality; see the myriad of framing effects discussed in chapter 1); toward the ones expressed when the patient is in a "hot state" or a "cold state"; toward preferences for the future self or the current self?[26] There is, as one can see, a lot to sort out under the misleadingly simple notion that the choice architect should nudge a patient toward what would "make the person better off," even if we add the caveat "as defined by herself." Defining and determining what is an "improved decisional outcome" turns out to be philosophically and methodologically quite complicated. To add one more point to this complexity before turning to responses to the general objection, consider that in medical decision-making patients are often, in a way, deciding between *lives* and not just between treatment A and treatment B. For example, an end-stage heart-failure patient may have to decide between life on a left-ventricular assist device (LVAD) and life without one. Life with one means that the patient can no longer be a fisherman, but he can do more of other things. Life without an LVAD means that the patient can continue to be a fisherman, but he cannot go on long walks because of his worsening heart failure. His life as an LVAD acceptor or as an LVAD decliner will play out very differently and involve many nuances beyond physical health, including impact on his social life, relationships, and personal identity. In nudging, the choice architect has to take account of life A versus life B, where the patient's life is "better" if he gets more of his preferences satisfied. As the philosopher David Sobel puts it, this would require people like the choice architect to "see to what extent her preferences are satisfied within a life, come up with a number such as 74 percent satisfied, and use that to determine the degree to which she is benefited by that life."[27] It is hard to fathom how a choice architect who is a physician is supposed to do that sort of calculating. In the context of nudging in medicine, some have argued that because of the difficulty in defining and identifying a stable "preference," we simply should not anchor on preferences at all and instead should anchor on some more objective interest assessment.[28]

I believe that this is one of the biggest objections to the idea of nudging or choice architecture in medical decision-making. While I understand that there is a tendency to throw up one's hands and abandon the idea of choice architecture in response to these tough cases, nuances, and complexities, I believe that this abandonment is too quick. For example, few people advocate abandoning the entire ethical theory of consequentialism, but it faces similar challenges in defining "the good" that it aims to maximize. In fact, medical ethics relies heavily on consequentialist assessments when it appeals to principles such as beneficence (maximizing benefits to patients) and nonmaleficence (minimizing harms to patients). This response to the "toward what" objection to nudging could be called the consistency response. If one wants to argue against the ethical permissibility of engaging in choice architecture of patient decision-making on the grounds that there are too many conceptual and methodological complexities in defining and determining "good or improved outcomes," then one must also argue against consequentialist reasoning (and the use of the principles of beneficence and nonmaleficence) on similar grounds.

A second response is that although defining and determining good decisional outcomes is incredibly complicated, there are clear-cut cases that most reasonable people can agree on. Consider, for example, a patient who is refusing a needed surgery because of the availability bias (her neighbor underwent a similar surgery, sustained a traumatic blood loss, and died). The patient needs the surgery to live, and it is a relatively straightforward procedure with a fairly easy recovery. Most of us would agree that we should nudge her toward the surgery. In the circumstances of the case, her undergoing the surgery and living is simply a better outcome than her dying. Another sort of case that most reasonable people can agree on involves treatment or prevention decisions that are strongly supported by clinical evidence as being of high benefit and low risk to patients (e.g., colorectal cancer screening for certain age groups).[29] Moreover, there will be cases where it is clear what a patient's individual values or goals are and what would make them as individuals "better off" given those. For example, it may be clear that for a particular patient, given her lifestyle and habits, oral medications are a better option for management of deep vein thrombosis than subcutaneous injections. Lest someone object that these examples occur only in routine or pedestrian medical decisions, let me give an example of an end-of-life case where we can imagine the best decision given the individual patient's preferences and values. Imagine that a family is deciding whether to proceed with LST for their seriously ill newborn who will very likely have a significant amount of neurological and developmental impairment. This family does not have the financial resources to care for a child with significant needs without major stress and distress for them and the child. We can also imagine that data indicate that a not-insignificant number of families who choose LST in similar cases come to regret their choice. It may be a tragic but perhaps better outcome if these parents do not proceed with LST.

The third response to the objection about the complexity of defining the good or improved outcome given the multitude of theories of welfare and well-being is that although these theories might sometimes provide different answers about what we should nudge toward, they will sometimes converge on one answer. Here we can draw an analogy with a point that the philosopher Derek Parfit made about different ethical theories reaching convergence around one principle, similar to climbers using different sides of a mountain but all reaching the top.[30] Consider, for example, the decision of a woman who is at high risk for breast cancer regarding whether or not to get screened. Her deciding to be screened is a better outcome regardless of the theory of welfare used to analyze the case. Preventing breast cancer–related mortality by detecting a breast cancer early (assuming certain clinical details of the case) will make her happier (a hedonic theory of welfare), satisfy more of her goals and preferences (a preference-satisfaction theory of welfare), and give her more objective goods such as health and time to develop relationships (an objective theory of welfare). Thus, if choice architects can use decision psychology techniques to nudge this patient and other similarly high-risk women toward screening, then they ought to do so, all else being equal. One way to do this might be by framing the risk of breast cancer in terms of relative risk rather than, or in addition to, absolute risk (e.g., "You are 24% more likely to develop breast cancer than most other women").[31]

The "toward what end" or "difficulty defining improved decisional outcomes" objection to choice architecture and nudging does, however, raise an important point: there will indeed be cases where it is unclear what would make a person better off, even according to themselves. In these cases, the expected utility gain of nudging is low. These cases fall into at least two categories: (1) preference-sensitive decisions in which there is significant variation in what different patients choose (e.g., many women will choose a lumpectomy for dealing with breast cancer and many others will choose a mastectomy; some women will choose termination in the face of certain fetal anomalies and others will choose fetal surgery or other interventions) and where we have little knowledge about the particular patient's preferences, values, and goals; and (2) cases where there is a significant amount of uncertainty about the consequences associated with each option, making it difficult to assess which choice is best for the patient. In these cases, it is tempting to take the normative position that physicians should refrain from nudging or engaging in choice architecture of any kind. The astute reader will see the problem with this response: as I noted in the beginning of this chapter, setting up choice in a way that will not influence patients' decision-making at all is most likely impossible. However, as I also noted, we can work to decrease the amount of nudging in a particular case. A good rule of thumb, then, is: the less expected utility gain from nudging, the more we should try to minimize engaging in choice architecture and nudging. We can call this the *principle of minimizing nudging with lowering expected utility gain*.

There is, however, a caveat to this principle. That is, there may be situations where we have little clarity about what would make a person better off (even according to themselves)—and thus we expect a lower utility gain from nudging—but where nudging is still ethically justified because of counterbalancing existing biases. We can call this *counterbalancing nudging*. Imagine a case where a patient is entering into a decision leaning toward a particular option not because of values and goals but because of decision-making biases or heuristics. Consider, for example, a man who has been diagnosed with early-stage prostate cancer and is faced with a decision between immediate treatment such as surgery to remove the prostate or active surveillance (AS) of the cancer. The man comes into the situation biased toward surgery because of a commission bias (doing something is always better than doing nothing) and as a result does not even consider the option of AS despite evidence that it is a viable option (mortality rates of both options are the same, and AS has lower morbidity). Physicians might engage in choice architecture to encourage the patient to more seriously consider AS even though they do not ultimately know what is most in line with his interests (e.g., they may not know how important the surgical risk of impotence is to him).[32] Here, nudging is used in service of balance (not to be confused with neutrality).

### The Problem of Adaptive Preferences for the Decisional-Improvement Argument

A third potential objection to the decisional-improvement argument in favor of nudging and choice architecture is that we will never truly know if we have made a patient better off by nudging because of the problem of adaptive preferences. *Adaptive preferences* are those that are formed in response to a person's restricted options.[33] The worry is that people minimize what they want or what they are happy with based on what they are able to get. For example, a patient may say she prefers one treatment protocol to another just because that is the only one she can afford. In the context of nudging, adaptive preferences might challenge our ability to know if we have truly improved a patient's decision, or if it just appears that we did because after the fact she has developed an adaptive preference for what she chose. Imagine that physicians nudge a woman with breast cancer away from a contralateral prophylactic mastectomy (CPM) of the unaffected breast because they believe that to be a bad decision (it does not lead to significant changes in mortality or chance of recurrence, nor does it reduce anxiety about recurrence even though women believe it will—a predictable affective forecasting bias).[34] After the fact, the woman is quite satisfied with her decision, reporting that she is better off not having undergone the CPM procedure. How do we know if we have really improved her decision, or if she is just expressing an adaptive preference for what she was nudged toward? This epistemic question is important because we do not want decisional-improvement claims to be unfalsifiable because of adaptive preferences.

In response to this concern, there are several points to make. First, it is in part an empirical question of how much a concern this is. That is, what is the likelihood that a patient nudged away from CPM but unhappy with her decision would respond by adapting and expressing satisfaction rather than by expressing discontent? We can change the example to make it impossible for her to go back and have the CPM (imagine that her window of insurance coverage has closed and the procedure is cost prohibitive)— such that her options are either to express a preference for non-CPM simply because she is stuck with it (the adaptive-preferences response) or to say that she wishes that she had in fact undergone CPM. Although the adaptive-preferences response is a risk, in which case we would incorrectly believe that we really improved her decision with our nudge, it is an open question how likely that would be. She might in fact express her discontent, in which case we would know that we did not succeed with what we intended as decisional improvement.

Second, those working with the problem of adaptive preferences are typically concerned that deferral to those preferences might result in the promulgation of injustice or bad circumstances, on the grounds that "the person wants them." For example, a laborer expresses a preference for a low-paying job, or a woman expresses a preference for an emotionally abusive relationship. But no one is proposing that clinicians nudge patients toward some horrible end that they then put up with because of adaptive preferences.

Nudging or choice architecture is to be directed toward the interests of the patient.

### Decisional-Improvement Arguments and the Problem of the Fallible Choice Architect

A fourth possible objection to the decisional-improvement argument in favor of nudging and choice architecture is that even if there were conceptual agreement about what it means to make a patient "better off," choice architects who are physicians are fallible in ways that make it unlikely they would accurately determine what would make a particular patient better off. For example, they may not be skilled at listening to patients or at figuring out (in the moment) what is best for patients based on what they say.[35] Indeed, one study of prostate cancer decision-making found that in 250 clinical encounters, less than 15% involved physicians asking patients how important sexual activity was to them ("preference diagnosing").[36] Physicians may, in the end, simply resort to aggregate theories of welfare, nudging patients toward what would make most people better off in their view.[37]

Second, some argue that physicians are subject to the same concerning decisional biases and heuristics as patients, making it dubious that they can improve patients' decisions. Indeed, a systematic review demonstrated clinician susceptibility to biases and heuristics in medial decision-making.[38] In addition, physicians may be biased toward, or focused on, their own specialty, which may cloud or narrow their judgment about what is best for a patient. For example, a psychiatrist may believe that a medication is best because it improves a patient's manic mood, but it may cause significant weight gain, which puts stress on bodily organs; an interventional cardiologist may believe that a ventricular assist device is best for her patient without realizing the financial and social burden of the device due to the patient's limited means and living circumstances. There are also general biases to deal with, such as racism, sexism, ableism, homophobia, religious discrimination, class bias, and weight bias.[39]

And finally, some evidence shows that physicians do not practice evidence-based medicine as much as we would like them to, and that they may practice defensive medicine much more than we would like.[40]

In sum, most physicians will genuinely and honestly believe that they are doing what is in their patient's best interests, but that may in fact not be true. How, then, can physicians expect to improve patients' decisions?

The first response to this family of objections deals directly with the concern about physicians being subject to the same problematic decision-making heuristics and biases as patients. Some evidence shows that people are less susceptible to predictable errors and biases in judgment and decision-making when they are deciding for or advising others. One study found that when advising a friend on buying a car, people were better able to focus on the most important thing (e.g., safety and reliability) than when they were asked to make the same decision for themselves and were distracted by various other attributes (e.g., legroom).[41] In other words, just because the choice architect is susceptible to making choices in his private life that are influenced by decisional heuristics and biases, this does not necessarily mean that when he helps other people make choices he is similarly susceptible. When we make a decision for another person, or assist them with their decision, we are capable of maintaining a distance that we are not capable of with ourselves. Decision-making for or advising others often generates a critical attitude that is not always present when we decide for ourselves.

The second response to the fallible-choice-architect objection is that even with errors and biases, choice architecture designed to improve choices is likely better than the alternative, which is to allow people's choices to be influenced by random and unstructured choice environments that unintentionally direct them to bad choices, or even worse, to let them be influenced by choice environments structured by choice architects with interests opposite of patient well-being. Consider, for example, direct-to-consumer advertising by drug or cigarette companies, in which advertisers subtly, creatively, and persuasively prompt people to buy their products, consume their goods, and adopt their way of life. In light of this, it would be preferable to have choice architects such as physicians concerned with structuring choices reflectively and responsibly in a way that makes patients better off, even if they are occasionally subject to biases and errors in judgment and decision-making.

Rather than not engaging in choice architecture, physicians ought to do so reflectively and responsibly. This means a couple of things in practice. First, physicians ought to take the time and effort to have discussions with patients about patients' values and goals (the sort of preference diagnosing that did not occur in the prostate cancer study). Preference diagnosing can happen by way of both ordinary conversations and more formal tools such as values clarification exercises, which are often embedded in decision aids. These exercises can supplement or serve as a starting point for conversations.[42] Second, physicians, and all choice architects, should check themselves and each other regularly. I recently met a palliative care physician who told me that his clinical team members regularly discuss potentially harmful decisional biases and heuristics in their own decision-making. He gave the example of discussing whether the team was falling prey to sunk cost bias when deciding to continue to treat a patient who was declining, or availability bias in thinking of only the "bad" cases since those are the ones they see the most. Having a common language of identifiable biases and heuristics helped the clinical team to be more self-reflective about their own decision-making. These sorts of self-checks can help minimize the chance that biases may lead choice architects to nudge patients in a way that they believe to be beneficial but that is really not. This is especially important given the phenomenon of bias blind spot, in which individuals fail to realize that they, too, are susceptible to cognitive biases.

A final possibility that could help alleviate some of the concerns raised in this section is what Robert Veatch has called "deep values pairing." This is the idea that patients and physicians who share similar "religious and political affiliations, philosophical and social inclinations, and other deeply penetrating worldviews" should pair up.[43] As Paul Hamilton has suggested, this could act as an additional safeguard in the context of physician-patient nudging and choice architecture.[44] The suggestion is limited, however, in that while it may help minimize deleterious effects of personal biases in nudging and choice architecture, it is unlikely to alleviate concerns tied to physicians' cognitive biases since deep pairing operates on the level of values rather than cognitive biases.

### The Moral Risk Objection to Decisional-Improvement Arguments

A fifth objection to the decisional-improvement argument in favor of nudging and choice architecture is the *moral risk objection*. According to this view, the mere risk that a person might be wrong in her judgment about an ethical issue, and as a result do something that is morally wrong, generates an important reason for her not to do that thing. For example, suppose a person believes that abortion is morally permissible. There is, however, a chance that this proabortion person could be wrong. After all, the arguments about abortion rest on complex moral and metaphysical principles.

Moreover, there are many examples where society has changed its collective mind on applied ethical issues over the years (e.g., gay marriage, racial equality). Finally, smart and reasonable people disagree on the morality of abortion. As a result, so the moral risk argument goes, there is a chance that the proabortion person might have it wrong. And having it wrong would risk a "deep" or "serious" moral wrong being committed. This risk provides a compelling, though not necessarily decisive, reason to avoid supporting abortion in practice or in policy.[45]

In order for the moral risk argument to apply to the case of nudging, it would have to be the case that if the decisional-improvement argument in favor of nudging happened to be wrong, then some deep or serious moral wrong would be committed.[46] I do not believe that the analogy holds, at least in most cases. Steering someone toward a certain medical decision is typically not a deep moral wrong (like wrongfully taking a life). Second, at least in many cases, assessing whether a nudge would improve decision-making does not involve complex principles such as those involved in the metaphysics and ethics of abortion. Essentially, moral risk objections are most defensible in cases where the risk of getting the answer wrong is significant and the effect of getting it wrong is grave. A lowering of those thresholds presents an undesirable ethical premise: whenever there is any chance that doing something might produce a wrong, we should avoid doing it. In fact, this premise is dangerously close to the omission bias described in chapter 1.

## Are Nudges Really That Effective Anyway? Another Challenge to Decisional-Improvement Arguments

The preceding objections have centered around whether choice architects can accurately identify what will improve patient decision-making in theory and in practice. Another sort of challenge exists, however, and that is to ask whether nudging or choice architecture is actually an effective mechanism for shaping decisions.

There is a healthy debate in the literature about the effectiveness of nudging, with some expressing skepticism. Some have argued that the evidence that nudging can improve population-level health (e.g., decrease alcohol, food, and cigarette consumption long-term) is weak.[47] As a result, some have advocated for more paternalistic or coercive approaches such as laws and bans. For example, due to effectiveness concerns, Sarah Conly argues for "coercive paternalism" (saving people from themselves by making certain courses of action such as using food stamps to buy soda or producing food with trans fats illegal) rather than choice architecture or nudging.[48] While bans and mandates may be applicable in public health settings, this approach is less applicable to medical decision-making between doctor and patient.

Luckily, evidence demonstrates that nudges *can* be effective, particularly in cases of one-time individual decisions (like medical decisions).[49] Nudges have been used effectively to shape decision-making around vaccination,[50] prescribing of antibiotics (for physicians),[51] completion of advance directives (even with explanation that a nudge is occurring),[52] CPR,[53] organ donation,[54] HIV testing,[55] breast cancer screening,[56] colon cancer screening,[57] and many more behaviors.[58] In fact, *all* of chapter 1 can be seen as evidence that nudging works, given that nudging is simply the application of insights about cognitive biases to shaping behavior and decision-making.

Finally, some evidence actually *does* indicate that nudging can be effective at the population level. For example, a recent review of nudge-driven policy interventions from 2000 to 2015 found that nudge interventions compare favorably to traditional interventions in terms of ratio of impact to cost.[59] Areas studied were retirement savings, college enrollment, energy consumption, health and well-being (e.g., flu vaccination), enrollment in job-training programs, reducing fraud/error/debt (e.g., compliance with paying required governmental fees), and crime reduction (e.g., mobile phone theft).

### The Sliding Scale Approach to Easy Rescue and Decisional-Improvement Arguments

The final issue I will briefly discuss with respect to the decisional-improvement argument has to do with the easy rescue part of the argument. Recall that the thrust of the previous argument was that if we see a patient about to err in decision-making, and we can fairly easily prevent it, then we ought to do so.

The reluctant choice architect might object: how bad does the predicted outcome have to be, and how easy does the rescue have to be in order to trigger the rule of easy-rescue obligation? This objection is prompted by a remark made by a cardiologist in the audience of a talk I gave on the ethics of choice architecture. The remark was, "I don't have time to figure out whether to phrase things like this or like that for each patient—percentage, frequency, first, last, using this wording or that—that's a million things to have to consider."

In response, I would argue that at least some minimal form of choice architecture is almost always easy. After all, the risks and the benefits of a medical intervention have to be presented, and it takes little time or cognitive effort to consider what order to present them in, whether to give frequencies or percentages or both, or whether to frame things as chance of occurrence or nonoccurrence or both. There is, however, some additional effort to bringing in "extras" or "additional lines" of nudges (e.g., creation of a video that vividly displays outcomes, gathering information on what "most" people decide and relaying it to the patient, gathering information on decisional regret and communicating it, etc.). There is also time in getting to know a patient and her particular values and goals. For these more substantial sacrifices (in terms of time or effort), we might adopt a sliding scale approach: the worse or more harmful we anticipate the outcome of the bad decision to be, the more obligation the physician has to engage in some additional forms of or attempts at choice architecture.

### Does the Decisional-Improvement Argument Prove Too Much?

A final objection to the decisional-improvement argument might be that it proves too much. That is, if nudge interventions are justified in part because they can get people closer to what their better-deciding self would choose, on either subjective or objective accounts of well-being, then might we be justified in intervening to nudge them toward what their "ideal" self would choose, even if it is totally alienating to their actual self? Imagine a person, Kevin, who does not comprehend the consequences of poor health, lacks self-control, and as a result has an actual desire to spend all his time eating pizza and playing video games. Objectively, and even according to himself in his better moments (i.e., subjectively), Kevin would be better off if he led a healthier lifestyle. So we nudge Kevin to be more physically fit by making it harder to order pizza (placing extra steps on the pizza app on his phone) and easier to exercise (blocking 30 minutes at the end of his workday and buying a stationary bike for his office). Let's imagine we are successful and Kevin grows healthier each day, but he retains his original desires to be lazy and eat unhealthy food. Thus, Kevin grows more miserable as his desire to sit around the house and eat pizza is consistently frustrated.

My response to this scenario is that it contains an ambiguity about what "better off" actually means. One could argue that even though Kevin is better off according to his informed desires, he is not better off according to his expressed or actual desires (all variants of subjective accounts of well-being). Nor is he better off according to whole-life subjectivism (having more of his desires satisfied rather than unsatisfied over his lifetime). These nuances and complexities were discussed earlier in this chapter, in the section titled "Concerns about Defining 'Improved' Decisional Outcomes," and also in chapter 2 (on different philosophical accounts of well-being or welfare). In the section from this chapter, I argue that in cases where it is unclear what would make a person better off, we ought to try to minimize nudging. These unclear cases can result from epistemic causes, meaning the person never made their values and preferences clear, or can occur for theoretical reasons, meaning that the various accounts of well-being conflict rather than converge on a clear answer. Kevin may be this sort of unclear case: he himself does not seem clear on what he wants, and different theories give us different results. In other words, we do not need to be forced to the conclusion to nudge toward ideal Kevin at the expense of actual Kevin.

The second way in which the decisional-improvement argument might prove too much is that if nudges are defensible in clinical health contexts, one might wonder whether we would be justified in nudging people in their personal lives—in, for instance, their dating and educational choices or wherever else nudging could be more effective than rational persuasion. Nudges have certainly been proposed in these realms. The entire book *Nudge*, by Thaler and Sunstein, is about using nudges to improve health, wealth, and happiness. Thaler and Sunstein explicitly discuss marriage, education, and finance. Their ideas include defaults in life situations where a deliberate choice must be made: couples must opt to have a traditional covenant marriage, workers must opt not to join retirement savings plans, high school students must opt not to complete a college application before they graduate, parents must opt not to send their children to the neighborhood school.[60]

The question is whether the arguments made so far in this book extend to those domains. Are those decisions ones where choosers are generally less autonomous than we might think, making choices that are poor quality, making choices that are harmful to them, and where we could intervene fairly easily to improve choice, and where doing so might be endorsed by the choosers? An important difference between these contexts and the health context, however, has to do with the nature of the relationships involved. The nature of the relationship between the parties determines, in part, the moral legitimacy of a nudge.[61] The role of the government in nudging in personal domains is debatable because of this.[62] In the case of health care, the reason that nudging might be even *more* easily justified is that there is an assumption of a fiduciary relationship between clinician and patient.[63] Thus, it is not necessarily the case that there is something about health per se that makes it normatively distinctive, but rather the relationship between doctor and patient. I turn to that argument next.

## Argument 2: The Argument from the Principle of Beneficence

So far, I have argued that we ought to use decision-shaping or nudging techniques because their use can improve patients' decisions. In medicine, this argument takes an additional form because of the ethical principle of beneficence.[64] The principle of beneficence calls for the protection and promotion of patient interests and well-being, including the prevention of harm. Harm is defined as the thwarting, defeating, or setting back of the patient's interests. As Beauchamp and Childress note, although the notion of harm is complicated and contested, almost everyone agrees that pain, disability, suffering, and death count as harms.[65] Failure to engage in choice architecture can, in some cases, be considered a failure to prevent a foreseeable harm. Consider the earlier quote from a physician who felt as if she let her patient's parents "walk off a cliff" by not being more directive about tracheostomy placement for their child with severe and devastating neurological injuries. Or consider some of the examples in chapter 2 of bad decisions resulting from predictable biases. For example, a patient does not get a vaccination due to an omission bias and contracts a disease; a woman does not get colorectal screening due to a focusing effect (on the disgust factor) and misses an early cancer diagnosis; a patient undergoes surgery for a slow-growing prostate cancer due to a commission bias and the surgery leaves him with sexual problems. In each of these cases, had the physicians engaged in choice architecture to combat the force of the biases leading the patients toward harmful decisions, they might have been able to prevent some of the foreseeable harms. For example, the physician could have made salient the harm of not vaccinating by use of a vivid video. In the colorectal-screening case, the physician could have asked the patient to think about the regret she might feel if she missed a cancer diagnosis, reshifting the focusing effect. In the prostate cancer case, the physician could have increased saliency around the harms of impotence or incontinence, or used normative messaging or defaults to make active surveillance feel like a normal or reasonable first approach.[66]

Some might wonder whether it makes sense to frame a failure to impact patients' decisions via nudging and choice architecture as a failure of beneficence.[67] The resistance might be something like this: failure to frame choices to patients in a way that might improve their decision-making is (1) merely a failure of omission and, moreover, (2) an omission that *might* result in an increase in risk of harm (thwarting, defeating, or setting back patient interests in some way) but is not itself a harm.

In response to point 1, consider James Rachels's famous example of the man who watches his young cousin drown and does nothing to save him.[68] Though the man did not cause the drowning harm, he failed to prevent it in an ethically problematic way. In response to point 2, an argument can be made that risk of harm is itself a harm. Adriana Placani has argued that what is harmful about putting someone else at nontrivial risk for harm is that it shows a lack of respect for them.[69] John Oberdiek has argued that what is harmful about imposing risk of harm is that it limits autonomy. He gives the fanciful example of a person who walks through a minefield without stepping on a mine. Still, her options were limited, and that was harmful.[70] Finally, Shelly Kagan has also argued that harm prohibition and prevention should include consideration of risk of harm. He gives the example of an electronic harpoon that has a fixture that lets the person pulling the trigger set the probability of it actually firing. According to Kagan, it is not just that pointing the harpoon at someone's heart, setting it to 100% probability, and pulling the trigger (i.e., causing harm) is problematic. So, too, is setting the device at *anything* beyond zero (i.e., risking harm).[71] Now, there may be debate about at what level (e.g., 30%, 70%) contributing to risk of harm is problematic in various contexts, but the main theoretical point is that beneficence considerations extend to working to minimize risk of harm.

In sum, the principle of beneficence stipulates that physicians have an ethical obligation to protect and promote patient welfare and interests. As argued in the section on decisional improvement, choice architecture can be used to improve the outcomes of patients' decisions—to protect them from unwanted harm, but also to help them further their own interests, goals, and values. Thus, the principle of beneficence, when applied correctly, also supports the use of insights from behavioral economics and decision psychology in the context of medicine.

**Argument 3: The Argument from Justified Soft Paternalism and Respect for Autonomy**

A third argument for the use of nudging is that we would *not* be interfering with autonomous decision-making or disrespecting patients' autonomy since patients do not act very autonomously to begin with (chapter 2). In intervening, we can actually prevent nonautonomous or nonvoluntary decision-making, potentially protect future autonomy, and prevent people from harming themselves from a not-so-autonomous decision. In essence, we can actually *respect* autonomy by thoughtfully constructing choice architectures, and nudging is a case of justified soft paternalism. There are several objections to this line of argument, which I now turn to.

**The "Disrespecting Potential Autonomy" Objection to Nudging**
Some might object that in using decision-shaping or choice-architecture techniques, we are *disrespecting autonomy by failing to foster or promote it*. There are several varieties of this objection, but they are alike in linking autonomy to rational deliberation. For example, Douglas MacKay and Alexandra Robinson argue that it is disrespectful of people's autonomy to take advantage of their cognitive biases since doing so involves bypassing, not engaging, their rational capacities.[72] Till Grüne-Yanoff makes a similar argument, as do Daniel Hausman and Brynn Welch.[73] Hausman and Welch object that when "pushing does not take the form of rational persuasion, [people's] autonomy—the extent to which they have control over their own evaluations and deliberations—is diminished. Their actions reflect the tactics of the choice architect rather than exclusively their own evaluation of alternatives."[74] Geoff Keeling argues that "the failure to respect autonomy lies in the assumption that *but for* the nudge, the [patient] would be incapable of making an informed judgement."[75] Nudging shows insufficient respect for people's capabilities as practical reasoners. Luc Bovens argues that nudging subverts rationality, which is a necessary condition of autonomy.[76] Thomas

Ploug and Søren Holm argue that nudges in medical decision-making fail to provide adequate protection to personal autonomy because, at a minimum, protecting autonomy involves giving people the opportunity to rationally form goals, plans, and values, and to decide what treatment is compatible with those. Nudges do not give people this opportunity since they bypass reasoning or trigger flawed reasoning.[77] In fact, in many cases of nudging, people are not even aware that they are being nudged, so there is no opportunity to rationally reflect on their decisions or to resist the nudge; autonomy is not fostered because rational deliberation is not fostered. This links to concerns about patient understanding, an important component of autonomous decision-making. Some have even gone so far as to suggest that nudging amounts to deceit or "bullshitting" by its apparent lack of concern for patients' processing and understanding the facts or realities of the situation.[78]

At the core of these objections is the idea that in using the very factors (e.g., decisional heuristics and biases) that were identified as potentially disruptive of autonomous decision-making in the first place, we are failing to respect or foster patient autonomy. In other words, choice architecture and nudging merely perpetuate patients' acting in nonautonomous ways (by heuristics and biases as opposed to deliberatively, intentionally, in informed ways, etc.).

To draw an analogy to John Stuart Mill's famous broken-bridge example (in which a person is about to cross a bridge she does not know is broken), soft paternalism permits us to intervene to prevent the person from nonvoluntarily doing something harmful (crossing the bridge). But what does soft paternalism permit after we stop the person from the immediately harmful activity of crossing the broken bridge? Soft paternalists would probably advocate that we inform the person that the bridge is broken. They would not, for example, advocate that we tackle the person over and over to stop them from crossing the bridge, or that we use knowledge of the person's fear of snakes to scare them into not crossing the bridge. Soft paternalism only justifies restricting or disrespecting autonomy when a person is acting nonvoluntarily and there is insufficient time or ability to restore their voluntariness (e.g., in the Mill example there is not time to inform the person that the bridge is broken). Thus, some might object, soft paternalism actually only justifies nudging or engaging in choice architecture when there is not time to return the patient to a more autonomous state before they make a harmful decision.[79] Otherwise, we ought to try to restore or foster more intentional and deliberative decision-making if we really want to respect and value autonomy.

I have several responses to this objection. One response to the objection that nudging disrespects autonomy by failing to foster it is to ask what exactly it would mean to "respect" or "foster" autonomy. I take it that what those who advance this objection have in mind is enabling people to decide less on the basis of heuristics and biases and more on the basis of intentionality, deliberation, and deeper values and goals. Thus, instead of *using* heuristics and biases to shape decision-making, we should aim to "debias" patients, perhaps by educating them about the influence of biases, heuristics, and other System 1 processes on their decision-making. This approach is difficult for at least three reasons: (1) there is little evidence that educating people about the phenomena in chapter 1 works to rid them of them (more on this below, in the section on debiasing strategies); (2) there are so many biases and heuristics that attempting to strip them away from a person's decisional processes is a bit like playing whack-a-mole— you could work very hard to identify one and eliminate it, and when you do so another may pop up;[80] (3) because there are so many framing effects and biases that are triggered by so many small and nuanced aspects of the choice architecture, it is difficult to avoid them all, since things must be framed one way or another. The physician must present options in a particular order and with a particular tone of voice, etc. This is not to say that certain types of nudging cannot be avoided—more on this in the sections "Why Not (and When) to Use Rational Persuasion" and "When Not to Nudge (or When to Minimize Nudging)"—but it is to press on the reality of the questionable dichotomy: either we foster autonomy or we have a decision-making process that involves heuristics and biases. As Shlomo Cohen notes in his defense of nudging,

> Think what a true commitment to minimizing nonrational influences on the patient's decision-making would entail: it would start from severe restrictions on possible locations for the clinic (e.g., a fancy location sends a nonrelevant message that biases decision-making), and continue with removal of awe-inspiring diplomas from the walls, severe restrictions on the doctor's attire, his forms of speech, the sense of urgency or calm or reassurance in his voice, and so on. All of those and many more contribute to nonrational influences to the patient's medical decision-making and so would be incongruous with the (hypothetical) duty to facilitate autonomous decision-making maximally. But thinking we could and

should standardize all such factors according to some ideal of neutral influence is frankly insane. Nobody expects or intends this; this would be an ideal of respect for autonomy going berserk.[81]

A second response to the objection about failing to respect potential autonomy by failing to engage or improve reasoning capacities is that, as George Sher argues, even if a person is nonautonomous with respect to a decision or action at time 1 (because of nonrational influence like a nudge), the person may become autonomous at time 2 as she becomes aware of the value-based reasons for the decision or action (or comes to value it "from the inside"). In other words, nonrational influence can enhance later capacity to respond to reasons—for those committed to reasons-responsive accounts of autonomy.[82] Sher gives the example of how a child might first act truthfully to please her parents but later (as an adult) might come to endorse the value of truth itself. Sher also argues that it is respectful of people to bring them to whatever they have reason to believe is good.[83] To this, I would add that even if the person's choice is not *grounded in* a good reason (i.e., the person does not come to see the value from the inside), their choice may still *reflect* a good reason—and in that sense be reasons-responsive. In other words, if a choice architect is guided by the patient's values, goals, and interests, then the nudged patient *is* acting *on the basis of* those reasons even if she did not conjure them up, insert them into her thinking, and make them the main cause of her choice in the moment. In this sense, (good) reasons *are* guiding her choice. In this way, nonrational influence can be compatible with autonomy in the immediate (nudged) decision, not just in future decisions, as Sher argues.

Adopting an account of autonomy that does not center on reasons-responsiveness is another way for nonrational influence to be compatible with autonomy, as I argue below in the section on endorsement. In this view, what matters for autonomy is the person's reflective attitude toward her decision-making processes. As long as she endorses the processes that drive her decision, she can qualify as autonomous regardless of whether those processes were particularly deliberative or reasons-responsive.

A fourth response to the objection that nudging disrespects autonomy by failing to restore or foster it (again, under a model of autonomy that prioritizes information acquisition, rational deliberation, and values clarification/goal setting) is that this *sort* of autonomy is often not desired by or valued by patients. Carl Schneider's seminal work, *The Practice of Autonomy:*

*Patients, Doctors, and Medical Decisions*, finds that patients often do not want to assume the full burden of decision-making and be "in power."[84] Patients do value being informed about what is going on, and they do not want to have their choices overridden or their physical or emotional privacy invaded (i.e., they value "negative liberty"). It is less certain, however, how much they value the notion of being self-legislating or in charge ("positive liberty"), or that they desire a significant amount of information or deep deliberation in medical decision-making. One study of 312 outpatients presented with various vignettes found that the mean score on a 0–100 scale was 33 (where 100 indicated a very high preference for being the one to make decisions, 50 was neutral, and 0 indicated a very low preference).[85] Similarly, studies of patients with cancer have consistently revealed that the majority of patients want physicians to make treatment decisions on their behalf, a minority prefer a roughly equally shared decision-making burden, and very few wish to take major decision-making roles themselves.[86]

Several factors about medicine and medical decision-making help explain these findings: patients are often in a vulnerable position (emotionally, cognitively) and are asked to make a lot of rapid-fire and heavy decisions in domains where they feel they have little experience and expertise. This is in contrast to other domains of decision-making such as career or whether and whom to marry ("life projects" sorts of decisions), in which people may be inclined toward more involvement in heavy deliberation and may value being in charge of decision-making—and where autonomy as the exercise of deliberative agency may be more normatively valuable. This is not to say that patients never value being drivers of decision-making and heavy deliberation; it is just to recognize that often they do not.

Fifth and finally, we also need to distinguish between scenarios and contexts in which being more autonomous (in the ideal self-reflective and controlled sense) is particularly desirable or valuable from ones where it matters less. Compare, for example, a decision about what to eat for dinner to a decision about where to attend college. The latter decision is a higher-stakes or higher-value choice in which the positive exercise of autonomy is more valuable and more important.[87] As a result, an autonomy violation such as forbidding one option (or a failure to foster autonomy) would be more harmful to the person in the college-decision case than it would in the dinner-decision case.[88] As Madison Powers and colleagues point out, even Mill, the great defender of individual liberty, distinguished between liberties that are immune from interference, liberties that warrant a presumption in favor of liberty, and liberties that do not deserve a presumption in favor of them when it comes to balancing them with public interests. The ones that deserve more protection are related to identity, expression, and life projects and plans.[89]

Thus, *even if* engagement in choice architecture or nudging disrespects autonomy by failing to foster it, this may only be morally problematic in the context of high-stakes or high-value choices. It is tempting to think that all medical decisions are by their very nature high-stakes or high-value choices, but this position is dubious both theoretically and empirically. For example, whether to get a simple screening test or take a blood pressure medication is probably closer to a decision about what to eat for dinner rather than a decision about where to go to college. A physician using nudging techniques rather than putting in time to restore and foster deliberative decision-making is less objectionable in these cases because they are not high-stakes or high-value choices. Other cases will involve more debate.[90] Consider, for example, deceased organ donation. Is the decision about whether to be an organ donor a high-stakes or high-value choice where the positive exercise of autonomy is particularly valuable and important, thus creating an obligation to try to foster it rather than engage in choice architecture that bypasses it?[91] An interesting argument has been made that autonomy is *not* valuable in these cases, since at the time when the choice is actually respected or overridden (the autonomy-relevant time point), the potential donor will be deceased and as such unable to experience the harm of an autonomy violation.[92] Although this particular argument is controversial, the main point here is that there are cases of various sorts—some in which fostering the exercise of deliberative, "positive" autonomy is more valuable and others in which it is less so.

Before moving on, I need to address a potential paradox in my argumentative strategy thus far. In chapter 2 I argue that behavioral economics demonstrates that when it comes to medical decision-making (or decision-making generally), people are not as autonomous as we typically assume them to be the various decisional processes, heuristics, and biases outlined in chapter 1. I am now arguing that the use of these very same phenomena by choice architects (which turns them into nudges) can be perfectly compatible with autonomy. Are these arguments incompatible?

First, we must remember that with nudging, the driving force behind the decision-making can still be the patient's preferences (the choice architect sets up the architecture to aim toward the patient's preferences and interests). This is not the case when heuristics and biases occur organically in the patient's decision-making. Rather, these shallow cognitive processes often orient the patient away from ends that are good for her or that she would endorse. In this sense, intentional nudging is more reasons-responsive than organically occurring biases that shape decision-making—and as such, the former can be less of a threat to autonomy than the latter.[93]

Second, in nudging, as discussed above, the patient may later see the value in (i.e., may become reasons-responsive to) what she is nudged toward (assuming the clinician nudges the patient toward what is in line with her values and interests). Conversely, random shallow cognitive processes take hold on their own, undirected and unchecked. They often bias the patient toward choices that are against her interests, obviating the opportunity to later come to respond to the value of those choices as required by reasons-responsive accounts of autonomy.

Finally, patients might endorse nudges (and associated shallow cognitive processes) when used by choice architects to benevolently shape and improve their decision-making, but not endorse them when they occur organically and thwart their interests or distort their decision-making. For accounts of autonomy that focus on endorsement of decision-making processes, the former would be compatible with autonomy and the latter would not. And, as I argue below in the section on endorsement, some empirical evidence supports the view that people *do* endorse nudge processes so long as their aims are important and legitimate, promoting their interests rather than thwarting them. While these remarks may not resolve the entire paradox, I believe they go a long way in showing that the two positions are not inconsistent; heuristics, biases, and other behavioral economics phenomena can both pose a threat to autonomy and be used to rescue or respect autonomy.[94]

I have spent a good amount of time arguing that nudging does not necessarily threaten autonomy. But it is also worth noting that there are goods and values other than autonomy *and* that autonomy comes in degrees. As Sher notes, "Even policies that do diminish autonomy may increase people's chances of living valuable lives."[95] Thus, even if one continued to think that nudging diminished autonomy, there would be further questions: to what extent does it do so, and do the other values (e.g., of an improved decisional outcome) outweigh those concerns?[96]

### The "Piling On More Autonomy Impairments" Objection to Nudging

So far, I have examined the claim that nudging disrespects autonomy by failing to try to restore or foster it. But there is a second way in which using decision-shaping or choice-architecture techniques might disrespect autonomy, even if one takes the view that they cannot "violate" it since the person is acting with autonomy impairments to begin with. That is, by adding more autonomy-impairing factors (more biases and heuristics), as choice architecture does, perhaps we are making it even more difficult for the person to recover and engage in more autonomous decision-making. I call this the "piling-on" objection to the soft-paternalism defense of nudging. One way to think about it is when a potential choice architect such as a physician encounters a patient who is significantly under the influence of the phenomena discussed in chapter 1, she is dealing with a person who is at zero or neutral in terms of autonomy (because of existing biases and heuristics), and by exposing the patient to even more biases and heuristics she is putting him in the negative.

In response, I believe that piling on is the wrong analogy. A more accurate portrayal of what the physician does in this context is switching or trading. Consider the example of someone who smokes because he has been nudged by tobacco companies to do so through advertisements showing "cool people like him" smoking, thus normalizing the behavior (through the use of social norm bias/bandwagon effect). Imagine that this man goes to his annual wellness visit with his physician, and the physician nudges him to stop smoking by emphasizing that nowadays most "highly educated people like you" do not smoke (again, using the social norm bias/bandwagon effect). The most accurate way to describe this situation and the psychology involved is that the physician has traded one bias for another (a social desirability bias toward smoking for a social desirability bias against smoking). In addition to the piling-on objection not being the best construct theoretically, I am aware of no empirical evidence that indicates a positive correlation between the number of System 1 factors influencing people's decision-making and their ability to dig through those factors to rationality.

### The Puppeteer Objection to Nudging

There is a third way in which using decision-shaping or choice-architecture techniques might be thought to disrespect autonomy, even if one thinks that autonomy cannot be violated since the person is not acting autonomously to begin with (the soft-paternalist defense of nudging). Someone might argue that a significant difference exists between accidental choice architecture that influences a person's decisions in a way that renders them nonautonomous and intentional manipulation of the choice architecture (puppeteering) that influences a person's decision-making. Even if a person is rendered nonautonomous (leaving room for justified soft paternalism), it is an entirely different matter to bring a puppeteer into the picture. This is more threatening to autonomy. As Hamilton argues, the use of nudges places physicians in a position of domination over patients. That is, it violates the republican freedom of patients because it grants physicians the power to arbitrarily interfere.[97]

Compare two cases. The first is a patient with localized, low-risk prostate cancer who chooses to undergo active surveillance of the cancer rather than immediate surgery to remove it because he happened to hear a story on the news about a man like him who made that decision. In other words, he made the decision based on an availability heuristic and the power of norms rather than making the decision in a more autonomous way (e.g., taking the time to really understand the facts and the figures and what they mean for his life and his values). Second, imagine that this same patient chooses to undergo active surveillance because he goes to a doctor who intentionally tries to get him to choose active surveillance by using his knowledge of decision psychology (the doctor just attended a lecture on behavioral economics). The doctor does this by telling the man stories about several patients who held off on immediate treatment, in an attempt to trigger an availability bias in favor of active surveillance. Maybe the doctor does this because he believes that the patient is coming in with a preexisting availability bias in favor of surgery. At one level, the cases seem the same with respect to the autonomy analysis—put simply, the man is not making a very autonomous decision (he is making it because of an availability heuristic). In the second case, however, it seems that something more troubling is happening with respect to autonomy: it is a case of another person (the physician) using their knowledge and power to intentionally steer the patient's decision-making and behavior.

I would make two points in response to this objection. First, several scholars argue that whether our actions are controlled (or heavily influenced) by another person or a random environment is not very significant. A lack of autonomy is a lack of autonomy, regardless of the source.[98] As Harry Frankfurt writes, "We are inevitably fashioned and sustained, after all, by circumstances over which we have no control. ... It is irrelevant whether those causes are operating by virtue of the natural forces that shape our environment or whether they operate through the deliberatively manipulative design of other human agents."[99]

Second, in the medical context, patients may not share the perspective that in utilizing insights from behavioral economics to improve their choices, physicians are acting like puppeteers in an objectionable way.[100] In fact, many philosophers have argued that a person acts autonomously (or "from herself" or "on her own accord") as long as she does not mind acting for the reasons that she does. Thus, we can imagine many cases where a patient has no objection to her decision being driven by her physician's recommendations and use of choice architecture. This intersects with a point made in the section "'Medical Decisions Are Different' Objection to the Endorsement Argument" later in this chapter about patients often not valuing positive autonomy as it is traditionally conceptualized (i.e., being rational, deliberative, and in control). This is ultimately an empirical question, but I hypothesize that many patients would not take issue with their physician's use of nudging. I turn to a more extensive analysis of the relevance of this point in the next section.

Before moving on, however, let me raise an objection that is related to but slightly different from the ones just discussed. Some might argue that even though nudges need not necessarily disrespect (and may even protect or promote) *autonomy*, they disrespect the *person* in some deeper way by, for example, infantilizing them, exploiting their weaknesses, or treating them unjustly. Nudges may be insulting or infantilizing to people, implying that they cannot handle more advanced, deliberative ways of improving their own decision-making. Nudges are the sort of thing we do with children who are not yet capable of rational deliberation. For example, rather than explain the benefits of eating vegetables to my two-year-old and leave it up to him as to whether he eats them, I ask if he wants to eat them like *either* a bunny or a dinosaur (a framing that works marvelously). The default I set is *that* he eats them; he only chooses *how*. Employing these sorts of insights about choice architecture with adults is infantilizing, so the objection goes, regardless of whether doing so necessarily impairs their autonomy. Relatedly, doing so takes advantage of or exploits identified weaknesses, which again, even if not necessarily autonomy-reducing, is disrespectful. And finally, Evan Riley has argued that nudges are a form of "epistemic injustice" in that they fail to support the development and/or exercise of reflective capacities for critical reasoning.[101] Thus, it is not just that nudges interfere with autonomy; it is that they are disrespectful or even unjust in some deeper (or other) way. Cass Sunstein has recently called these concerns "dignity related concerns."[102]

There are several responses to these concerns. First, as we will see below, in the discussion of endorsement, patients may simply not feel infantilized or disrespected by their physician who employs a beneficent nudge. To insist that nonetheless such nudges *are infantilizing* or disrespectful to patients as persons (more generally, apart from autonomy concerns) would require quite a bit of argument. And as Gerald Dworkin has argued (and I discussed in chapter 2), it is unclear why it is insulting to say that someone has made a mistake or is prone to make a mistake (or, I would add, to say that judgment and decision-making do not typically work in the ideal way that some economists and philosophers have presumed—and to respond accordingly).[103] Second, as I have argued at various points throughout the autonomy section, nudges can be used to help protect and promote what is most important to people and most in their interest. In this sense, the use of nudges and choice architecture is extremely respectful of persons; the opposite of disrespectful. To care about how patients' lives go and to want them to make choices that reflect their interests and values is a way of respecting them as persons. Third and finally, this will depend in part on *how* the nudging is done. It is easy to imagine cases where it is done in a condescending way, but it is equally easy to imagine cases where it is not. It is also easy to imagine cases where the clinician doing it believes that the patient is not as smart or is somehow lesser, but it is equally easy to imagine cases where the clinician harbors no such beliefs.

### Argument 4: Patients Don't Mind and the Principle of Endorsement

The fourth and final argument for why we ought to use decision-shaping, choice-architecture, or nudging techniques to bolster good decision-making is that patients may often have no objection to acting because they were benevolently nudged by their doctor. Rather, they would accept this method by which they came to their decision. I call this the *principle of endorsement*, and it can be used to argue that the resulting choice is autonomous.[104] Many philosophers have argued that as long as a person endorses the reasons for which she acts rather than resists those reasons, and as long as that endorsement is not under the controlling influence of another, she is autonomous with respect to the corresponding action.[105] The principle of endorsement also can be used more generally, simply to justify the ethical permissibility of a nudge.

To bolster the argument, consider the general point that quite often people do not mind acting from processes that are emotional, intuitive, heuristic-like, etc. As philosopher Sarah Buss points out, many well-informed, self-governing agents would endorse a policy that involved being influenced by nonargumentative forms of influence. We should simply remind ourselves of the wide range of circumstances where nonargumentative influence occurs and by which we are not the least bit threatened. In fact, we often welcome or value it, such as when we are seduced by a lover.[106]

Some concrete empirical evidence shows that people might not mind nudges influencing their decision-making processes. Although this evidence is not about medical decisions in particular, it is instructive. In a chapter titled "Do People Like Nudges? Empirical Findings" in Cass Sunstein's *The Ethics of Influence: Government in the Age of Behavioral Science*, Sunstein discusses the results of a nationally representative survey that tested 34 nudges with 563 Americans. Sunstein concludes that the survey shows that "most people have no views, either positive or negative, about nudging in general; their assessment turns on whether they approve of the purposes and effects of particular nudges. ... So long as people believe that the end is both legitimate and important, they likely favor nudges in its direction." People reject nudges when the ends include political or religious favoritism, nudges that are inconsistent with the interests or values of most people, and nudges in which people's decisional biases are used against them to get something from them (e.g., their organs for donation). The main point is that people do not have a general objection to being nudged in their decision-making. Sunstein notes, "This is an important finding, because it suggests that most people do not share the concern that nudges, as such, should be taken as unacceptably manipulative or as an objectionable inter-ference with autonomy."[107]

The more general point here is about the moral relevance of the relation-ship between the nudger and the nudged, which will likely play a critical role in answering the endorsement question. For example, people may not be fine with the government nudging them to stop smoking, but they may be fine with their doctor doing so. The underlying question is what the person who is nudged could reasonably expect and view as appropriate in the con-text of the relationship. I have discussed the moral relevance of the relation-ship between the two parties elsewhere.[108]

### The "Medical Decisions Are Different" Objection to the Endorsement Argument

It is one thing to endorse your romantic choices as the result of emotion or your recycling choices as the result of the government engaging in a social-norming campaign. When it comes to medical decision-making, though, some might argue that most people would not endorse having their choice be the result of their doctor's intentionally using a reason-bypassing strategy to get them to make a particular decision. In medical decision-making in partic-ular, people want to "act for reasons" rather than have their decision driven by a reason-bypassing process such as choice architecture. We can call this the "medical decisions are different" objection to the endorsement argument.

But the claim that people often want their medical decisions to be rooted in reasons rather than choice architecture is not necessarily true. One study showed that patients whose decision-making was driven by a feature of intentional choice architecture (a default option set in their advance direc-tive) were just as content with their decision-making processes as those who chose more "autonomously" (were forced to make an active choice about life-sustaining treatment).[109]

There is, however, a framing effect to the endorsement question that makes it difficult to determine the truth about the patient's attitude regard-ing whether her decision is being driven by a process of nudging or by nonargumentative influence.[110] For example, if the process were described as follows, the patient might object to the circumstances under which she came to consent to a surgery: "Your decision to consent to surgery was formed by a process in which your physician framed it in a certain way (i.e., survival rates instead of mortality rates) to increase the likelihood that you would consent to surgery." But if it were explained in the following way, the patient may be less likely to object: "Your decision to consent was formed by a process wherein your physician decided to frame things in terms of survival because she did not want to frighten you, and she thought the surgery was most in line with your values and goals."

To add to the complexity of this empirical task, consider that when we are asking if a patient endorses their decision-making process, there are subparts to that question, some of which the patient might endorse and others not. For example, we need to assess whether the person minds acting because of the *nudge* or *heuristic* that is triggered (e.g., the patient doesn't care that she acted because of a default effect), and also whether the person minds acting because of that heuristic *in the particular context* (e.g., the patient doesn't care that she acted due to a default effect because her doctor intentionally used the default effect to get her to choose some treatment). Even further, we may receive different answers if we describe the *broader context* (e.g., noting that the patient is also likely nudged by lawyers, advertisers, and a wide variety of others in life).[111] The general point, however, is that we may reasonably think there are cases where a patient would have no objection to, or would even welcome, acting because of a benevolent nudge from her doctor. We may not know with certainty whether a patient would endorse such nudging in a particular case,[112] but we may be able to make well-reasoned guesses.

### Why Not (and When) to Use Rational Persuasion

In chapter 2 I argue that behavioral economics shows that patients' decisions can fail to be autonomous or improve their well-being in ways beyond what has been appreciated, and that this permits, or even requires, that something be done. Enter the justification for nudging and choice architecture (this chapter). Some may agree that *something* must be done but may argue that the preferred approach is one of rational persuasion rather than engaging in shaping, nudging, and choice architecture. Persuasion, or what is sometimes called "rational persuasion," is defined as inducing someone to do something through reasoning or argument.[113] Thus, if we find a patient making a bad decision (e.g., a decision to not vaccinate her child) because of a decisional bias (e.g., the omission bias), we ought not to employ nudging techniques such as framing vaccination as the default

("We're going ahead with the following vaccinations today" and waiting to see if the parent objects or interjects with questions) or making salient the harms of not vaccinating by using vivid videos of children with the diseases in question.[114] Rather, we ought to provide the parent with reasons for vaccinating her child. These might include the following: vaccination is recommended by the American Academy of Pediatrics; it reduces the risk that children will contract serious diseases that can cause significant morbidity and mortality; the evidence shows that vaccination is not associated with autism; you have an obligation to protect and promote your child's well-being, and vaccination is most in line with those values; you have an obligation to other children and society to vaccinate in order to reach herd immunity against terrible diseases. This more persuasive approach aims to provide reasons to convince a patient to make a choice that the physician believes is best rather than to trigger shallow cognitive processes such as the default bias or the emotions of fear or disgust.

There are two reasons someone might give for opting for rational persuasion rather than using behavioral economics techniques to improve patient decision-making. First, someone might argue that rational persuasion effectively achieves all the goods aspects of the choice-architecture approach without the potentially negative aspects. For example, the use of rational persuasion can improve decisions (both outcome *and* process elements); it fulfills the rule of easy rescue (providing reasons to someone is an easy way to prevent an anticipated harmful decision); it discharges the duty of beneficence (to protect and promote patient interests by advising them against harmful choices); it prevents patients from making autonomy-impaired decisions that might be harmful (justified soft paternalism); and it avoids potential "disrespect" of patient autonomy (it respects autonomy—or traditional views of autonomy—by fostering decision-making that is driven by reasons, reflection, goals, values, etc.).

Second, someone might point out additional reasons to prefer rational persuasion to other modes of influence. Philosophers dating back to Plato have been critical of approaches that rely on modes of influence other than rational persuasion. Plato's argument is presented in several of the dialogues. In *The Republic* he distinguishes between philosophy and poetry (a form of rhetoric). Poetry (and rhetoric) affects "the soul" by way of emotion. What is troubling about these forms of influence is that they can create difficulty in judging truth from falsehood.[115] Emotions can cause us to lose our critical stance. In the dialogue *Gorgias*, Plato makes the point that in rhetoric (often practiced by the Sophists) the goal is simply to win arguments, whereas in philosophy the goal is better understanding, or knowledge.[116]

In response to this line of argument, first, it is not clear that rational persuasion does sufficiently achieve all the goods of the choice-architecture approach. If behavioral economics has taught us anything, it is that giving people information is often insufficient to improve their decisions. Rational persuasion is often up against the more powerful System 1 decision influences discussed in chapter 1 (e.g., psychological drivers such as fears, anxieties, biases, and heuristics).

Imagine a patient who is considering a CPM to reduce the risk of breast cancer recurrence. If she decides to keep her noncancerous breast, there is a 6% probability that she will develop a new breast cancer within 10 years, but a 1% probability if she decides to have the noncancerous breast removed. Even though this woman recognizes the reasons to keep her breast (the odds of recurrence are very low, and surgery for removal has undesirable risks and side effects), her decision-making is driven by fear and anxiety, which she feels would be alleviated if she had her other breast removed. Her physician even provides her with another reason to consider, which is that the evidence indicates that most women do not experience a significant reduction in anxiety with removal. This rational-persuasion approach has little impact on the woman's psychological levers and processes. A behavioral economics approach that recognizes and uses decision psychology could help her make a better decision. Using such an approach, the physician might frame her odds in a positive rather than a negative light (e.g., 94% of women who decide to keep their noncancerous breast do *not* develop a new breast cancer), might use the power of social norms to inform the patient that most woman in her situation (93%) do not elect CPM, and might also make more salient the potential harms and side effects of CPM. Aristotle made the point that the art of persuasion involves rhetorical tools that are an important supplement to the use of reason and argument.[117] Most of us are not rational robots, driven purely by reason and argument, and this is why rhetoric or choice architecture is necessary. In sum, it is not clear that rational persuasion as a response will effectively or reliably prevent patients from making bad decisions, and thus it is not clear that it fulfills the rule of easy rescue, the obligation of beneficence, or the expectations of justified soft paternalism.

Second, the rational-persuasion argument makes the dubious assumption that there is such a thing as "pure argument" or "pure reason" that is unaffected by framing effects, emotion, etc. We could say that the rational-persuasion approach lacks authenticity because it ignores the realities of how decision-making works. We can pretend that we are offering patients "just the arguments" or "just the facts," but we know from behavioral economics and decision psychology that things are rarely so simple. In the dialogue *Phaedrus*, Plato wrote about how difficult it is to separate rhetoric (e.g., the use of moving figures of speech that induce emotion) from more purely philosophical dialogue. Rhetoric is present to some extent whenever people speak.[118] So, too, are the effects of framing and choice architecture.

That being said, it is certainly true that one can use behavioral economics techniques more or less, and that some amount of rational persuasion (an appeal to reasons, considerations) is possible and sometimes effective. And there may be some reasons to prefer a rational-persuasion approach since it poses no threat to autonomy.[119] Thus, all things being equal (i.e., if either choice architecture or rational persuasion could lead to the patient's making a good decision as defined in chapter 2), a rational-persuasion approach might be preferable because it carries less *risk* for autonomy-related harms.

In that context, I offer some remarks on when to prefer one approach over another. First, consider whether a rational-persuasion approach is likely to be effective at improving bad decision-making. If the patient's bad decision-making is heavily driven by biases, heuristics, or emotions, then perhaps a rational-persuasion approach is unlikely to be effective. We must counter like with like.

Second, consider the feasibility of a rational-persuasion approach, including the issue of how much time such an approach would take. One cost of rational persuasion is that it may take significantly more time than an approach that uses some tools from behavioral economics and decision psychology. Compare the amount of time a physician might spend explaining all the recent studies about vaccinations that say they are not linked to autism or other harms to an approach where the physician persuades a parent to vaccinate by saying that 92% of parents opt to vaccinate their infants. From a consequentialist point of view, this time burden is morally relevant (though not determinative, of course).

Third, consider the cognitive or emotional burden that a rational-persuasion approach might put on the patient. This relates to the larger issue of patient preference for such an approach. If we have reason to think the patient would feel strongly about or prefer one approach or another, then we ought to take that into consideration. If, on the other hand, we believe that the patient would feel offended by something other than rational persuasion, then that might speak in favor of it.

Fourth, consider whether there is a knowledge-based reason for a rational-persuasion approach rather than a nudge approach. For example, perhaps it is important that a patient be able to recite reasons for one course of action rather than another. Perhaps it is important that a parent really understand why vaccination is important in the case of her first child so that she will choose to vaccinate her future children. Or perhaps it is important that a patient understand the arguments and reasons for a particular treatment because there is a link to better compliance, etc. Consider whether it is a situation where deliberation or the positive exercise of autonomy is particularly valuable or important (what I described earlier as a high-value or high-stakes choice).

In sum, if the outcomes are the same (e.g., improved patient decisions that better protect and promote their interests and values), a rational-persuasion approach *might* be morally preferable because it does not even carry the *risk* of autonomy-related harms that the nudge approach does. But the rational-persuasion approach might, in certain circumstances, carry other morally relevant costs (e.g., time burden on physicians, emotional and cognitive burden on patients) that outweigh small risks to autonomy, especially in low-stakes choices where the positive exercise of autonomy is not particularly valuable or important.

### Why Not (and When) to Use Coercion

Some might agree that patients making bad decisions as a result of decisional biases and heuristics permits, or even requires, that something be done, but they might also argue that I have proven too much. The arguments that I have made in favor of nudging and choice architecture could also be made to justify various forms of coercion.[120] Coercion includes overriding patient choices, not giving them a choice to make them in the first place, or threatening them if they fail to make the preferred choice. For example, instead of nudging a patient to vaccinate by framing it as the default or making salient the harms of not vaccinating, vaccination would be mandated, and the physician might threaten the parents that if they fail to vaccinate their child, care will no longer be provided. Someone might argue that based on my arguments thus far, these forms of coercion are acceptable. After all, coercion can improve decisions (at least the outcome elements); it fulfills the rule of easy rescue; it discharges the duty of benefi-cence; and arguably a coercive intervention could be a form of justified soft paternalism since it prevents a patient from making nonautonomous deci-sions that might be harmful.

Of course, coercion has other costs that nudging does not have, which is why nudging is more ethically justifiable than coercion. First, coercing patients causes harms that nudging does not because of coercion's actual or potential negative consequences (i.e., being "forced" to do something in the case of overt coercion—through either the use of physical force or threats of harmful consequences or loss of rights if one does not do the desired thing—is a negative experience). Second, coercion is much more disrespectful of autonomy than nudging. Whereas nudging *could* be con-sidered disrespectful of autonomy (e.g., by failing to foster more delibera-tive decision-making or by making it very difficult for the person to go her preferred way), coercion certainly violates autonomy by blocking someone from doing something they want to do.

All this is not to say that coercion is never ethically justified. Sometimes it is—for instance, in situations where it is a last resort, after other types of attempts have failed, where it is reliably expected to prevent an imminent, highly probable, serious, far-reaching, or irreversible clinical harm, or if it is the only means for protecting a patient's future autonomy from significant or irreversible impairment. In these circumstances, coercive interventions might be more ethically appropriate than nudge interventions.

Someone might even argue that there is a way in which coercion could actually be *more* ethically justifiable than nudging and choice architecture— and that has to do with the issue of transparency. Coercion does block cer-tain choices, but at least it interferes with decision-making in a way that is transparent. Nudging, on the other hand, although it does not block choices, directs and shapes choices in a way that is often not obvious to the chooser. For that reason, perhaps coercive interventions are a more ethi-cally desirable response to patients' bad decision-making.

While this is true, I again note the negative aspects of coercion that are not present with nudging, and also the practical difficulty of coercion in many medical decision-making scenarios. Often a physician cannot legally ban a choice, threaten a patient if she makes the nonpreferred choice, or even decide against presenting a certain option since patients are likely to be aware of all options from a simple internet search. The underlying qualm about different types of nudging (some are less transparent than others) and their ethical relevance is important, however, and are discussed more in the next chapter in the analysis of transparent and nontransparent nudges.

### When Not to Nudge (or When to Minimize Nudging)

This section addresses the issue of when to be more or less in nudge or persuasion mode versus less (again, recognizing that complete neutrality is impossible). Obviously, *if a patient is making a decision that is well thought out and in line with her values and goals, physicians should avoid engaging in attempts to change or reshape her decision through either nudging or old-fashioned rational persuasion.*[121] An example of this might be a Jehovah's Witness patient who refuses a blood transfusion due to her beliefs about the religious prohibitions on transfusions. Additionally, *the less the expected utility gain from nudging or influencing patient decision-making, the more we should try to minimize it.* This may be due to significant uncertainty about the outcomes and their utility for the patient. In these cases, we may aim as much as possible for information delivery that focuses on "just the facts" and work to help the patient think critically about identifying the options and how their values fit into each. We need to acknowledge our own blind spots and that we too (as choice architects) are susceptible to our own biases in judgments. Clinicians should thus check themselves and each other for identifiable biases and have conversations with patients to determine what would make them better off according to *their* values and interests.

It is also important to note that *if patients object to their decision being the result of triggering System 1 processes such as biases and heuristics, this is a reason to try to minimize the nudge approach. If patients take issue with their doctor's attempts to shape their decisions (even benevolently, even using their own goals and values as an end), there is reason to try to avoid doing so as much as possible.* This is in part due to autonomy-related concerns and in part related to consequentialist-based concerns about damaged physician-patient relationships.

Finally, and a bit differently, *if trying to improve patient decision-making by devising creative and effective choice architecture takes too much time and effort, the physician is justified in avoiding such approaches if the outcome of the patient's decision is not expected to be particularly harmful.* The more harmful the patient's decision, the greater obligation there is to intervene in the most likely effective way (which will often involve use of insights from behavioral economics and decision psychology).

### Nudging Alternatives? The Promise of Debiasing Strategies, Bumps, and Boosts

One obvious objection to the use of nudges and choice architecture is that other strategies exist that are morally preferable. *Debiasing strategies*, for example, aim to rid decision-makers of potentially harmful heuristics and biases. *Bumps*, a new "sister" category of nudges, aim to alter behavior via rational learning mechanisms (e.g., by providing regular feedback or reminders to patients about the cost of their insurance plan compared to alternatives—"bumping" them to change to a better plan).[122] Bumps fall somewhere in between nudges and rational persuasion. *Boosts* aim to increase the competence of decision-makers by increasing their skills, strategies, and knowledge (e.g., by presenting risks in absolute instead of relative terms, by using frequencies instead of percentages in order to lead people to "better understanding," or by training individuals to structure their environments in ways that are "conducive to a better use of [their] temptations and impulses").[123] Boosts, like bumps, fall somewhere in between nudges and rational persuasion.

Each of these approaches has its limitations. Debiasing strategies have mostly been found to be effective at eliminating or reducing statistics-related heuristics and biases (thus addressing only a narrow set). One study examined the impact of debiasing training on ten different biases (outcome bias, sunk cost fallacy, base rate neglect, insensitivity to sample size, regression to the mean, covariation detection, framing effect, anchoring bias, overconfidence bias, planning fallacy). The strategy only held up for statistical biases but not for the others.[124] Other studies have generated similar results.[125] Second, successful debiasing strategies tend to involve programs that span over some period of time. As Croskerry and colleagues write, "Cognitive debiasing involves changes that rarely come about through a discrete, single event but instead through a succession of stages—from a state of lack of awareness of bias, to awareness, to the ability to detect bias, to considering a change, to deciding to change, then initiating strategies to accomplish change, and finally, maintaining the change."[126] A recent systematic review of strategies to debias health-related judgments and decisions (a total of 87 studies were examined) found that 86% of studies addressed only one bias and that the biases that were most addressed were framing effects (e.g., survival versus mortality), base rate neglect, and optimism bias. Two major types of debiasing strategies were tested: cognitive strategies that aimed to train people to improve their critical thinking (e.g., "consider the opposite" exercises—used in 41% of the studies) and "technological" strategies to restructure the way information was presented (e.g., visual displays of information to eliminate framing effects or base rate neglect—used in 38% of the studies). Technological strategies were effective at debiasing in 88% of cases, and cognitive strategies were found effective in 50% of cases.[127] While these results show some promise for debiasing strategies, it should also be emphasized that, again, the studies focused on a narrow set of biases that were mostly related to how people understand and use numbers (perhaps with the exception of debiasing unrealistic optimism).[128]

Bump approaches have similar limitations. As Victor Kumar, originator of the notion of bumping, has admitted, the sort of feedback required by bumps often takes a long time to begin to affect behavior (e.g., a "bumper" may need to remind a patient about the cost of her insurance plan compared to other alternatives several times before the patient actually makes a change). Bump approaches, Kumar admits, are often costly, protracted, or unfeasible/unavailable. As such, he argues that choice architects need to carry out a cost-benefit analysis to determine whether bumping is possible and worth the effort compared to nudging.[129] Given that bumps are somewhat similar to rational persuasion, I refer the reader to the previous section for remarks on when to prefer bumps and rational persuasion to nudging.

Boosts face similar issues. Grüne-Yanoff and colleagues, originators of the notion of boosting, have admitted that there is a high cost to boosting.[130] This is because "boosts aim to teach the right application of simple heuristics, which must be trained in repeated applications in order to be learned."[131] They write, "Boosts are most effective in domains where simple and effective rules of thumbs can be identified or simple ways exist to teach a more complicated strategy. Hence, when teachability is low, nudges tend to be the better choice."[132] Thus, boosts may not be the best approach to improving patient decision-making unless the proposal is to put patients through long training programs or to focus on repeat-decision situations where patients might benefit from training and feedback on their decision-making over time. The other thing to note about boosts is that, conceptually, they seem very much defined by the *intention* behind them. Grüne-Yanoff and Hertwig give an example of presenting frequencies instead of percentages to patients as a "boost" that improves their understanding of the odds.[133] They acknowledge that someone might view this example as a nudge that employs the frequency bias (frequencies feel more real or salient to people). They respond that although the effect on choice might be the same, in the boost case, the intention is to use frequency framing to better engage understanding, whereas in the nudge case the intention is to "use a cognitive bias" to "take advantage of faults." I am not sure the distinction between these two cases is entirely clear. Moreover, intention is often opaque, not only from the outside, but also, sometimes, from the inside. Most importantly, if the effect is the same (influencing patient choice in the direction of the frequency frame), it becomes further unclear wherein the meaningful distinction lies. Finally, it is less than clear why the frequency frame represents "better understanding" than the percentage frame. In any case, even if we could work out some of the particulars of this example, the larger issue is that there is doubt about whether boosting strategies are really feasible or applicable in patient decision-making. Or, even, whether they work. While Grüne-Yanoff's main point was that there are, theoretically, alternatives to nudging and choice architecture, he defers, "Let the psychologists decide whether nudging or boosting works."

## Conclusion

In this chapter I have made four arguments in favor of the use of choice-architecture and nudging techniques in patients' decision-making: decisional improvement and the rule of easy rescue; the ethical obligations associated with the medical principle of beneficence; justified soft paternalism and respect for autonomy; and patient endorsement (summarized in table 3.3). I have defended these arguments against several objections, although some caveats remain with respect to each argument to ensure ethical acceptability. I also have drawn some conclusions about when to try to minimize the use of choice architecture and nudging techniques (summarized in tables 3.1 and 3.2). In the next chapter I turn my attention to some remaining philosophical and ethical issues.

**Table 3.1**

When to avoid* or limit persuasion and nudging in medical decision-making: anti-intervention cases.

| When to avoid any persuasion (rational or nudging) | Ethical justification for anti-intervention stance | Example |
|---|---|---|
| 1. Patient's medical decision is well thought out and/or in line with her values and goals. | Respect for patient autonomy. | A patient who is a Jehovah's Witness is refusing blood products. Note that this is contrary to the situation in which a patient is refusing blood products because her neighbor received a blood transfusion and died, so she believes it is likely that she will die (availability bias). |
| 2. Lowered expected utility gain from nudging, due to, for example, uncertainty about what choice would be best for the patient.[†] a. Preference-sensitive decisions in which there is significant variation in what different patients choose and little knowledge about the decision-making patient's preferences, values, and goals. b. Uncertainty about the consequences associated with each option. | Consequentialist: attempts to shape choice will not (are not likely to) lead to improved decisional outcomes for the patient because it is unclear what the best option is. | A patient is deciding between implanting one and two embryos during a cycle of in vitro fertilization (IVF) and is undecided about what matters most to her (increasing the odds of a live birth or avoiding the risks associated with carrying twins). |
| 3. The patient would object to attempts, even if beneficently motivated, to shape her choice. | Respect for patient autonomy. Consequentialist: attempts to shape choice will (are likely to) harm the patient-physician relationship. | A patient makes it clear that his preferred decision-making role is to make the decision on his own without considering his doctor's opinion. |

* By "avoid persuasion," I mean attempt to present just the facts/information associated with each option without employing reasons, arguments, intentional framing, or other techniques to influence choice in one direction or another. It is, of course, impossible to avoid influencing choice altogether, but one can work to limit it.

[†] There is a caveat to this: persuasion or nudging to *counterbalance* existing bias toward one option might be justified even if there is uncertainty about which choice is best.

**Table 3.2**
When to prefer rational persuasion to nudging/choice architecture.*†

| When to prefer rational persuasion | Ethical justification | Example |
|---|---|---|
| 1. Rational persuasion would likely achieve all of the goods of choice architecture; it is likely to be just as effective at improving a patient's decisional processes and outcomes.<br><br>Note: if a patient's decision-making is heavily driven by biases, heuristics, and emotions, rational persuasion may be ineffective. | Respect for patient autonomy (fosters deliberative and reflective decision-making). | A pediatrician is discussing treatment options with a parent who prefers and is responsive to facts and arguments. Instead of just employing a default ("We're going to do the following vaccinations today, okay?"), the physician presents the parent with reasons why the American Academy of Pediatrics recommends the vaccination.<br><br>This is in contrast to communication with a vaccine-hesitant parent whose hesitancy is due to a strong fixation on a case of a child who suffered harm from a vaccination. |
| 2. Rational persuasion is reasonable in terms of the time and effort required to employ it. | Appeal to consequences. | An oncologist is treating a patient with a newly diagnosed inflammatory breast cancer. There is time over multiple visits in which the physician can present reasons and discuss with the patient why she should proceed with chemotherapy and mastectomy.<br><br>This is in contrast to situations in which a family physician is dealing with a patient who presents for a fifteen-minute routine office visit and is due for blood work, or an emergency room physician is dealing with a situation where a fairly quick decision needs to be made. |

*(continued)*

**Table 3.2 (continued)**

| | | |
|---|---|---|
| 3. A rational-persuasion approach would place an acceptable emotional and cognitive burden on the patient. | Appeal to consequences. | A fetal surgeon is communicating with a couple who are both emotionally calm and come to the consultation with accurate facts and figures from PubMed studies about the outcomes of fetal surgery for their child's condition. The physician believes the surgery is not in the child's or pregnant woman's interest given the severity of the prognosis. He lays out six reasons why he believes this (three based on an explanation of the statistics from the trials and how the analysis is not as straightforward as it might seem, and three based on the values he has heard the patient clearly articulate during the consultation). He ends with, "But this is your decision." <br><br>This is in contrast to a neonatal intensive care physician communicating with a family who is emotionally overwhelmed and looking for guidance about whether to proceed with tracheostomy placement for their terminally ill child. More facts, figures, and reasons would further exhaust them and provoke anxiety, but a story about parents in a similar situation who chose to forego the tracheostomy would give them peace. |
| 4. It is important for the patient to be able to recite the facts and the arguments for a particular option (e.g., because that ability is linked to adherence to a treatment plan). | Appeal to consequences. | A parent needs to understand *why* vaccination is important (not just decide to do it) so that she will choose vaccination for her future children. |
| 5. The decision in question is a high-stakes or high-value choice in which reflection and deliberation is morally or practically desirable. | Respect for patient autonomy (fosters deliberative and reflective decision-making). <br><br>Appeal to consequences. | A patient is making a decision that plays a vital role in self-identity, expression, or life's projects—e.g., a decision to implant one or two rather than all five available embryos in the case of IVF. |

\* In cases where *some* form of persuasion (either rational persuasion or nudging) is justified. For cases where it is not, see table 3.1.

† "Rational persuasion" is defined as inducing someone to do something through reasoning or argument. "Nudging" or "choice architecture" refers to the use of insights from behavioral economics and decision psychology to shape people's decisions or guide them toward a particular choice without forbidding other options. It works by triggering shallow cognitive processes such as decisional heuristics, emotions, and intuitions.

**Table 3.3**
Key arguments for nudging in medical practice.

| Key argument | Explanation | Objections | Potential replies |
|---|---|---|---|
| Unavoidability* | *Some nudging is unavoidable.* Decisions will be shaped by the order, tone, and frame in which options are presented—as well as by who presents them. Even the smell in the room can shape choice. We should, however, admit that nudging can be minimized—which it should be when the expected utility gain from nudging is low. | Neutrality can be achieved by framing information and options in multiple ways. | Impractical (e.g., requires providing information as percentage and frequency, as percentage survival and mortality, with risks first and then repeated with benefits first, etc.). Patients will be confused. Sometimes neutrality requires nudging to counterbalance an existing (starting) bias. Framing in multiple ways would not combat this existing bias. |
| | | Neutrality can be achieved by informing the patient that nudging is occurring. | This has been shown to have no effect and sometimes even a countereffect (patient trusts physician even more, and influence is more powerful). |
| Decisional improvement and the rule of easy rescue | Nudging can improve people's decisions, and if we can fairly easily improve patients' decisions with little to no cost to ourselves, then we ought to do so. We should, however, take care to recognize and prevent our own biases via self-reflection exercises and discussion with colleagues. We should also take care and time to identify what matters to patients. | Nudging improves only decisional outcomes, not processes. | Processes are only instrumentally valuable because of their link to outcomes. In certain cases, nudging can improve processes. |
| | | There is no agreed-upon definition of "improved" or "better" choice. | There are cases in which different theories of "the good" (hedonic, subjective, objective) converge to provide an answer, or where reasonable people agree. |
| | | Decisional-improvement claims will be plagued by the problem of adaptive preferences. | There is no empirical evidence to support the concern that patients are happy with their decision simply because they adapted their preferences to whatever outcome they were nudged toward. |

(continued)

**Table 3.3 (continued)**

| Principle | | Objection | Response |
|---|---|---|---|
| | | Choice architects are themselves susceptible to concerning decisional biases and heuristics. | There is evidence that we are less subject to errors when deciding for others. Even with potential errors and biases, this is better than the alternative of leaving patients susceptible to random or ill-intended nudges. |
| | | The mere risk that we could be wrong in our judgment provides us with a powerful reason not to nudge (moral risk objection). | This objection does not apply to most cases of nudging in this context because no serious or deep moral wrong would occur if we were wrong in our judgment. |
| | | Nudges are ineffective. | There is evidence that nudges can be particularly effective in individual decisions such as medical decisions. |
| Obligations of beneficence | Failure to engage in nudging can, in some cases, constitute a failure to prevent foreseeable harm and a failure to protect, promote, and prioritize patients' welfare and interests. | There exist other professional obligations with which nudging conflicts (e.g., protection and promotion of autonomy). | Nudging need not disrespect, and may even protect, autonomy. |
| Justified soft paternalism | Nudging can protect people from acting nonautonomously. It does not violate autonomy in cases where decisions are not being made autonomously to begin with due to decisional biases and heuristics. Nudging can actually respect and preserve future autonomy. | Nudging disrespects autonomy by failing to restore or foster it, and rather perpetuates nonautonomy by making use of decisional biases and heuristics. | If restoring autonomy means debiasing patients and returning them to purely rational deliberators, this is unrealistic. Patients often do not value the sort of autonomy idealized by medical ethicists (highly deliberative and being "the" main agent or decision-maker). This sort of autonomy may be valuable in some contexts (decisions central to one's identity or life projects or plans), but less so in others. Nonrational influence can enhance later capacity to respond to reasons. |

| | | |
|---|---|---|
| | Nudging disrespects autonomy by "piling on" more autonomy-impairing factors, making restoration of autonomy more difficult. | There is no empirical evidence for this effect. Restoration of idealized autonomy is unrealistic (see above). Rather than piling on, nudging is often counteracting (e.g., marketers nudge a patient to smoke, a physician nudges a patient not to smoke). |
| | Nudging involves intentional manipulation of choice, which is more threatening to autonomy than organic impairments to autonomy. | A lack of autonomy is a lack of autonomy, regardless of the source. Patients may endorse the use of nudges by their physicians, thus avoiding threats to autonomy and respecting it on process views of autonomy. |
| The principle of endorsement | Many patients would not mind being benevolently nudged by their doctor. | |
| | It is difficult to empirically study and support this claim. | It is reasonable to think that many such cases exist. There is evidence from other contexts that people view nudging as acceptable when the end is viewed as important and legitimate. |
| | Even if we have population data, we do not know for certain whether a particular patient would endorse nudging in a particular case. | The physician can make well-reasoned guesses, especially in cases where there is reason to think the patient would object, based on her knowledge of the patient (or similar patients in her situation). |

* As discussed in the text, unavoidability is not an argument per se but rather an important preface to the arguments.

# 4   Are All Nudges Ethically Equal?

In chapter 1 I review findings from behavioral economics and medical decision-making showing that patients' decision-making is often driven by heuristics, habit, instinct, and impulse. In chapter 2 I argue that these findings demonstrate that patients make decisions that are autonomy impaired, potentially harmful, and of poor quality more often than has been appreciated in medical ethics. In chapter 3 I make several arguments in favor of the use of choice architecture and nudging in patients' decision-making, defend them against objections, and offer caveats to ensure ethical acceptability. I also provide arguments for when the use of nudging and choice architecture should be minimized and when rational persuasion should be preferred, noting that the effects of choice architecture can never be entirely eliminated.

This has been the ground covered thus far, but several issues and puzzles remain related to the use of nudging and choice architecture in medical decision-making. For example, are some types of nudges more morally defensible than others? Which ones and why? Are some types of nudges a form of manipulation, and if so, what does this imply about their ethical acceptability? What is the relationship between nudging and shared decision-making—a topic of growing importance in medical practice and policy? At what point in clinical decision-making can nudges be used? Namely, is it ethical to use nudges in anticipation of bad decision-making, or only after evidence of bad decision-making? Finally, what if a nudge makes most patients better off, but some worse off? It is these remaining issues and questions that I now turn my attention to. I will divide the discussion, roughly, into two overarching categories: more on *types* of nudges and whether some types are more or less morally problematic or "manipulative" than others, and more on *when* nudging is justified (e.g., before or after bad decisions, in relation to shared decision-making, and when some patients are harmed but others are benefited).

## Additional Questions Related to Types of Nudges

### Are All Nudges Created (Ethically) Equal?

Thus far in this book, I have argued that the use of choice architecture and nudging techniques in patients' decision-making is ethically permissible and perhaps even ethically required. But, as we have seen in chapter 1 and in the examples discussed throughout the book, there are many different types of nudges. This raises an important question: are some types of nudges ethically superior to others? I have elsewhere developed a taxonomy of various types of influence.[1] Here I present a revised version of that taxonomy and then make remarks on the moral relevance of two different types of nudges (in figure 4.1, "nonargumentative influences"): transparent and nontransparent nudges.

I refer to broader parts of this taxonomy later in the chapter when I discuss where nudging fits with other forms of influence and whether it counts as manipulation, but for now, let us focus on the category of nonargumentative influence, for this is the category where nudges reside (force or threats are not nudges, nor are omissions or the use of reason and argument). Recall that nudges are defined as "any aspect of the choice architecture that alters people's behavior in a predictable way without forbidding any options or significantly changing their economic incentives."[2] Nudges operate by triggering shallow cognitive processes such as biases, heuristics, emotions, and intuitions. Nudges are easy to avoid, and they preserve choice sets, which is why omission of options, threats, and force are not nudges.

### Transparent and Nontransparent Nudges

It seems to me, then, that there are two important categories of nudges: those that the person is aware of and those that she is not—*transparent* and *nontransparent nudges*. This terminology illuminates the fact that some nudges operate by bypassing a person's awareness. Often, but not always, defaults and certain framing effects powerfully influence choice without the person's being at all aware that they are being influenced by these phenomena. On the other hand, sometimes people's choices are powerfully influenced

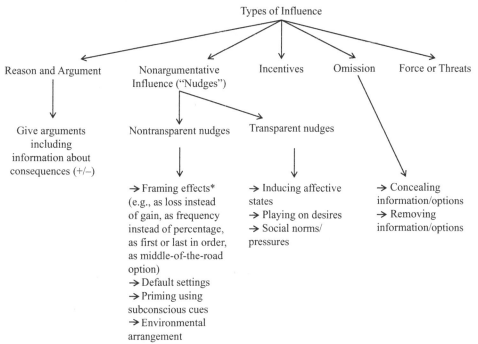

* Note: This is a rough categorization. Some of these examples, such as framing effects, might be quite obvious (transparent) to some individuals (e.g., if they have studied behavioral economics). And vice versa, some of the more "transparent" examples might be things that some people are oblivious to. Also, "bumps" and "boosts," discussed in chapter 3, fall between rational persuasion and nudges.

**Figure 4.1**
Types of influence.

by shallow cognitive processes that the person is very aware of—such as when they are nudged by having risks made salient (inducing fear) or by being given information about what most other patients choose (inducing a powerful desire to be within the social norm). In these cases, the patient is likely aware of being influenced (or nudged) in a certain direction. Both transparent and nontransparent nudges bypass deliberative capacities, but they do so in different ways.[3]

At first glance, it may seem as if nontransparent nudges are more ethically suspect. After all, in order for something to count as a mere nudge, it must be easy to avoid (substantially noncontrolling), and it is hard to see how someone could easily avoid something they are unaware of. For example, if a physician is nudging a patient to select surgery by giving her the odds of survival instead of the odds of mortality, it is not easy for the patient to avoid being influenced by this nudge since she is not even aware that it is occurring. So, one could argue, "If a person is aware of a nudge, then at least she has the opportunity to resist or avoid it."

This conclusion is too quick, however. First, nontransparent nudges may be easy to avoid in the sense that it is easy for the person *to choose another option* if she wants, even if it is not easy for her *to notice* the nudge itself—and ease of choice is the core concern in preservation of liberty. For example, in the above case, it is easy for the woman to avoid the nonsurgical option. She merely has to say so, as opposed to having to jump through hoops or paperwork to make that choice. Second, transparent nudges can be quite *difficult* to avoid because of their impact on what Saghai has called "inhibitory capacities."[4] That is, ease of resistance is in part about the ability to inhibit whatever urge or propensity is triggered by the nudge. Return to our example of using the power of social norms to nudge a patient toward one decision rather than another (e.g., "*Most* patients in your situation will elect to try a medication to reduce their anxiety"). Certainly the patient may be well aware of the nudge, but she may find the propensities being triggered (i.e., the desire to be socially normal) difficult to resist. Indeed, this occurs in marketing all the time. We are well aware of the marketers' nudges to get us to buy certain products, yet we find them difficult to resist.

But, someone might ask, might there be other reasons besides the link to ease of resistibility that transparent nudges are morally superior to non-transparent ones? Indeed, in their original work on nudging, Thaler and Sunstein develop a "Rawlsian publicity principle" for ethical nudging, where they stress that nudgers should be willing and able to defend their nudges to the public.[5] Sunstein focuses in his later work even more on the ethical importance of transparency, writing, "At a minimum, [this means that] no nudging should be hidden or free from public scrutiny."[6] He argues that the government or policymakers who utilize nudges (e.g., establish a particular default rule) need to explain and defend themselves (i.e., they have a justificatory burden).[7] Thus, one reason that transparency is important is to help ensure that the ends and rationale for particular nudges are not objectionable.

Imagine the following case of a potentially nontransparent nudge: a physician makes use of defaults to nudge a pregnant woman whose fetus has significant genetic abnormalities toward termination. He does this by presenting termination as the default for "cases like these," offering her an appointment time but leaving her the choice to "opt out" if she disagrees or feels differently. Imagine that the nudge operates in a nontransparent way, as the patient simply goes along with the default without really realizing there is another reasonable option (to continue the pregnancy) and without realizing what the physician is up to. This nudge is not transparent to the patient, nor to anyone else, and so the physician is not accountable for it. He flies under the radar, so to speak, with respect to the nudge itself and his reasons for doing it. If, on the other hand, he was using transparent nudging, the patient would notice it, and he would be more likely to be held accountable for it in terms of both the nudge itself and his rationale. For example, imagine that the physician nudged the patient away from termination by having her listen to the heartbeat of the fetus on surround-sound speakers for two minutes. Here, the physician is attempting to induce affect and to signal disapproval in a way that is likely transparent to the patient. Because of this, he is more likely to be held accountable for this act by the patient, his colleagues, his institution, and his community. Thus, we see how transparency serves an additional function beyond purported necessity for ease of resistibility: transparent nudges allow for more accountability and public scrutiny than nontransparent ones. We might think that it is *this* way that transparent nudges are morally superior to nontransparent ones.

While this is true in general, there are several remarks to make in response. First, we must ask what *exactly* needs to be transparent toward the ends of accountability and justification. I would argue that it is the physician's *reasons* for employing a nudge in one direction or the other. We want to know, for example, why the physician in the first case presented termination as the default. What was his underlying justification for believing that termination should occur in this case? It is his reason that we want to know about and subject to moral evaluation. Transparent nudges (e.g., the use of a more obvious affective nudge) are not going to give us *that*. For this point, see the second case. Here, there is a transparent nudge (listening to the heartbeat), but that tells us nothing about the reasons *why* the physician is nudging in that direction. If, for example, it is because he has a personal objection to abortion, we want to know that for public accountability purposes—and we might find it an objectionable reason for why he is employing a nudge. In other words, what seems ethically important is physicians being willing and able to justify their actions and rationale to the public. This is an expectation that we have of physicians independent of the use of nudges—for example, even in cases of rational persuasion it seems important. Thus, it is not clear that the normative work desired can be carried heavily or predominantly by simply employing nudges that are transparent (rather than nontransparent) to the patient.

In sum, we should resist generalizing conclusions that some categories of nudges (e.g., transparent) are inherently more or less morally problematic than others. Much depends on context and on considerations outlined in earlier chapters of this book. Similarly, specific types of nudges (e.g., messenger effects, norms, defaults, framing, priming) also resist easy categorization. Consider, for example, messenger effects in which patients are easily influenced by who delivers the information. Some patients may be well aware of this sort of effect (the potential nudge) and be easily able to avoid it, while other patients remain oblivious. Or a patient might be aware that something is operating as a nudge (e.g., the power of social norms) but not be aware of how *much* it is influencing her. All this is to say that the ethics of a nudge and its level of transparency cannot easily be inferred from its type or category.

### Educative and Noneducative Nudges

Some types of nudges are what Cass Sunstein calls "educative nudges," meaning nudges that attempt to inform people.[8] These are in contrast to nudges that attempt to help people without increasing understanding or knowledge; Sunstein gives defaults as a type of nudge that lacks educative features. What Sunstein calls educative nudges are similar to what others have called "bumps" or "boosts." I discussed these at length in the previous chapter, but briefly, bumps are similar to nudges in that they aim to influence choice without formal argument, but they are unlike nudges in that they employ rational learning mechanisms such as reminders and feedback when a poor choice is made.[9] Boosts are similar: they aim to influence choice by increasing self-competencies (e.g., structuring one's environment differently) or presenting choice more clearly (e.g., risk in absolute versus relative terms).[10] In short, educative nudges promote learning and help people become better choosers.[11]

Here, I will simply refer to lengthy discussions in the previous chapter on when to prefer rational persuasion to nudges, and on the promise and limits of boosts and bumps. Briefly, there I map out conditions under which rational persuasion is preferable to nudging, but I also argue that rational persuasion will never be entirely free of nonrational influence, and that boosts and bumps are often not practical in the context of patient decision-making, nor is it always clear how or why boosts and bumps are tied to understanding and truth in ways that nudges are not. The issue of nudges' relationship to the truth is an important one, however. Might certain types of nudges be morally preferable to others—namely, ones that bring choosers closer to truth or understanding?

### Nudges to Truth and Nudges to Mislead

To see what is meant by this distinction, consider the following points. Neil Levy refers to some types of nudges as "nudges to reason," meaning nudges that make salient relevant facts.[12] Similarly, Andres Moles points out that some nudges make salient relevant facts that should be appreciated.[13] Robert Noggle argues that ethical nudges are ones that call attention to something that is both true and important to the decision at hand.[14] Noggle compares two types of cases. In one, patients' pictures are attached to X-rays to nudge radiologists to take extra time and care when interpreting the images. Noggle characterizes this as a nudge to remind the radiologist of something "both true and important"—that is, behind the images are human beings whose lives can be ruined by careless interpretation. In the second case, a doctor nudges a patient to stop smoking by reminding the patient that cigarettes come from tobacco plants, which often contain bird droppings (the doctor knows that this patient has a fear of contamination). Noggle characterizes this as a nudge to boost the salience of an irrelevant fact, and indeed, to induce a faulty mental state, since the doctor knows that bird droppings are regularly washed away by the rain.[15] Similarly, William Simkulet gives an example of a physician who is treating a patient who has been exposed to rabies, but discusses both options (vaccine and continued life versus no vaccine and possible painful death) "with the same level of optimism."[16] While this is not a nudge, the point is that, in Simkulet's view, doing this hides a relevant truth from the patient—namely, that one option is far better than the other. This is what Simkulet believes is morally wrong with most nudges: their use shows little concern for patient understanding. According to him, at best, those who employ nudges aim only for nudgees to have partial understanding. At worst, they aim to mislead those whom they nudge. Simkulet draws on Harry Frankfurt's conditions for truth-telling to make his point. Summarizing Frankfurt, Simkulet writes that an agent tells the truth if and only if (1) she believes X, (2) she acts to convey X to an audience, and (3) she intends the audience to come to believe X.[17] In Simkulet's view, the physician who nudges fails to satisfy conditions 2 and 3 since she cares little about what her audience (the patient) *believes* or if it matches what she believes—she only cares about getting the patient to choose or do Y.[18] Again, at worst, the physician, by her nudge, gets her patient to believe something very different from what she believes; at best, she gets the patient to believe only some subset or partial amount of what she believes.

While I disagree with Simkulet that all or most nudges involve *only* an intent to persuade *rather than* an intent to tell the truth or promote understanding, there is a morally relevant distinction at play here.[19] That is, some instances of nudging such as the bird droppings example will seek to mislead or to hide or mask some relevant fact. These types of nudges are in contrast to those that do not operate in these ways or that seek to make salient relevant facts that should be appreciated. These boundaries will of course be gray, but there will be clear cases that fall into the morally concerning category of nudges to mislead. This is not to say that these types of nudges can never be justified, but it is to mark a wrong-making feature of certain types of nudges that counts as a pro tanto reason against them.

### Nudges with High and Low Friction Costs

Another morally relevant way to categorize various types of nudges is recognizing those that involve low versus high friction costs. Recall that in order for an intervention to count as a mere nudge, it must be easy to avoid (according to Thaler and Sunstein) or substantially noncontrolling (according to Saghai). It is clear that avoiding a nudge can be more or less "easy" or "costly" in various ways (e.g., cognitive effort, time, emotion, willpower, economic resources, etc.), and that some nudges are easier to avoid than others factoring in all these considerations. As Chris Mills has put it, many nudges do not impose traditional social or economic costs but rather psychological ones. Mills labels these *friction costs* and suggests that nudges can be categorized according to how they employ them. According to him, nudges that impose high friction costs to avoid them will likely be very effective, but they will not be "easy to avoid." Nudges that impose low to moderate friction costs will be easy to avoid but will either be ineffective or indistinguishable from other, more traditional forms of influence such as rational persuasion. Mills refers to this as the "choice architect's trilemma."[20] While I disagree with the trilemma characterization (tension is a more accurate description), the distinction between nudges with low(er) versus high(er) friction costs is a morally important one. To see the point, consider an example that I discuss further in chapter 5, where a physician nudges a man to take an antidepressant by informing him about what "most other patients do." Compare this with the example of a physician who nudges the man to take an antidepressant by stressing that the patient's wife, if alive, would have wanted the patient to take the medication, triggering guilt and social norms of a different sort.[21] The first sort of case may have a relatively low friction cost. While social norms are influential, it would not be *too* difficult for this man to simply dismiss the impulse to do what most people do. The second case, however, likely has a much higher friction cost. Ignoring the nudge would require the man to put aside complex feelings of guilt, duty, and approval with respect to his deceased wife. One thing to notice about friction cost assessments is that they are, in part, tied to individual psychology rather than to the type of nudge per se. That is, the use of social norms may have relatively high friction costs for some individuals and low ones for others. This is to repeat the earlier point I made with respect to transparency/nontransparency and individual differences. Thus, the categorization is less about types of nudges per se (e.g., that default-type nudges are more or less ethically defensible than social norm–type nudges), but rather about a morally relevant heuristic for assessing individual instantiations of nudges. Those with lower friction (psychological) costs may be more ethically defensible.

### Are Nudges a Type of Manipulation? Does It Matter?

One of the common objections to all or most types of nudging is the charge of manipulation.[22] But what exactly is manipulation, and why is it bad? Anne Barnhill, relying heavily on Robert Noggle,[23] offers the following definition: "Manipulation is directly influencing someone's beliefs, desires, or emotions such that she falls short of ideals for belief, desire, or emotion in ways typically not in her self-interest or likely not in her self-interest in the present context."[24] "Ideals" for beliefs, desires, or emotions goes largely undefined here. Claudia Mills has defined manipulation as trying to "change another's beliefs and desires by offering her bad reasons, disguised as good, or faulty arguments, disguised as sound—where the manipulator himself knows these to be bad reasons and faulty arguments."[25] Ruth Faden and Tom Beauchamp define manipulation more broadly as "any intentional and successful influence of a person by noncoercively altering the actual choices available to the person or by nonpersuasively altering the other's perceptions of those choices."[26]

While Barnhill's, Mills's, and Noggle's accounts are quite narrow, Faden and Beauchamp's is quite broad. In Faden and Beauchamp's account, manipulation includes influence by incentivizing, offering, increasing or decreasing options, tricking, using (resistible) threats of punishment, managing information, presenting information in a way that leads to predictable inferences, deceiving, lying, withholding information, slanting information, and exaggerating it in a misleading way.[27] Manipulation can also involve misleading packaging or misleading images, trading on fear, subliminal suggestion, flattery, guilt, appealing to emotional weakness, and initiating psychological processes that are difficult to reverse or that lead to predictable behaviors or decisions.

As these definitions demonstrate, there is little agreement on what counts as manipulation. In some accounts, nudges count as manipulation; in other accounts they do not. As I have argued elsewhere, this is largely irrelevant.[28] Whether a particular act of nonargumentative influence is ethically permissible depends on the answers to certain normative questions (about impact on autonomy, legitimacy in light of the relational and situational context, and whether it aims at and achieves good ends or bad ones), and not on whether it is called manipulation. Labeling something as manipulation does not settle the question of normative status; there may be instances where "manipulation" is morally acceptable or even desirable. Throughout the book I outline some of these guiding questions—for example, whether the patient would object to or endorse benevolently motivated attempts to shape her choice through choice architecture; whether such attempts would harm the patient-provider relationship by implying a breach of trust or respect; whether it is more or less clear what choice would be best for the patient in light of her goals, values, and interests; whether the patient is making or is likely to make a choice that is well thought out and in line with her goals, values, and interests; whether the nudge will improve choice; whether there is instrumental value in the patient's being able to recite facts or arguments for a particular option; or whether there is a practical or moral reason that the choice result from substantial reflection and deliberation.

For all of these reasons, I reject the standard taxonomy of influence often appealed to in bioethics of rational persuasion, manipulation, and coercion. The category of manipulation is too broad and carries a misleading negative connotation. Instead, to motivate a more serious conversation, as outlined in figure 4.1, I find the following to be a more helpful taxonomy: rational persuasion (inducing someone to do something through reason and argument), nonargumentative influence (inducing someone to do something through triggering shallow cognitive processes such as decisional heuristics, emotions, and intuition), incentives (inducing someone to do something by offering them something, commonly monetary), omissions (inducing someone to do something by removing or concealing information and options), and coercion (inducing someone to do something by threatening harm or loss if they do not, or by use of force).[29]

## Additional Questions Related to When Nudging Is Justified

In addition to questions about types of nudges and whether some types are more or less morally problematic, several questions remain regarding the timing, context, and circumstances under which nudging is ethically justified.

### Prophylactic Nudging versus Nudging after, or in Anticipation of, a Bad Decision

One such question is whether we *wait* for a patient to make a bad decision, or at least see *indicators* that a patient is making a bad decision, before intervening with decision-shaping techniques. Or are we justified in prophylactically using such techniques if we believe that doing so is likely to improve patient decision-making? Recall my argument in chapters 2 and 3: (1) behavioral economics demonstrates that patients make bad decisions more often and in more ways than has been appreciated, and (2) this justifies using nudging and choice-architecture techniques to improve decision-making. Since (1) justifies (2), one might argue that *only* when (1) is in fact the case is (2) justified. In other words, only when a patient has made a bad decision are we justified in implementing nudging and choice architecture to redirect her decision.

Recall from chapter 3 that the principle of soft paternalism justifies intervening only if a person is *in fact* acting involuntarily and harmfully (not simply because they *might*) and until the person's voluntariness is restored.

If we apply this principle narrowly, then clinicians should always aim to be as neutral as possible in initially presenting options, and only upon witnessing a biased or bad decision-making process should they integrate tools of decision psychology to attempt to improve patient choice.

In response, I believe that the question here is really about where we set the default assumption. And one must be set. Is our default assumption that patients are generally making good decisions as defined by the indicators in chapter 2, *or* that they are generally not? Based on evidence from the decision sciences, the answer seems to be the latter, thus justifying a *presumption* in favor of the "prophylactic" use of insights from decision psychology when engaging in decision-making with patients. The goal of such intervention, after all, is to help patients make decisions that are in line with their interests. All the caveats discussed in the last chapter apply, however, regarding when to back off from that assumption and from the use of nudges as much as possible.

### What about Shared Decision-Making?

One might wonder, what is the relationship between nudging and shared decision-making (SDM)? Is there a tension between the two? Can nudging be part of SDM, and can behavioral economics inform SDM? If there is a tension, is one approach preferable to the other, and in what circumstances/why? This section attempts to deal with these questions because I receive them often, especially from clinicians who are interested in the role of nudging and behavioral economics in patient decision-making.

SDM is increasingly becoming the gold standard for decision-making between physicians and patients, especially in cases that have multiple options involving value-laden trade-offs where different patients might make different decisions depending on those values (i.e., preference-sensitive decisions). It is endorsed by several professional societies and increasingly mandated or incentivized at the policy level, including being required by Centers for Medicare and Medicaid Services for reimbursement for care in some cases. *Shared decision-making* occurs when the physician and patient engage in a process of decision-making together; the physician informs the patient about her medical condition and the reasonable options, the patient shares information about her goals and values, and together they discuss and deliberate the options.

SDM includes three key conceptual components: (1) information exchange (about medical facts and the patient's values and goals), (2) collaborative or assisted deliberation between the health care provider and patient, and (3) patient voice or centeredness.[30] Now let us return to the definition of nudging discussed earlier in the book. Nudging involves triggering shallow cognitive processes (e.g., decisional heuristics and biases, emotions, intuitions) that make it more likely that a patient will choose one option over the other. This occurs by use of knowledge and insights from fields such as behavioral economics and decision psychology about how decisions are made and shaped. In nudging, no options are taken away or forbidden, patients are not threatened or punished for their choices, and choices are not substantially controlled. It must be easy for patients to get around the nudge.[31]

Given these descriptions, in what ways are nudging and SDM in tension, and in what ways are they compatible?

## Nudging and the Information-Exchange Part of Shared Decision-Making

Nudging and behavioral economics can and should be *part of* and *inform* SDM. Here is how: SDM involves information exchange. The physician must think about how to explain the patient's condition, her options, and the risks and the benefits of those options. The way in which this is done will trigger various shallow cognitive processes that are likely to tip decision-making in one direction or the other (i.e., it will "nudge" the patient). And if the physician is aware of this fact (e.g., if she has read chapter 1 of this book, or studied texts in behavioral economics and judgment and decision-making), she will need to make decisions about how to construct the choice architecture in ways that may influence choice.[32] So, for example, if a physician is discussing amputation versus a third attempt at revascularization for an ischemic leg (an example of a quintessential preference-sensitive decision that calls for a shared decision-making approach),[33] then she will need to decide which option to discuss first, whether to present the benefits first or the risks first, whether to describe each option via words or via images/video, and whether to include patient testimonials for either or both options and how many for each and which ones. All of this will impact patient choice in predictable ways via various shallow cognitive processes (e.g., order effects, availability bias, focusing effects, framing effects).[34]

A second part of the information-exchange component of SDM involves discussion of the patient's values and goals. This *very process* can be considered to involve nudging. In other words, values elicitation can trigger certain heuristics and emotions that will have predictable impacts on decision-making. Asking someone to write down what is important to them or what their goals are triggers what behavioral scientists have called commitment effects: people have an intense desire to be consistent with public promises and proclamations.[35] Moreover, the way in which values are discussed and elicited may induce certain shallow cognitive processes. Consider, for example, a standard values clarification exercise that a patient may go through during shared decision-making. Figure 4.2 is an adapted version of a values clarification exercise in a decision aid about breastfeeding.[36]

We can see that one of the values clarification statements asks the patient to indicate how important it is to her to "follow the advice of experts, who recommend breastfeeding." This may trigger a social norm bias and an authority bias whereby the evaluation becomes less about the patient's values and more about a drive to do what is socially acceptable or endorsed by those with power. In other words, it may nudge a patient toward breastfeeding.

### Nudging and Collaboration in Shared Decision-Making

Beyond its role in the information-exchange aspect of SDM, nudging and the use of behavioral economics insights can also be an important and ethically justified part of the collaborative and assisted decision-making component of SDM. During this part of SDM, the physician and patient weigh the options in light of the trade-offs and the patient's values, with the aim of arriving at a decision. The physician does not simply excuse herself and hand things over to the patient. Rather, she engages in the process too. One important role that the physician can play during this process is nudging the patient toward the option that seems best aligned with her goals and values in light of the medical likelihoods. For example, if, in the earlier example of amputation versus a third attempt at revascularization for an ischemic leg, the physician hears the patient say that she is tired of repeated surgeries and hospitalizations, is unmotivated to control the factors affecting ischemia (e.g., diabetes), has a strong support system, and is generally adaptable, then the physician might nudge the patient toward amputation by, for example, having the patient meet a similar patient who elected amputation. Or by saying to the patient, "Based on what you have told me about your values, it sounds like amputation might be the right decision for you at this point." Of course, this statement is in part a direct appeal to

## What matters most to you?

Your personal feelings are just as important as the medical facts. Think about what matters most to you in this decision, and show how you feel about the following statements:

Reasons to choose breastfeeding           Reasons to choose formula

I want to breastfeed.            I prefer to bottle-feed my baby.

| < | < | < | < > | > | > | > |
|---|---|---|---|---|---|---|

More Important       Equally Important       More Important

I want to follow the advice of experts,
who recommend breastfeeding.       My baby can be healthy on formula.

| < | < | < | < > | > | > | > |
|---|---|---|---|---|---|---|

More Important       Equally Important       More Important

Formula is too expensive for my budget.       I can afford formula.

| < | < | < | < > | > | > | > |
|---|---|---|---|---|---|---|

More Important       Equally Important       More Important

I don't have family or friends around
who have breastfed and can help me.
I have support from family and friends    I don't want to ask for help from
who can teach me about breastfeeding.      strangers.

| < | < | < | < > | > | > | > |
|---|---|---|---|---|---|---|

More Important       Equally Important       More Important

I'm confident that I can find the time    My type of work and my schedule don't
and a place to breastfeed or pump     give me the time or place to breastfeed
breast milk.          or pump breast milk.

| < | < | < | < > | > | > | > |
|---|---|---|---|---|---|---|

More Important       Equally Important       More Important

**Figure 4.2**
Sample values clarification exercise.

reason, but this speech act from the doctor also works as a nudge in that it is likely to impact decision-making at the level of shallow cognitive processes due to phenomena such as the authority bias, social norm bias, and desire to appear consistent.

### Nudging and Patient Centeredness in Shared Decision-Making

A third core conceptual component of SDM involves patient voice and centeredness. SDM is contrasted with a "paternalistic" approach in which the physician makes all the decisions, does not involve the patient, and makes medical considerations central (or makes assumptions about what is and is not important to the patient), rather than actually exploring what is important to the patient and evaluating the options in light of that. Nudging in medicine can and should put patients' interests at the center. As I argued in the previous chapter, ethically justified nudges will aim to protect and promote patient interests and autonomy, not just abstractly construed but as voiced and informed by patients and their experiences.

In sum, I believe there is a way to think of nudging as compatible with or part of SDM. That having been said, it is not *always* compatible; whether it is depends in large part on its forms and its ends in particular cases. Consider the example of a physician who hands a patient an advance directive form that is designed to nudge the patient away from life-sustaining treatment (LST) in situations of terminal or irreversible illness by making non-LST the default. The physician and patient certainly did not make a shared decision. In that case, the nudge approach was a *substitute* for a SDM approach rather than part of it. Or consider the case of a physician who enters into the decision-making situation determined to get the patient to consent to a surgery without having had any conversations with the patient about her goals and values—and who uses nudging techniques to make that happen. Certainly that is not SDM, as it is missing very central components such as patient voice and centeredness.

### Objections and Replies to the Role of Nudges in Shared Decision-Making

Some might object that a fundamental tension remains between SDM and nudging. The philosopher Michael Bratman has developed an account of shared agency according to which deciding or acting together requires that each individual have a "participatory intention," meaning that each intends that "we" make this decision together. These participatory intentions involve what Bratman calls the "meshing of subplans": each individual's intentions and plans have to work with the other's and be developed in consideration of the other's. Bratman gives the example of sharing the decision to paint a house (and the activity of painting it). The two parties cannot intend different things—for example, one to paint it purple and the other to paint it green. Sharing an intention or a decision puts certain constraints on individual intentions, according to Bratman. These constraints include that neither party can intend to be overly manipulative, and the two parties must come to agreement about the weight of certain things (e.g., they may need to agree to give highest weight to quality of life when deliberating about a treatment together).[37]

Given this account of shared agency, there might be reason to think that engaging in intentional nudging and choice architecture is *not* compatible with shared decision-making.[38] Bratman identifies manipulation as something that is incompatible with truly shared agency. Although earlier in this chapter I argue against calling nudging "manipulation," the thrust of Bratman's argument is that if one party aims to get the other to come to what she has *already* decided on, then the decision is hardly shared. This is what happens in intentional nudging or choice architecture—the *patient's* subplan is to gather information, discuss values, and come to a decision with her doctor, whereas the *physician's* subplan is to consider the patient's values and interests and present information in a way that will increase the likelihood that the patient will consider or choose one option over another.

While I think there is some truth in this view of a tension, I offer two responses. First, as Bratman suggests, two people can share deliberation by deciding together on a *policy or procedure of authority*, whereby they decide to defer to one of the two deciders. In this way, nudging could be compatible with shared decision-making, but only if the physician and patient decided together on the procedure of choice architecture or nudging. In practice, this is very unlikely and unwieldy, although it is a theoretical possibility. A second line of response is to argue that the intention to nudge and the intention to engage in the elements of SDM are not mutually exclusive. That is, the physician may have a subplan to inform the patient about the options and their risks and benefits, to understand the patient's values, and to reach agreement with the patient about next steps (the exact same subplan as the patient), while also having an intention to reflectively frame the options in a way that decreases the chances of a bad choice in light of what she knows about choice architecture and human psychology.

A second possible objection is that nudging does not add anything of value or substance that SDM does not achieve by way of potentially morally superior means. That is, SDM can help improve patients' decisions and fulfill physician obligations of beneficence, all the while promoting trust, patient autonomy, and respect. Why prefer nudging? After all, SDM has been shown to improve patient experiences, support patient autonomy, and improve health outcomes.[39] Patient decision aids, which are tools that facilitate SDM, have been shown to increase knowledge, decrease decisional conflict, increase accurate risk perceptions, and increase match between values and choice.[40]

I have several responses to this objection. First, we do not know whether the SDM interventions tested involved nudges. Perhaps some of them did. For example, one study found that some decision aids induced cognitive biases (e.g., order effects) that nudged women either away from or toward taking medication to prevent breast cancer.[41] Second, the studies showing that SDM improved patients' decisions in various ways (e.g., increased accuracy of risk perception) were mostly done in research settings. It is much more debatable whether clinicians practicing SDM in the real world have the time, enthusiasm, or expertise to do SDM and to do it well. And finally, one thing nudges do that SDM often does not do[42] is meet decision-makers where they are. In other words, the nudge/choice-architecture approach recognizes and deals with the patient as a System 1 thinker who makes decisions based on "irrelevant" factors such as how the choice is presented, what she has just heard or saw on television, what she is focusing on at the moment, what her mood is (e.g., hot state or cold state), what she has heard other people do in this situation, etc. The physician using a nudge/choice-architecture approach seeks to understand these processes and work *with* them. For example, a physician trained in behavioral economics/choice architecture will understand that a parent considering tracheostomy (versus comfort care) for her child who is in the ICU with a devastating neurological injury has likely seen other patients receive a tracheostomy and do well— thus inducing an availability bias that causes the parent to be overly optimistic about the outcome in her child's case. To deal with this, the physician makes sure to make salient the harms, risks, and quality-of-life issues that will be raised by proceeding with a tracheostomy. The physician does this by talking about the challenges first, prior to talking about the potential benefits and good outcomes. She also shows the parents a short video of a family who is dealing with a tracheostomy-dependent child in their home. The video offers a realistic snapshot of the burdens of day-to-day life. The physician will also understand that the parents do not want to do anything that causes harm to their child, or to make an active decision to limit life-sustaining treatment (e.g., she will understand the omission bias), and that the parents may have a drive to do something like a tracheostomy for the sake of doing something (e.g., she will understand the commission bias). Thus, instead of asking the parents to make an active choice about the tracheostomy ("Do you want to proceed with a tracheostomy or move to comfort care only?"), the physician will frame limitation of treatment as an acceptable default that the parents can either go along with or speak up against.

This is in contrast to a physician who is trained to take an SDM approach where she sees herself as coming into the situation as a neutral provider of information, trying hard not to influence the parents' decision in either direction; instead she asks them questions about their values, answers questions about the medical facts, helps them weigh the options (perhaps through administration of a values clarification exercise that asks them to list the pros and cons of each option), and generally supports them and gives them voice throughout the process. This approach is limited in that it does nothing to recognize, match, or work with the psychological processes at play within the patient or within the choice setting and context. Parents may be able to accurately recite the risks and benefits of tracheostomy (counting as "knowledgeable") and list or rank their values (counting as "values clarified"), but they are still likely to believe that their child will do well because their optimism and availability biases were never addressed. And they may be forced to make decisions that they do not want to make (e.g., to "actively choose" whether to forego a tracheostomy). Or they may find themselves going down the road of tracheostomy because *it* becomes the default—a road that is hard to turn back on for many parents. In this sense, a nudge/choice-architecture approach *can* achieve something of value that a "pure" SDM approach does not.[43]

Perhaps what SDM proponents who object to the use of nudging and behavioral economics really object to (or object to the most) are situations where nudges are used as *shortcuts* to the work of SDM. As I have argued throughout the book, nudges can be used more or less. So, the SDM proponent might buy my arguments that nudging will be and can be part of SDM, but take issue with nudging techniques being used very heavily to shortcut the work of SDM. To see this, let us consider a case of what I will call *extreme masterful nudging*. My primary care doctor knows that I am a medical ethicist. I only see her for annual checkups, but every year we make chitchat about work. She's collected some nuggets from our conversations, which she has written down in my chart. Apparently, over the years, I've made several comments about valuing quality over quantity of life, never wanting to wind up like some of the end-of-life cases I've seen in the hospital, valuing independence, being liberal in my views on death and physician aid in dying, etc. Now, let's say I develop advanced heart failure and things decline rather rapidly. I'm hospitalized, and the physician on service sees my chart and makes several assumptions about what I would or would not want. He comes to talk to me, and being very highly trained in the psychology of judgment and decision-making and the science of choice architecture, he does a couple of things. First, he flashes a toothy smile and tells me that he, too, studied philosophy as an undergraduate and enjoys spending time hiking at the local state park (apparently that was in my chart too). By so doing, he immediately gains my trust and becomes a "person like me," increasing his propensity to become an influential messenger. Then he tells me that I have two options—one is to wait it out for a while and see what happens, and the other is to immediately have a heart device called a left-ventricular assist device (LVAD) placed inside my body to take over the function of my heart. He says he is going to leave a decision aid with me, which goes into the risks and benefits of the LVAD, but, he says, "Most people like us who are young and active would never get the device, at least until it is a last resort. But I don't have to tell you that, you've seen a lot" (he uses social norms and appeal to ego). He says that he will tell the rest of the medical team to hold off before going in that direction, but that I should let him know if I feel differently after I have had a chance to review the decision aid (setting a default). He leaves a form with me that has "decline LVAD" checked as the default and asks me to sign it, but lets me know that if I want to, I can scratch it out and change the selection.

In this hypothetical scenario, the *entire* encounter between the physician and me was just a series of nudges; no conversation ever took place between the two of us. There was no exploration of my goals and values, why I have them, and what they mean in this context; there was no encouragement to express questions; there was no attempt to give me a voice—all aspects of the SDM process that its proponents prize. It is this sort of nudging—the sort that cuts out those components and *substitutes* them with decision-shaping techniques—that is objectionable in preference-sensitive decision-making contexts.

The conclusion, then, is that nudging sometimes is and sometimes is not in tension with SDM. And in some ways it is, and should be, a part of SDM. This is a complicated answer, but one of my professors once said that the answer to any philosophical question is almost always "yes and no." That is, "In some ways yes, and in some ways no."

### The Problem of Mixed Recipients: When Nudging Benefits Some but Not Others

Another issue that emerges concerns cases where a minority of patients may be harmed by a nudge. Imagine that *most* patients in some medical decision-making context are biased in some predictable way that causes them to make poor choices. The physician knows this and believes he can use behavioral economics insights to create a choice architecture that improves choice whenever he discusses the choice with patients. In most cases, this nudge improves individual patients' decision-making, but in a small handful of cases, it actually makes it worse: it nudges a patient in a different direction, away from what would have been good for him or most in line with his values.

This problem is particularly present for those who design *patient decision aids*—tools that aim to inform patients about a medical choice and present information about the risks and benefits of each option. While such tools traditionally aim for neutrality, as mandated by the International Patient Decision Aids Standards Collaboration, we have recently understood that complete neutrality is likely unattainable, and that nudging may, in some circumstances, be desirable.[44] Thoughtful choice architecture can be useful in decision aids that deal with medical decisions that many patients enter into with some existing bias. For example, choosing active surveillance is a viable option for men with early-stage prostate cancer, but many men come in with a bias toward surgery, often because of their doctor or because of what they have seen in the news. Since the developer of a decision aid has to choose whether to describe the potential harms of surgery such as impotence and incontinence as plainly stated where men may be swayed toward surgery, or in detail where men may be swayed away from surgery, then she may justifiably decide on the latter given the preexisting bias. There is a risk in doing so, because a *particular* man who may have been better off receiving surgery is swayed away from that treatment option.

We can call this the *problem of mixed recipients*—people are different, and the consequences of a prophylactic nudge might be good for some and bad for others. As much as a physician tries to tailor choices to individual patients, the reality is that a population-based approach to nudging will often be the default. A physician will reason, "Most of my patients are subject to biases that steer them toward immediate treatment for early-stage prostate cancer, which is often against their interests; thus I will design a choice architecture that nudges my patients to give active surveillance a try." Moreover, sometimes a population-based approach is unavoidable, such as in the case of decision aids that are designed for a population of patients and not individuals.

In response, I think we must simply accept this fact and use as our justification the utilitarian view that more individuals will have their decisions improved in the sorts of cases I have been discussing, especially when we consider that the complete absence of any nudging is impossible. This utilitarian justification does, however, involve some deontological constraints—meaning, it is not the case that so long as a nudge makes more people better off than it harms then it is justified. I discuss several additional constraints and limits to nudging in chapter 3, summarized in the tables at the end of that chapter.

### Social Nudges: Distinguishing Libertarian Paternalism from Libertarian Welfarism

A final theoretical question to be addressed is the distinction between nudging to improve the well-being of an individual, or some subpopulation of individuals, and nudging to maximize social welfare. The former is labeled libertarian paternalism (LP) and the latter libertarian welfarism (LW).[45] The focus of this book is primarily libertarian paternalism, but libertarian welfarism is relevant for medical ethics as well. Take, for example, a situation where patients tend to choose an expensive medical intervention when a less costly approach would be just as effective. Here, the patient makes a decision that is bad for her, assuming she bears some of those higher costs, but that is also bad for society in that it wastes health care resources. The patient could be nudged toward a cheaper alternative, and in this case the theoretical justification would be a mixture of LP and LW.

The Choosing Wisely campaign, where patients and providers were discouraged from selecting low-value care options, is a prominent example of this sort. Other examples where the theoretical justification is likely a mixture of LP and LW include nudging people toward vaccination, nudging toward exercise and healthy eating, nudging patients to enroll in certain health insurance plans, and nudging patients in private insurance plans to avoid overusing them. There are some nudges whose theoretical justification lies more squarely in the realm of LW. These include nudging people to donate their organs, nudging people who are sick to wear masks or avoid spreading their illness to others, and nudging individuals to participate in research.

Being clear about these differences is important, and often discussions of nudging in medical ethics are not careful enough and lump these different examples (LP, LW) together. The differences are important for ethical analysis, however, since patient/physician ethics and public policy/public health ethics are different in important ways.[46] For example, individual physicians are thought to have fiduciary obligations primarily to their patients and would be more ethically justified in nudging for the purposes of LP than for LW. In mixed cases, where a particular nudge benefits both patient and society (e.g., vaccination), matters are likely to be less controversial. In pure LW cases, however, the physician may be less ethically justified in nudging—*especially if* the nudge harms the individual patient. Imagine a physician who nudges her patient to withdraw life-sustaining treatment to free an ICU bed for a patient who is expected to have a better outcome. Or the physician who does this in order to save the health care system money given the high expense of ICU care. Such "bedside rationing" outside of emergency times, as opposed to rationing at the policy level, has been met with ethical condemnation because of the unique moral features of the physician-patient relationship.[47]

Social welfare is a broad category, and it is worth distinguishing between pro-social nudges that have a direct impact on health (e.g., nudging vaccination to achieve herd immunity), those that have a loose tie to health (e.g., nudging organ donation to increase the number of transplants), those more closely related to health systems issues (e.g., nudging to reduce health care spending), and those related to social or political projects at large (e.g., nudging toward environmental protection). Arguably, those cases lie on a spectrum where physicians are more or less justified in using nudges for the benefit of society (LW as opposed to LP). Of the latter sorts of nudges, as Mark Navin argues, following Robert Nozick, individual members of a society do not have a political duty to contribute to all the valuable public projects being pursued. And physicians should take care not to treat their patients as instruments for promoting political projects.[48]

Indeed, empirical evidence shows that pro-self (LP) nudges are perceived as more acceptable than pro-social nudges. One study presented 962 subjects with vignettes of different types of nudges, some pro-social (e.g., a nudge to donate organs, consume less energy, reduce tax evasion) and some pro-self (e.g., a nudge to stop smoking or reduce consumption of highly caloric foods). Respondents were from Sweden and the United States. The rate of acceptance ranged from 54% to 86% and was, on average, 11 percentage points higher for pro-self nudges than for pro-social nudges.[49]

## Conclusion

In this chapter I examine several additional theoretical issues related to the ethics of nudging. Digging deeper into different types of nudges, I argue that nontransparent nudges are not necessarily more ethically problematic than transparent ones, and I draw attention to several wrong-making features of certain types of nudges: namely, nudges that mislead and nudges that impose high friction costs. Further, I argue that nudging is best conceptualized as a form of nonargumentative influence rather than as a type of manipulation, a term that is value laden and unclearly defined. I argue for a presumption in favor of the prophylactic use of insights from behavioral economics (nudging) when engaging in decision-making with patients, and that nudging can be compatible with a shared decision-making approach. I argue that in cases of mixed recipients, where a few might be made worse off by a nudge that makes many better off, the nudge is justified on utilitarian grounds, although deontological considerations and constraints such as autonomy should be part of the calculation. And finally, I identify important theoretical and justificatory differences between libertarian paternalism and libertarian welfarism. In the next chapter I turn my attention to several case studies of nudging in real-life clinical practice and apply the arguments and analyses developed in the book thus far.

# 5 Nudging in the Weeds: Case Studies of Nudging in the Clinic

This final chapter analyzes the use of various forms of influence, including nudges, in several real and varied clinical contexts: specifically, psychiatry, pediatric critical care, fetal surgery, and prostate cancer. I focus on these examples because they are ones in which I have conducted empirical work to investigate whether and how insights from decision psychology and behavioral economics are used (knowingly and unknowingly) to impact patient choice. Often, case examples of nudging come from purely hypothetical examples or from investigations in which a researcher studies the impact of a behavioral economics intervention on choice or behavior. The examples I discuss here come mostly from the actual use of nudges and various other forms of influence by physicians in medical decision-making.[1] Some examples do not fall into the strict definition of nudges enumerated in earlier chapters, or they fall into the category in some ways but not others.[2] Where this occurs, it is noted.

## Nudging in Psychiatry

### Clinical Examples

Between 2009 and 2011 I attended weekly rounds in an inpatient neuropsychiatric unit. Of interest to me was how psychiatrists presented choices and recommendations to patients. The attending psychiatrist and I collaborated to catalog the types of influence that we noticed in our experience. We identified several examples and seven distinct varieties of influence (table 5.1): direct recommendations, appeals to patients' values and goals, appeals to norms, intentional framing of information or options, concrete incentives, concrete threats, and deception.[3] For each type, we specified a clinical example.

Table 5.1
Influencing patients' decision-making in psychiatry.

| Type of influence | Clinical example |
|---|---|
| **Direct recommendation\*** | The physician recommended to a sexually active female patient with bipolar disorder who used contraception inconsistently that she discontinue Depakote (a drug to treat bipolar disorder) because of potential harms to the fetus in the event of a pregnancy. |
| **Appeal to patient's values and goals\*** | The physician called a severely depressed patient's attention to the positive effect that treatment (medication) could have on her ability to continue to parent her child in her own home (the alternative was calling CPS per reporting requirements). |
| **Appeal to norms (nudge/ part nudge)** | The physician said, "Most patients in your situation choose ..." and "Your deceased wife would have wanted you to ..." |
| **Intentional framing of information or options (nudge)** | The physician framed the risk of tardive dyskinesia (involuntary facial movements that can result from psychiatric medications) to a patient who was obsessively concerned about appearance as a percentage instead of frequency (percentages are less influential) and sandwiched this risk between the benefits of treatment (recency and primacy effects) in order to get her to take the medication. |
| **Offering of concrete incentives\*** | The physician told patients that taking medications, participating in groups, practicing good hygiene, etc., would result in outdoor, phone, or snack privileges. |
| **Leveling of concrete threats\*** | The physician told patients that failing to follow treatment recommendations would result in removal of outdoor privileges, longer hospital stays, reports of dangerous behavior to employer, etc. |
| **Deception (e.g., concealing, misleading, or lying)\*** | The physician omitted the option of going home to a patient who had been living in self-neglect, and told a psychotic patient that medication would remove a spirit. |

\* Not nudges.

## Ethical Analysis

One point to make at the outset is that of the types of influence identified, the ones that most clearly fall into the category of nudging or choice architecture are framing and appeal to norms.

My colleagues and I analyzed the ethical permissibility of each of these types of influence,[4] but here I will focus my comments on framing and appeal to norms, since those categories involve nudges. One important ethical consideration is that in the context of psychiatry, we are dealing with patients who have two sorts of vulnerabilities that are in tension with each other. On the one hand, they are vulnerable to impediments to decision-making, which might argue in favor of using choice architecture to improve their decision-making. On the other hand, they are vulnerable to excessive paternalism and coercion, which might argue against attempts to shape their decision-making via the use of nudges or behavioral economics strategies.

The first question to ask is whether clinicians should be in any sort of persuasion mode (rational persuasion or nudging). In chapter 3 (see table 3.1) I argue that there are three situations in which clinicians ought to try to avoid any form of persuasion: (1) the patient's decision is well thought out and in line with her goals, (2) there is uncertainty about what choice would be best for the patient (because of either lack of evidence regarding clinical efficacy or effectiveness of proposed options, lack of information about the patient's interests and values, or unchecked and distorting biases in the physician's own judgments), or (3) the patient would object to any attempts to shape choice, resulting in damage to the therapeutic alliance. Based on these factors, I cannot make any determinations about whether it is *generally* good or bad to influence patient decision-making in psychiatry, but there does not seem to be anything prima facie prohibitive. In fact, in psychiatry in particular, there may be more cases where, due to symptoms of an underlying mental illness, a patient's decision is not well thought out and in line with her goals, even if these concerns do not rise to the level of calling into question the patient's decision-making capacity.

The second question to ask is about the ethical acceptability of nudging in particular as a form of influence. In chapter 3 I argue that there are certain cases when a nudge approach should be avoided or minimized in favor of a more direct appeal to reasons-type of persuasion. These include cases where it is important for the patient to act on the basis of reasons (e.g., she needs to internalize and apply those reasons to future decisions, or doing so is morally or practically desirable because those reasons relate to overarching life plans or identities). I also include cases where a nudge approach would subvert autonomy by blocking options or triggering processes that the patient would resist or regret acting on. And finally, if a very direct (dry) listing of appeals (reasons) for why a patient should choose one option over another does not place an undue cognitive or emotional burden on the patient and is likely to be effective, it might be considered before the integration of behavioral economics–inspired nudges. Again, at the theoretical level, nothing here seems prohibitive of the use of nudge techniques in psychiatry.

If, however, we examine some of the concrete examples observed, things become more muddied. For example, consider the psychiatrist who utilized the power of *social norms* and told his patient that he *should begin medication to treat his depression* because his recently deceased wife would have wanted him to. This example involves a mixture of rational persuasion and nudges, in the sense that it uses both appeal to reason and established values, but it also triggers shallow cognitive processes such as emotions and the desire to adhere to social norms for the sake of norms. Several ethically relevant considerations point in favor of this particular nudge.

First, the norm appealed to was true and not merely made up in an attempt to get the patient to do something. Second, strong evidence supported the effectiveness of the medication that was suggested to treat this man's depression and showed that the benefits outweighed the risks. Most importantly, there was reason to believe that the goal of treatment of the depression was in the patient's interests and in accord with his own goals (e.g., to be free from suffering, to function better in his daily life and family).[5] There was no reason to think that this (partial) nudge would fracture his relationship with his clinical team or that he would feel that it compromised his autonomy or triggered a decision-making process that he wished not to have. Further, the patient's ambivalence or hesitancy to start treatment was not the result of a reflective, deliberative, volitional process whereby he was exercising his autonomy. Rather, it was largely the result of a malaise and depression, due in part to his wife's death. Thus, this nudge could be viewed as an *ethically justified* instance of justified soft paternalism.

Another example of how psychiatrists used nudges in clinical practice involved *framing effects*. More specifically, they nudged a patient who was very concerned about her appearance *to begin an antipsychotic medication* by sandwiching discussion of the risk of tardive dyskinesia (a condition causing involuntary movements of the face and jaw) between the potential benefits of treatment.

On the one hand, the medication would likely have decreased her psychotic symptoms, which was certainly in her interest. She did not enjoy the symptoms, and they interfered with her achieving what was important to her (she was a student, and they impeded her academic functioning). On the other hand, the importance of physical appearance was a long-standing priority for her. The questions then become at how much risk does the medication put her for tardive dyskinesia, and can it be reversed if it occurs. Essentially, if the nudge is successful and she consents to the medication and it successfully rids her of her psychotic symptoms, but it results in damage to her facial appearance, has it really improved her condition? Both freedom from psychotic symptoms and physical appearance are important to her, but which is *more* important? In this case, the answer was physical appearance. This gets to a deeper philosophical point discussed earlier in the book about different views on well-being. The nudge, if successful, might make her better off from the psychiatrist's perspective, but not hers.

A second consideration in this case is how autonomous the process was by which she came to her decision or inclination to protect her physical appearance. Was her prioritization of physical appearance a preference that the patient came to authentically and autonomously, or rather one that she arrived at by some sort of distortion in understanding or reasoning—or by some external or unwanted set of influences? We might, as a general matter, wonder how much society has "brainwashed" her into caring so much about her physical appearance, although we could ask this about almost any value or preference. Without convincing evidence that she wished she did not care so much about her appearance, her "value" of maintaining physical beauty is one that is hers. It had been quite important to her for much of her life. Thus, it is problematic to make the argument that she is not acting autonomously in prioritizing her physical appearance and that a nudge in the other direction is merely an instance of soft paternalism to prevent her from enacting a nonautonomous but dangerous decision. In other words, a nudge toward medication in this case is *ethically problematic* because it seems to be in tension with her preferences and values as she has defined them. Thus, such an attempt potentially threatens *both* her autonomy and her decisional outcome. Moreover, in this case, the patient would have likely not endorsed the process by which she came to consent to the medication if it were made transparent to her.

## Nudging in Pediatric Critical Care

### Clinical Examples

The next set of examples of nudging in the clinic comes from pediatric critical care. My colleagues and I conducted qualitative interviews with 18 pediatric critical care physicians to explore how they approach consent for tracheostomy placement with parents of children with conditions such as incurable neuromuscular disease and devastating neurological injuries. A tracheostomy is a surgical procedure that creates a hole in the neck to allow for the placement of a breathing tube that provides an airway and allows for removal of lung secretions. Physicians were asked (1) how they perceive parents' decision-making ability, (2) whether physicians use (knowingly or unknowingly) "nudges" or "choice architecture" techniques during the decision-making process, and if so which ones, and (3) about their attitudes toward the ethics of using these more subtly directive approaches. In table 5.2 I outline some of the examples provided by clinicians.

### Ethical Analysis

The first question to ask is whether clinicians should be in any sort of persuasion mode. Of central concern is how certain the clinicians are about the patient's poor prognosis. Prognostication is particularly difficult in the case of pediatric neurological injury; much depends on the location of hemorrhage, presence of brainstem involvement, and presence of additional brain abnormalities. Even more concerning, clinicians frequently overestimate poor outcomes. Before attempting to shape choice in the direction of nonintervention, physicians should consider whether their judgments about poor prognosis are based on objective and accurate evidence and not on a biased sample (e.g., the physician sees only bad cases that require readmission and not patients that do well).[6]

Related to this, clinicians considering nudging in this case need to assess how certain the negative impact will be on the child's and family's quality of life if the family proceeds with the tracheostomy. And the clinicians should be aware of their own personal and occupational biases. It is true

**Table 5.2**

Influencing patients' decision-making in pediatric clinical care.

| Examples of clinical nudges provided by physicians | Types of nudges |
| --- | --- |
| "I try to be realistic to where almost any mom is in tears. ... I paint a really harsh picture." "I try to emphasize how having an ICU in their house will impact their life." | Appeal to salience and affect; loss framing. |
| "I am very explicit: you can't just get a babysitter, you can't go get your hair done, you can't run to the grocery store. And I talk about what it means to the family, to the other children. I have gone so far as to cite the higher divorce rates." | Appeal to salience and affect; loss framing. |
| "If you were able to show videos of all the kids who have gone through this ... and here is the data on divorce rates and on families that are broken up ... that would be more informed in terms of the decisions they make." | Appeal to salience and affect; loss framing. |
| "I say, this is what I think will happen next, from recovery to PCU [progressive care unit] to home nursing, and how they call in sick and can't get to your home. And how will you keep your job? And what about your other kids? And I always add the phrase: I am a doctor and I don't think I could handle this at home; I don't think I could do this. My recommendation is not to trach. I say it is up to you, but my recommendation is not to do this." | Appeal to salience and affect; loss framing; power of messenger; defaults. |
| "I say he will need help breathing, may experience some pleasure and pain, maybe recognize a face. ... [I] give them a developmental level of about four months. That sets it up quite well. I could come out and say, could you live with this outcome? And once the family agreed that was not an outcome they found acceptable, I could say, listen, a trach will increase hospitalizations and not improve neurological outcomes. Maybe it was biased from the beginning, but it was all true." | Appeal to salience and affect; loss framing; power of messenger; appeal to social norms. |
| "I tell them my recommendation is to not let the child suffer. ... I have experience with this more than you, so from what I have seen and know, I can tell you I would not choose for me or my child to live like that. I say I do understand your perspective as a parent and would never want to be in your shoes." | Appeal to salience and affect; loss framing; power of messenger; appeal to social norms. |

that caring for a technology-dependent and/or profoundly neurologically impaired child is a demanding, all-consuming experience, but it can also bring joy, and even severely impaired children can have meaningful interactions with loved ones. Despite the possibility of such joy, many families foresee more negative rather than positive impacts. The clinicians we interviewed reported seeing families torn apart by their efforts to care for such children as well as by the children's suffering, experiences that motivated them to "nudge" parents away from these bad outcomes. One remarked,

> The benefit of being a mid- or late-career intensivist is that I have had the opportunity to see some of the children in these scenarios who I have given a trach to come back to the hospital multiple times, and I have seen their lack of progress and the burden it places on families. So I am much more comfortable now than I was earlier in my career with a higher degree of assurance and conviction that what I predict is a most likely outcome … and my own opinion that a trach will not fix or change anything.

However, overall it must be noted that this decision is a very high-stakes preference-sensitive decision with a lot of variation in choice, and, as noted, some evidence shows that clinicians are disposed to personal and cognitive biases in this area. Some physicians in our sample (specifically, two) were even aware of their biases. One said, "What I worry about is that we know we have bias, we pretend that we don't, and we do not disclose to the family our inherent biases. Like in SMA [spinal muscular atrophy], my experience and views are colored by the fact that I have met families that have regretted a trach every single day of their lives." Another said,

> We do not spend enough time to understand families' inherent values and beliefs. I typically tell them it is a personal decision, and they have to live with the decision for the rest of their life. At the end of the day, I go home. And so it is not necessarily fair for me to tell a family what is best for them, because the truth of the matter is none of us has a vested interest even though we think we do. And that is why I have never felt very strongly that we should influence them one way or another.

Thus, on the whole, there may be concern about whether one of the normative justifications for a more persuasive approach is met—namely, certainty about what choice would be best for the patient and their family.

Another question is whether, in nudging, the clinicians are directing the parents away from decisions that are well thought out and in line with their goals. This did not appear to be the case in our study. First, in most cases, parents had not yet made a final determination about the best course of action. Second, the clinicians testified that in their view, many factors were biasing parents *toward* a tracheostomy—which is one reason that they saw their nudges away from tracheostomy as justified. One factor that clinicians believed was biasing parents toward a tracheostomy was present bias. As one clinician put it, "In my experience, the families have a hard time looking at the future because this is an immediate solution that solves an immediate problem. They never say, tell me more about what will happen. They say, so can you save my child if you put in a trach?" Another factor cited in defense of nudging was loss aversion: "They are tired and scared and about to lose the one thing they love most. I don't know what I would do. I might make some really dumb choices." A third was cascade effects: "The parents have been through a period with us where things are just done. The kid gets intubated, lined up, end of story. At that time, our goal was to save the child's life. Now we have a much murkier situation." A fourth factor cited was affective forecasting errors: "I have a personal belief that the majority of these parents would not put their child and family through those last 10 years if they had known what it would have been like." As another physician put it, when the child is an infant,

> You can hold him and care for him and change him. But as he gets older, scoliosis happens, they cannot feed themselves, they can't feel pleasure, can't cough. They get very difficult to care for. And that is something we see happen, but for families they just can't capture it. They haven't experienced it and just can't comprehend it. It's hard to play out thàt feelings component.

And finally, several clinicians pointed to the availability bias and social norms as factors that likely bias parents toward intervention. They talked about how parents have often heard of only the good outcomes of tracheostomy—be it from other parents, the internet, or even hospital staff. As one physician said, "Any family that reads anything, or talks to family [about] Uncle Joe who had a trach and got better—whatever, there is always someone who knows someone." In essence, in the clinicians' views, parents are often predisposed to make decisions that are not so well thought out and in line with their goals—and that are biased toward intervention—thus, employing nudges in the other direction is a way to even things out.

All these views on the state of parents' decision-making were tempered by the recognition that while parents' wishes matter, the clinician's primary ethical obligation is to protect and promote the well-being of the child. And that might involve nudging the parents. One clinician said,

> All of these six patients [I have had] did eventually die and had no good quality of life, and neither did the families. That has influenced me in certain situations like bad neurological injuries. I think many of our decisions are based a lot on what the parent thinks and that we don't want to upset the parents. We should put more importance on the patient. We are physicians for the child, not the parents.

But this brings us back to the initial question of whether there is in fact clarity about which option is best for the patient.

A final consideration regarding whether the clinicians are justified in taking a persuasive approach of any kind (be it rational persuasion or choice architecture/nudging, as they did here) involves the question of whether the patient (in this case, the parents) would object to any attempts to shape choice, resulting in damage to the therapeutic alliance. I cannot make a blanket statement here, as of course each case and each parent will vary, but in the physicians' experience, parents actually desire more direction from the physicians in their decision-making. As one physician put it, "I think they want direction. My personal approach is very direct in terms of information and guidance. In many cases parents will say they are so appreciative that I was direct with them from the get-go." Another physician said, "I think a large majority of families would like more direction and/or saying it's okay not to do it. And I think the, for lack of a better word, permission to not opt for further treatment is all the family needs sometimes."

One major reason for this desire is the relief from the cognitive and emotional burden of end-of-life decision-making for a child. As one physician said, "I have become convinced that it is unfair to families to force them to choose between letting their child die or keep going. I firmly believe now it is our responsibility to tell them what is best." Another said,

> If you as the doctor are the one to say or tell them, no, this is not appropriate, most families won't argue against that. But if you put open-ended questions, though they would not want the child to suffer and maybe not opt for trach, they don't want to take that decision on themselves because they feel guilty about it.

Another emphasized, "When you tell a family you can choose or not choose a trach, that burden of decision-making is going to almost always make them veer toward choosing a trach. Because to ask a family to choose to let go is impossible." Another said, "I think they appreciate heavy guidance, if that is a term, and that it takes away their guilt." Finally, another reasoned,

"We give them three options and ask them to tell us what they want to do. I have decided I feel that is wrong."

The second big-picture question to ask more explicitly is about the ethical acceptability of *nudging in particular* as a form of influence or persuasion. In chapter 3 I argue that there are certain cases in which a nudge approach should be avoided or minimized in favor of a type of persuasion that is more of a direct appeal to reason. One of the factors is consideration of whether the nudge approach would subvert autonomy by blocking options or triggering processes that the patient would resist or regret acting on. None of the nudges discussed here involve blocking options. It is, however, worth noting that we did find examples of persuasive techniques that went beyond nudging and involved the *omission* of options—namely, the option of a tracheostomy. Three clinicians admitted to this. As one said,

> There are times I leave it [a tracheostomy] out. If I think it is clear the kid is going to be in a vegetative state and [there will be] no interaction [with others]. ... I don't know if that is necessarily right because it is supposed to be informed consent, so technically you should be offering all of their options ... but if I think it is futile I will not.

Another said, "Oftentimes they are on BiPAP [bilevel positive airway pressure] at home, get intubated, have a failed extubation, we intubate again. ... I think it is going to continue to get worse. ... Sometimes in those cases I don't offer trach." And finally, one explained,

> Cases where they've been intubated for a long period of time or they are neurologically devastated after a prolonged cardiac arrest or something like that—I would typically just talk about withdrawal and would not bring up a tracheostomy. ... I do not offer a trach when I am sure that it will in no way enhance the quality of life for the child or the family.

Whether these omissions are morally acceptable and why are important questions, but these instances are in a different category from the nudge examples we found, none of which involved blocking or significantly burdening the choice of a tracheostomy. If parents chose a tracheostomy, their choice was respected.

Autonomy is not just about not blocking options, however. As we have seen, of equal relevance is whether the nudge triggered processes that the patient would resist or regret acting on. There are two reasons to think that these nudges did not trigger such processes. First, as discussed earlier, there is reason to believe that parents were happy to be spared the cognitive and emotional burdens of involved deliberative processes and "active choice" scenarios. Second, as I discuss in chapter 3, empirical research has shown that people's assessment of a nudge depends on its purposes and effects. People favor nudges when their ends are seen as legitimate and important. They reject nudges that use heuristics and biases *against them* to get something *from them*. None of the cases examined were of this sort. On the contrary, they were all cases of using heuristics and biases to help parents make decisions that they would *not* regret and that would be best for their child and family in the long run.

One additional consideration is whether these are cases where it is important for the parent to act *for* or *from* particular reasons in the traditional sense. Examples discussed earlier involve cases where a parent or patient might need to internalize or apply such reasons to future decisions (e.g., vaccinations over the course of the first two years of a child's life). This is not such a decision. Another example involves cases where acting "from reasons" is morally or practically desirable because those reasons relate to overarching life plans or identities. Acting "for reasons" when it comes to choosing a college is more important than acting for reasons when deciding what to have for dinner. One might be tempted to say that choosing whether and when to withhold a life-sustaining treatment from a child is more like (and in fact, even more significant than) choosing where to go to college. This may in fact be true, which may be one consideration that points in favor of working to foster parental decision-making that is more deliberative in nature—that is more of a positive exercise of agency and autonomy. However, as I emphasize earlier in the book, that decision-making style may or may not be valuable to every person. Even for these higher-stakes decisions, what seems especially relevant is how an individual does feel, and will feel, looking back on the way she made that decision—or on the way that the decision-making around the major event or situation happened. So there is still room to back off from the normative force of a deliberative model even in these sorts of cases.

The second thing to say is that, as discussed in chapter 3, there is a sense in which a parent who is nudged away from tracheostomy is still acting "from" or "on the basis of" reasons. Reasons are what is driving the physician to engage in a certain kind of choice architecture that nudges parents to seriously consider not proceeding with tracheostomy. In that sense, reasons underlie and have causal force in ultimate decisions made. The final decision is not devoid of reason.

## Nudging in Maternal Fetal Surgery

### Clinical Examples

In 2014, my colleagues and I recorded and analyzed 15 hour-long conversations between fetal surgeons (n = 5) and pregnant women (n = 15) whose fetuses had been diagnosed with a rare and serious abnormality, making them candidates for maternal fetal surgery. Many were cases of fetal spina bifida. A woman could undergo a surgery in which her uterus would be opened, the fetus partially exposed, the open lesion on the fetus's spine covered and repaired, and the uterus closed again for the duration of the pregnancy. Another surgery offered was to correct fetal congenital diaphragmatic hernia (CDH), a condition in which the muscle that holds lower abdominal organs in place is herniated, causing the organs to move up and press on the fetus's heart and lungs. During this surgery, a balloon is temporarily inserted into the fetus's trachea to allow the lungs to grow. This procedure is called a fetal tracheal occlusion (FETO).

These procedures afford potential benefits for fetal survival and morbidity. In the case of CDH, surgery can reduce the risk of death and the chance of the baby's needing extracorporeal membrane oxygenation (a pump that circulates blood through an artificial lung and back into the bloodstream) once born.[7] In moderate to severe cases, CDH mortality can be upwards of 60%.[8] Fetal surgery for spina bifida can reduce the chance that a child needs a permanent cerebral shunt from 80% to 40% and can increase the chance that the child walks from 20% to 40%. But the surgeries are not without risk to the pregnant woman and the fetus. Risks include preterm delivery (which can lead to increased risk of morbidity and mortality for the infant), fetal demise (rare), obstetrical complications from the uterine incision, risks to future pregnancies, the need for a blood transfusion, and maternal pain and suffering.[9]

We analyzed these consultations for how prognosis was discussed and also how the risks and benefits of fetal intervention were presented. We have presented the findings elsewhere,[10] but the major findings were that when prognosis was unfavorable, it was discussed qualitatively rather than quantitatively (e.g., "the odds are against her" rather than "30% chance of survival"). We also found that risk was framed more often in terms of percentage of survival rather than percentage of mortality. There were limited discussions of quality of life or values, and physicians talked the majority of the time. In table 5.3, however, I present for the first time examples of "nudges" found in the transcripts.

### Ethical Analysis

As in the other case studies, the first question to ask is whether clinicians should be in any sort of persuasion mode, be it rational persuasion or nudging. Indicators that they should *not* be are that the expected utility gain from the nudge is low, perhaps because we have little understanding of what would be best for the patient. Here, we have the added ethical complexity that there are two patients: the pregnant woman and the fetus (arguably, depending on views on fetal moral status—complicated by the fact that in the CDH intervention cases, the gestational age of the fetus is in the gray zone of viability). One could take the view, as Laurence McCullough and colleagues have argued, that a sufficient condition for the fetus being considered as a patient with interests is that the pregnant women has conferred that status on the fetus (e.g., by viewing it as such, by presenting for potential treatment, etc.).[11] The majority of the women in this study did in fact seem to view their fetus as a person, or a "patient" whose interests mattered: there was significant concern about, and desire for, fetal benefit. Of course, what is best for the pregnant woman is also important, but in these cases, the risks to the pregnant woman herself (especially risk of significant harm) were relatively minimal.

There are, however, risks to the fetus from fetal intervention, as mentioned. The most significant risk is that of early delivery. This, however, must be weighed against the risks of not intervening. In the case of CDH, without intervention there is significant risk of death (60–75%) in the severe to moderate cases. Thus, there is reason to think intervention would be best for the fetus. *However*, at the time of these consultations, FETO was still considered an experimental procedure for CDH. Thus, one *could* make the argument that no solid evidence base exists, and that there is thus significant lack of clarity about whether intervention is best for the fetal patient, meaning that the clinicians should very much try to avoid any persuasion (be it rational or nudging). But again, in the moderate to severe cases, the

**Table 5.3**

Influencing patients' decision-making in maternal fetal surgery.

| Examples of clinical nudges: quotes from physicians observed during the clinical encounter | Types of nudges |
| --- | --- |
| "Even if we do this trachea occlusion and you decide to go through with that, there's still a chance ... that she ... you know she might not make it. In fact the odds are probably against her—overall. But um. We tried on one patient ... and we couldn't do it ... and then *on two it was successful and ... those were babies very much like your fetus*—as best we can tell. And they seemed to do awfully well." | Use of availability heuristic (create focus on vivid examples rather than actual likelihoods). |
| "You know, we think we have a center here that, um, we think can take care of these babies as good as anyone in the world. We've been studying this problem for a long time, and we've, um, helped teach other doctors about this, and you know we think our results are as good as anybody's. ... You came here because your doctor was talking about fetal treatment and options. And, um, Dr. X is actually *one of the world's experts* on these treatments." | Power of the messenger. |
| "Our hope—all of us that are caring for these children—[we] believe that this is the right thing to do. *I wouldn't offer it to you if I didn't believe it's the right thing to do*. But we haven't— you know—we're just hoping. I believe that—everything I've done and known and animal work we've done for 20 years— that it's the right way to help these children with diaphragm hernia. But there's no proof about this. But the good thing is the procedure has been improved so much that the *risks have gone way way way way down* and now it's just a darn minimal procedure. *One guy in the world does this in his office*. Like right here [gestures to couch]." | Salience; affect; power of the messenger; normalizing (social norms). |
| "We don't want to talk you into it, but we want to just offer it as a treatment option. We want you to make a good, informed choice as to what's best for you and your family. We wouldn't offer it if we thought it was real risky to you or the fetus. ... *So far, in our experience, just to be practical—you know—9 mothers out of 10—you know—I think they would say that they had benefit to it*. But one mother so far would say for them it wasn't the right thing to do. Actually they don't say that. *They say that they knew there were risks, and they were happy with their decision*, is what they actually say." | Power of the messenger; social norms. |
| My—our whole team is sort of concerned, and what we want you to know is even if you do a fetal closure it does not guarantee that there is going to be a benefit. And there are a lot of risks that are associated with it to you and to the baby. And so I always tell families that if you are considering that the thing to remember is *the safest thing—just in* | Defaults (presents not choosing fetal surgery as the default); salience (emphasizes risks |

**Table 5.3** (continued)

| Examples of clinical nudges: quotes from physicians observed during the clinical encounter | Types of nudges |
|---|---|
| *terms of safety—for you and the baby is a postnatal closure. That is clear because there is not all the risk that you get from the operation.* There is not the risk of prematurity from the fetal procedure. There is not the risk to the baby from doing the operation and then reclosing the uterus. So in terms of safety for you and the baby—postnatal closure. But—so—that is the most important. So that is an important thing for you to understand. And *I do not want you to feel like as a mom or as a parent that if you want to do everything possible for your child you should choose fetal surgery* because it is not right for everybody." <br><br> Note: Patient then says, "It is changing my mind. ... You are making me feel like it is not worth going in there and doing." | of surgery); affect and social norms (appeals to role as mother). <br><br> Note: example of nudge *away* from fetal intervention. |
| "I'm worried at this point that the likelihood of her needing—if after birth it turns out she had a bunch of features that made us worry about a significant syndrome. ... In those cases, um, the—the most—those children do die within a period of time, and their quality of life is horrible. And *so usually we counsel just comfort measures ... but sometimes* we also can offer a trial of treatment, where we start treating aggressively and then we keep reassessing." | Defaults (set against intervention). |
| "Now the problem is that that is a lot for you to go through, and there are risks. And the problem for her is that it can lead to early delivery. Basically will lead to early delivery unless—you know—a miracle happens. And there is even a *horrible risk of her dying from the surgery. That risk is really small like 2 to 5%, but that can happen* from complications from her just not being strong enough or from infection or just being born severely early and then dying from complications of the prematurity." | Salience (risks of fetal intervention), loss framing. |
| "Yeah, I think we should— *I'm recommending that delivery approach [a procedure known as EXIT*—ex utero intrapartum treatment]. *I think it's the safest for her. It is—it's more or less like a C-section for you, except for the risks are a little bit higher. ...* Maybe a 1 in 10 chance of needing a blood transfusion because of it, but that's, I guess, *only 10 percent or so.* And then your recovery is kind of very similar to a C-section." | Default (toward procedure); framing (of risks to percentage); affect (safest for baby). |
| *You might ask me, Well, what would I do if it was my own baby? And I guess what I'm thinking is probably I would let him try poking it [the balloon in FETO], and if—if like—if every-*thing was all lined up right and everything looked okay, then we could try it that way. And if we couldn't or there seemed to be too much risk or something, then we would have to do the other thing." | Power of messenger; defaults (proposes to plan on FETO, but can change path later). |

**Table 5.3 (continued)**

| Examples of clinical nudges: quotes from physicians observed during the clinical encounter | Types of nudges |
|---|---|
| "Surgery would improve it from 10% chance of survival in this situation to 56%. So it's almost *five times more.*" | Framing (odds of survival, relative benefit). |
| "It [fetal surgery] seemed to *reduce hydrocephalus by about half,* so it doesn't make it go away. It doesn't prevent it like to zero, but it seems to reduce the risk of that happening."<br>   Note: hydrocephalus/need for shunt goes from 80% to 40%—so 60% will still need a shunt. | Framing (relative benefit). |
| "Doing the surgery early does seem to improve things, and what it does is it seems to decrease the risk of the baby developing hydrocephalus and needing a shunt. And *it seems to cut it in half,* so that's pretty high improvement." | Framing (relative benefit). |
| "We can tell you ... that in the study patients, their legs—their ability to walk independently, was *twice as high* as those that didn't have the surgery."<br>   Note: goes from 20% chance of walking to 40% with fetal surgery—so 60% still will *not* walk. | Framing (relative benefit). |

alternative is death, and so even absent the strong evidence base of a randomized controlled trial, it seems reasonable to say with certainty that trying FETO is better than not trying FETO (assuming the pregnant woman's goals are to do whatever she can, within reason, to benefit the fetus).

The case of fetal surgery for spina bifida is more complicated. On the one hand, a randomized controlled trial (high-quality evidence source) demonstrated that fetal repair is "best" for a certain defined group because it lowers the chances of the child needing a cerebral shunt and increases the chances of the child walking. But even with the surgery, 40% of children still needed a shunt and 60% did not walk. These data need to be weighed against the risks of early delivery and the maternal pains and burdens of the procedure. As it turns out, the median delivery after fetal repair of spina bifida is 34 weeks, which is not as dangerously early as it is in CDH cases (in the range of 22–27 weeks). But there is also a risk to future pregnancies and potentially very early delivery or uterine rupture since the uterus has been opened and stitched; the precise nature of that risk is unknown. Second, there may be lack of understanding about patient (family) values; clinicians may have a tendency to misattribute (in both directions, i.e., underemphasizing or overemphasizing) the importance of certain physical abilities to parents. To ensure ethical acceptability, care must be taken to make sure this is not the case.

The second relevant major indicator that clinicians should work to avoid any form of persuasion (be it rational persuasion or nudging) is if there is reason to believe that the patient (in this case the pregnant woman) would object to any attempts to shape choice and that such attempts would damage the therapeutic relationship. While we did not talk explicitly with the women about their views on this point, my sense was that the majority of women were not opposed to physician input and guidance about what to do in this difficult situation. In one exception, a woman who was herself an academic came into the consultation with an in-depth understanding of the peer-reviewed literature on the topic. She seemed quite confident in her understanding of the situation, weighing of the risks and benefits, and decision—even before the long encounter with the physician began.

But even if persuasion is justified in some cases of maternal fetal surgery, one might ask whether a nudge approach in general, or the particular types of nudges used in the examples provided above, is ethically permissible. One relevant consideration is whether the nudge approach subverted autonomy by blocking options or by triggering processes that the patient would resist or regret acting on. None of the nudges in the examples involved blocking or omitting options. It is, however, worth asking whether they triggered processes that the patient would resist or regret acting from. As in the pediatric critical care context, maternal fetal surgery is often a situation in which the pregnant woman (and her partner, to the extent she involves him/her) experiences a high emotional and cognitive burden. Thus, she may be relieved to have more System 1 processes triggered, rather than resisting or regretting such processes. And again, empirical evidence has demonstrated that people endorse rather than reject nudges so long as their own ends are seen as legitimate and important. The aim, conscious or unconscious, of nudges in these cases was to set up parents to make decisions that they would not regret and that were best for their child based on the severity of their condition and prognosis. We would need an empirical study to analyze the pregnant women's attitudes toward these examples, but without that we can hypothesize based on other empirical research that they are likely to accept, approve of, or endorse them. It is also worth noting that in these examples the nudges were probably to some extent transparent to the pregnant women—e.g., in hearing the stories of success cases, she knows the physician is pro-surgery and thinks it could be a good idea for her fetus and her, given her own goals and risk profile. And while we did not explicitly interview the women, none gave any negative reactions or indications.

Now, a way in which some of these examples *might* subvert autonomy is if they negatively affect the woman's understanding. As discussed, in many accounts of autonomous decision-making, sufficient understanding is a key criterion. One might argue that several of the nudges, particularly the ones involving framing of benefit in relative rather than absolute terms, might distort understanding of the risks and benefits of intervention. For example, to say, "it reduces the risk of cerebral shunt by *half*" may lead a woman to think that it reduces it by 50%, or it may cause her to feel as if there is a great chance that her child will not need a shunt if there is a fetal intervention. In reality, 40% of children will still need a shunt. A similar concern is telling a woman, "Their ability to walk was *twice as* high." This can also be misleading. In fact, one could almost see the "aha" moment in a mother when one physician reframed things. The physician said, "And so you know, again, there was 20% walking in the postnatal group versus 40% in the fetal surgery group. So that's double. That's great. But still, 60% weren't walking, right? So almost two-thirds weren't walking. So probably the most likely outcome is you're not walking and you have a shunt."

One final consideration in the ethical analysis is the importance of the patient's acting *from* or *for* particular reasons or, more formally, deliberatively. This is not a case where the woman will need to internalize and apply these reasons to a similar future decision. But there is another example where acting "from reasons" might be considered morally or practically desirable, and that is when those reasons relate to overarching life plans or identities (to repeat an earlier example, acting for reasons when it comes to choosing a college is more important than acting for reasons when deciding what to have for dinner). I think that here we can say what we said in the pediatric case, which is that this may in fact be true, but it may also be true that even though this is more like a college decision than a dinner decision, a very reasons-based or deliberative style may not be valuable to all women—either in the moment or looking back at the decision years later. Finally, I note what I noted in the pediatric case, that even if the woman doesn't sit down and write out her values and how they point in one direction or another, reasons still play a role in some of the examples provided above in the sense that they drove the physician to engage in a certain kind of choice architecture based on a belief about what the woman had best reason to do. So, all things considered, some factors point toward ethical acceptability in these cases, but some factors cause concern, particularly around patient understanding/misunderstanding and misinterpretation (e.g., "twice as high," "cut in half"). Moreover, the ethical acceptability depends significantly on the premise that these women's values and trade-offs have been considered and point in the direction of fetal intervention.

### Nudging in Prostate Cancer Decision-Making

### Clinical Examples

The final example I give has to do with the use of nudges in decision-making with men diagnosed with localized prostate cancer. Men with early-stage, localized prostate cancer are at low risk for dying from their disease; treatment is not likely to improve prognosis and may result in adverse effects such as impotence and incontinence.[12] In these cases, the UK National Institute for Health and Clinical Excellence Guidelines indicate that active surveillance (in which the cancer is monitored for growth) is the preferred approach.[13] Nonetheless, active treatment, including surgical removal of the cancer, remains the norm, with only 20–30% of eligible men on active surveillance protocols.[14]

We conducted a survey of over 300 men living with prostate cancer (only 24% of whom were on active surveillance protocols) to test several "nudges" that might encourage men to try active surveillance. The two general types of nudges tested were incentives with framing effects and normative messages.[15] For the incentives condition, we asked half the men to imagine that their copays would be covered for their active surveillance visits if they gave active surveillance a try (they could stop and choose treatment at any time), and we asked the other half to imagine that they would be given a $100 incentive per visit for giving active surveillance a try. Presenting these results for the first time here, we found that 31% of men said they would have *likely* given active surveillance a try, and 19% said they *might* have given it a try *(for a total of 50%) if their copays were covered*. Ten percent were unsure, and 40% said it would not have affected their decision. In regard to the $100 incentive, 27% of the men said they would have *likely* given active surveillance a try, and 16% said they *might* have (*for a total of 43%*). This is interesting in part because the $100 incentive per visit would likely be worth more than the copay coverage per visit (~$20–50), but our results indicate that the copay coverage framing is more influential.

For the normative messages condition, we tested several messages that presented active surveillance as a normal, reasonable, or desirable thing for men to try. The results of this study and the contents of the messages tested are reported elsewhere.[16] However, a few messages were rated by men as things that would have made them more likely to have given active surveillance a try had they heard the messages during their decision-making process. One message was, "As long as I'm keeping a close eye on it with my doctors, I can possibly prolong this for a number of years until the treatment options have improved"; 77% said that if men heard this, they would be more likely to choose active surveillance. Another was, "With active surveillance, my life goes on in a perfectly normal fashion, and I am interested in continuing that until I absolutely have to do something else"; 76% said that if men heard this, they would be more likely to choose active surveillance. A third was, "It depends on your age. If you're young and you have a sexual life, I would definitely wait and just watch and see if it spreads, and then you can always make that decision, but I just wouldn't jump into it"; 74% rated this message as making men more likely to choose active surveillance. An example that was rated very low in terms of its nudge potential was, "Regretfully, I never gave active surveillance a second thought when I was considering my treatment options. I was from the old school of thinking that says, if it's cancer, I want it out!" Only 45% of men rated this message as making men more likely to choose active surveillance. By studying these messages, we see ones that would be more effective at nudging men to try active surveillance and ones that would not be.

### Ethical Analysis

My analysis here is briefer than the other case examples because I have used the prostate decision-making example at various points in the book and I refer the reader to those. One important point to note is that in this case, even though the mortality rates associated with immediate treatment and active surveillance are the same, vastly more people choose surgery (or radiation) even though it presents with increased risks (impotence, incontinence). One explanation for this may be that men's decision-making is driven by several identifiable heuristics and biases. In fact, my colleagues and I have argued that the following biases likely play a major role: the commission bias (doing something is better than doing nothing even if the something causes more harm) and the availability bias (reliance on anecdotal stories). These biases play a role—in addition to fear, heavy reliance on physician recommendations, pressure from family members, and lack of awareness that treatment does not guarantee improved survival. All these factors skew decision-making in favor of immediate treatment.[17] Therefore, one way to view the ethical justifiability of various active surveillance nudges is to see them as counterbalancing existing biases, as discussed in chapter 3. One can also view them as instances of justified soft paternalism in that they prevent, or try to counter, a nonautonomous or autonomy-impaired decision that can result in harm (impotence, incontinence).

One might press the point that, although the clinical outcomes are clear (active surveillance has the same mortality rate as immediate treatment without the risks of impotence and incontinence), there may be missing information about patient values. In fact, one study finds that physicians did *not* take the time to have values-based discussions with men about whether/how they value sexual ability in this context.[18] Thus, it is true, care must be taken to ensure that any use of nudging is based on some grounding about what would, in fact, make a patient "better off." As discussed in chapter 2, on many accounts of welfare, a person's preferences, desires, values, and goals are part of that answer.

One might also object that although active surveillance does not carry risks of impotence and incontinence, it does carry a risk of increased anxiety or other negative psychological impacts. In response, interestingly, five-year outcomes reveal that both groups (immediate treatment and active surveillance) experienced equal amounts of health-related distress, worry, feeling low, and insomnia.[19] A systematic review of the impact of active surveillance on quality of life found that patients reported good quality of life, and another study found that choosing active surveillance did not produce decisional regret.[20] Thus, it is likely that active surveillance may be in the interest of many men with low-risk, localized prostate cancer despite the fact that they often do not consider it a viable option nor is it presented as one. Ethically responsible choice architecture may favor nudges in favor of active surveillance in this context.

## Conclusion

This chapter shows a view of nudging in the weeds. That is, what sorts of nudges are used in clinical care, with some of the ethical considerations that go into the assessment of their appropriateness in the context at hand. Through these examples, one gets a sense that the ethical analysis is extremely nuanced: one has to know much about the context. Thus, there is no simple answer about the ethics of nudging. Whereas bioethicists like to make general presumptions about the ethics of nudging (pro or con), so much is case specific, and we need to be willing to dig into the weeds of individual cases to do good ethical analysis.

# Conclusion

This book's core argument has been that findings from behavioral economics challenge some of our fundamental assumptions about patient decision-making and autonomy, and raise concerns about negative effects on patient decision-making and protecting and promoting patients' interests. At the same time, clinicians and ethicists who understand these effects can begin to use them to improve choice and to shape patient decision-making for the better through nudges and choice architecture. Under certain circumstances, clinicians have an obligation to do this because of their moral duty to protect and promote patients' interests. Shaping decision-making in this way need not interfere with patient autonomy; in fact, in certain ways it can respect and promote it.

That having been said, I hope this book has made clear that there is no single, simple account of the ethics of nudging. Much depends on the nuances and contextual factors of each case. Along with the book's philosophical arguments and ethical analyses, I have offered some concrete guidelines for clinicians who are considering when and how to shape patient choice through the use of behavioral economics insights and nudges.

To recap some of that guidance, situations where clinicians should work to minimize nudging (or rational persuasion for that matter) include those where a patient is making a decision that is well thought out and line with her values and goals; where there is lowered expected utility gain from nudging, due to, for example, uncertainty about what choice would be best for the patient; and where the patient would object to attempts, even if beneficently motivated, to shape her choice. In these cases, clinicians should work as much as possible to present "just the facts" and the information associated with each option. This book acknowledges that it is probably impossible to avoid influencing choice altogether, but such influence can be limited.

Situations also exist where influence is acceptable but where rational persuasion as a mode of influence might be preferable to nudging. These include cases where rational persuasion is likely to be just as effective at improving choice, where rational persuasion is reasonable and feasible in terms of the time and effort required to employ it, and where rational persuasion places an acceptable emotional and cognitive burden on the patient. Other situations where rational persuasion might be preferable to a nudge-based approach include high-stakes or high-value choices in which reflection and deliberation are morally or practically desirable, as well as cases in which it is important for a patient to be able to recite the facts and the arguments for a particular option (e.g., because that ability is linked to adherence to a treatment plan).

One of the main messages of the book, however, has been that avoiding influencing patients' choices altogether is often impossible. Thus, clinicians and ethicists need to think about how to do so in an ethically responsible way. As Richard Thaler and Cass Sunstein note in their book *Nudge*, "If you are a doctor and must describe the alternative treatments available to a patient, you are a choice architect."[1]

The work of a choice architect is ethically complex but important. It is imperative for ethicists and philosophers to continue to think about the challenges and paradoxes that behavioral economics and decision science present for our ideas about autonomy, informed consent, and even decision-making capacity. It is also imperative for clinicians to continue to learn about decision science and to consider how they might use these insights in their own work with patients.

I look forward to continuing to work on these issues and hope that I may have gained some new collaborators from readers of this book.

# Notes

## Chapter 1

1. Daniel Kahneman, *Thinking, Fast and Slow* (New York: Farrar, Straus and Giroux, 2011), 20–21.

2. J. S. Blumenthal-Barby and Heather Krieger, "Cognitive Biases and Heuristics in Medical Decision Making: A Critical Review Using a Systematic Search Strategy," *Medical Decision Making* 35, no. 4 (May 1, 2015): 539–557, https://doi.org/10.1177/0272989X14547740. This chapter is not meant to serve as a review of *all* the heuristics and biases or related phenomena, nor does it provide an underlying theory of the heuristics and biases research program. While I do discuss some of the underlying theoretical issues and debates later in this chapter, there are deep and interesting questions in psychology and philosophy of science that are beyond the aims of this book. The fundamental aim of this book is to consider how some of the work coming out of the science of judgment and decision-making challenges fundamental assumptions in medicine and medical ethics about patient decision-making and autonomy.

3. Blumenthal-Barby and Krieger, "Cognitive Biases and Heuristics in Medical Decision Making."

4. Buster Benson, "Cognitive Bias Cheat Sheet," Medium: Better Humans, September 1, 2016, https://medium.com/better-humans/cognitive-bias-cheat-sheet-55a472476b18. I am not wedded to this framework or to which category Benson assigns particular biases. It is simply a useful organizing framework for discussion of these effects and examples.

5. Noreen C. Facione and Peter A. Facione, "The Cognitive Structuring of Patient Delay in Breast Cancer," *Social Science & Medicine* 63, no. 12 (December 1, 2006): 3137–3149, https://doi.org/10.1016/j.socscimed.2006.08.014.

6. Daniel D. Matlock et al., "Evidence of Cognitive Bias in Decision Making around Implantable-Cardioverter Defibrillators: A Qualitative Framework Analysis," *Journal*

*of Cardiac Failure* 23, no. 11 (November 1, 2017): 797, https://doi.org/10.1016/j .cardfail.2017.03.008.

7. Peter A. Ubel, Christopher Jepson, and Jonathan Baron, "The Inclusion of Patient Testimonials in Decision Aids: Effects on Treatment Choices," *Medical Decision Making* 21, no. 1 (2001): 60–68, https://doi.org/10.1177/0272989X0102100108.

8. J. S. Swindell, Amy L. McGuire, and Scott D. Halpern, "Beneficent Persuasion: Techniques and Ethical Guidelines to Improve Patients' Decisions," *Annals of Family Medicine* 8, no. 3 (May 1, 2010): 260–264, https://doi.org/10.1370/afm.1118.

9. Jennifer Amsterlaw et al., "Can Avoidance of Complications Lead to Biased Health-care Decisions?," *Judgment and Decision Making* 1 (2006): 64–75.

10. Some might take issue with psychologists calling this effect a "bias" if the term is meant to imply some sort of error in judgment. These objectors might argue that omission bias is normatively defensible (in Kantian ethics, omission is better than commission in some cases—e.g., in allowing versus causing a death). I will have more to say about this in the section on normative and theoretical issues later in the chapter, but I acknowledge it here.

11. Katrina F. Brown et al., "Omission Bias and Vaccine Rejection by Parents of Healthy Children: Implications for the Influenza A/H1N1 Vaccination Programme," *Vaccine* 28, no. 25 (June 7, 2010): 4181–4185, https://doi.org/10.1016/j.vaccine.2010 .04.012; Ilana Ritov and Jonathan Baron, "Reluctance to Vaccinate: Omission Bias and Ambiguity," *Journal of Behavioral Decision Making* 3, no. 4 (1990): 263–277, https://doi .org/10.1002/bdm.3960030404.

12. Angela Fagerlin, Brian J. Zikmund-Fisher, and Peter A. Ubel, "Cure Me Even If It Kills Me: Preferences for Invasive Cancer Treatment," *Medical Decision Making* 25, no. 6 (November 1, 2005): 614–619, https://doi.org/10.1177/0272989X05282639.

13. Fagerlin, Zikmund-Fisher, and Ubel, "Cure Me Even If It Kills Me."

14. Brian Wansink, Robert J. Kent, and Stephen J. Hoch, "An Anchoring and Adjust-ment Model of Purchase Quantity Decisions," *Journal of Marketing Research* 35, no. 1 (February 1, 1998): 71–81, https://doi.org/10.1177/002224379803500108. I found this study in Kahneman, *Thinking, Fast and Slow*, 127.

15. Kahneman, *Thinking, Fast and Slow*, 119–128.

16. Jennifer C. Chen et al., "Measuring Patient Tolerance for Future Adverse Events in Low-Risk Emergency Department Chest Pain Patients," *Annals of Emergency Medicine* 64, no. 2 (August 1, 2014): 127–136, https://doi.org/10.1016/j.annemergmed.2013.12.025.

17. J. Richard Eiser, "The Influence of Question Framing on Symptom Report and Perceived Health Status," *Psychology & Health* 15, no. 1 (February 1, 2000): 13–20, https://doi.org/10.1080/08870440008400285.

18. Amy J. Keenum et al., "Generic Medications for You, but Brand-Name Medications for Me," *Research in Social and Administrative Pharmacy* 8, no. 6 (November 1, 2012): 574–578, https://doi.org/10.1016/j.sapharm.2011.12.004.

19. David J. Malenka et al., "The Framing Effect of Relative and Absolute Risk," *Journal of General Internal Medicine* 8, no. 10 (October 1, 1993): 543–548, https://doi.org/10.1007/BF02599636.

20. Itamar Simonson, "Choice Based on Reasons: The Case of Attraction and Compromise Effects," *Journal of Consumer Research* 16, no. 2 (1989): 158–174, https://doi.org/10.1086/209205; Janet A. Schwartz and Gretchen B. Chapman, "Are More Options Always Better? The Attraction Effect in Physicians' Decisions about Medications," *Medical Decision Making* 19, no. 3 (August 1, 1999): 315–323, https://doi.org/10.1177/0272989X9901900310.

21. R. Mendel et al., "Confirmation Bias: Why Psychiatrists Stick to Wrong Preliminary Diagnoses," *Psychological Medicine* 41, no. 12 (December 2011): 2651–2659, https://doi.org/10.1017/S0033291711000808.

22. As with omission bias, some might take issue with psychologists calling this effect a bias. These objectors might argue that the ostrich effect is normatively defensible.

23. Akiva Liberman and Shelly Chaiken, "Defensive Processing of Personally Relevant Health Messages," *Personality and Social Psychology Bulletin* 18, no. 6 (December 1, 1992): 669–679, https://doi.org/10.1177/0146167292186002.

24. Robert T. Croyle, Yi-chun Sun, and Douglas H. Louie, "Psychological Minimization of Cholesterol Test Results: Moderators of Appraisal in College Students and Community Residents," *Health Psychology* 12, no. 6 (1993): 503–507, https://doi.org/10.1037/0278-6133.12.6.503.

25. Gary H. McClelland and Beverly H. Hackenberg, "Subjective Probabilities for Sex of Next Child: U.S. College Students and Philippine Villagers," *Journal of Population* 1, no. 2 (June 1, 1978): 132–147, https://doi.org/10.1007/BF01277598.

26. Another example of a phenomenon that some may disagree should be considered a bias. Objectors might argue that deference to authorities and experts is normatively defensible.

27. Again, an argument can be made that this response is normatively defensible. I don't disagree, but I point out ways in which the bandwagon effect and the power of norms can negatively impact patient choice (in chapter 2) but can also be harnessed to improve choice (chapter 3).

28. Jennifer D. Allen et al., "Stage of Adoption of the Human Papillomavirus Vaccine among College Women," *Preventive Medicine* 48, no. 5 (May 1, 2009): 420–425, https://doi.org/10.1016/j.ypmed.2008.12.005.

29. Brian J. Zikmund-Fisher et al., "'I'll Do What They Did': Social Norm Information and Cancer Treatment Decisions," *Patient Education and Counseling* 85, no. 2 (November 1, 2011): 225–229, https://doi.org/10.1016/j.pec.2011.01.031.

30. Jason Riis et al., "Ignorance of Hedonic Adaptation to Hemodialysis: A Study Using Ecological Momentary Assessment," *Journal of Experimental Psychology: General* 134, no. 1 (2005): 3–9, https://doi.org/10.1037/0096-3445.134.1.3.

31. Dylan M. Smith et al., "Misremembering Colostomies? Former Patients Give Lower Utility Ratings than Do Current Patients," *Health Psychology: Official Journal of the Division of Health Psychology, American Psychological Association* 25, no. 6 (November 2006): 688–695, https://doi.org/10.1037/0278-6133.25.6.688.

32. Dylan Smith et al., "Mispredicting and Misremembering: Patients with Renal Failure Overestimate Improvements in Quality of Life after a Kidney Transplant," *Health Psychology: Official Journal of the Division of Health Psychology, American Psychological Association* 27, no. 5 (September 2008): 653–658, https://doi.org/10.1037/a0012647.

33. Colin F. Camerer, George Loewenstein, and Matthew Rabin, eds., *Advances in Behavioral Economics* (Princeton, NJ: Princeton University Press, 2004), 21.

34. Eric J. Johnson and Daniel Goldstein, "Do Defaults Save Lives?," *Science* 302, no. 5649 (November 21, 2003): 1338–1339, https://doi.org/10.1126/science.1091721.

35. Laura M. Kressel and Gretchen B. Chapman, "The Default Effect in End-of-Life Medical Treatment Preferences," *Medical Decision Making* 27, no. 3 (May 1, 2007): 299–310, https://doi.org/10.1177/0272989X07300608.

36. Enrico Rubaltelli et al., "Strengthening Acceptance for Xenotransplantation: The Case of Attraction Effect," *Xenotransplantation* 15, no. 3 (2008): 159–163, https://doi.org/10.1111/j.1399-3089.2008.00474.x.

37. Brian J. Zikmund-Fisher, Angela Fagerlin, and Peter A. Ubel, "'Is 28% Good or Bad?' Evaluability and Preference Reversals in Health Care Decisions," *Medical Decision Making* 24, no. 2 (March 1, 2004): 142–148, https://doi.org/10.1177/0272989X04263154.

38. Sara M. Banks et al., "The Effects of Message Framing on Mammography Utilization," *Health Psychology* 14, no. 2 (1995): 178–184, https://doi.org/10.1037/0278-6133.14.2.178.

39. Hitinder Singh Gurm and David G. Litaker, "Framing Procedural Risks to Patients: Is 99% Safe the Same as a Risk of 1 in 100?," *Academic Medicine* 75, no. 8 (August 2000): 840–842, doi: 10.1097/00001888-200008000-00018.

40. Carla C. Braxton, Celia N. Robinson, and Samir S. Awad, "Escalation of Commitment in the Surgical ICU," *Critical Care Medicine* 45, no. 4 (April 2017): e433–c436, https://doi.org/10.1097/CCM.0000000000002261.

41. Richard Thaler, "Toward a Positive Theory of Consumer Choice," *Journal of Economic Behavior & Organization* 1, no. 1 (March 1, 1980): 39–60, https://doi.org/10.1016/0167-2681(80)90051-7.

42. Martin D. Coleman, "Sunk Cost and Commitment to Medical Treatment," *Current Psychology* 29, no. 2 (June 1, 2010): 121–134, https://doi.org/10.1007/s12144-010-9077-7.

43. As with a few of the other examples, some might take the view that illusion of control, optimism bias, and overconfidence are normatively defensible.

44. Douglas B. White et al., "Prevalence of and Factors Related to Discordance about Prognosis between Physicians and Surrogate Decision Makers of Critically Ill Patients," *JAMA* 315, no. 19 (May 17, 2016): 2092, https://doi.org/10.1001/jama.2016.5351.

45. Neil Weinstein, "Unrealistic Optimism about Future Life Events," *Journal of Personality and Social Psychology* 39, no. 5 (November 1, 1980): 806–820.

46. Larry A. Allen et al., "Discordance between Patient-Predicted and Model-Predicted Life Expectancy among Ambulatory Patients with Heart Failure," *JAMA* 299, no. 21 (June 4, 2008): 2533–2542, https://doi.org/10.1001/jama.299.21.2533.

47. White et al., "Prevalence of and Factors Related to Discordance about Prognosis."

48. Stephanie J. Lee et al., "Discrepancies between Patient and Physician Estimates for the Success of Stem Cell Transplantation," *JAMA* 285, no. 8 (February 28, 2001): 1034–1038, https://doi.org/10.1001/jama.285.8.1034.

49. Val Morrison et al., "The Impact of Information Order on Intentions to Undergo Predictive Genetic Testing: An Experimental Study," *Journal of Health Psychology* 15, no. 7 (October 1, 2010): 1082–1092, https://doi.org/10.1177/1359105310364171.

50. Peter A. Ubel et al., "Testing Whether Decision Aids Introduce Cognitive Biases: Results of a Randomized Trial," *Patient Education and Counseling* 80, no. 2 (August 1, 2010): 158–163, https://doi.org/10.1016/j.pec.2009.10.021.

51. Eran Chajut et al., "In Pain Thou Shalt Bring Forth Children: The Peak-and-End Rule in Recall of Labor Pain," *Psychological Science* 25, no. 12 (December 2014): 2266–2271, https://doi.org/10.1177/0956797614551004.

52. Donald A. Redelmeier, Joel Katz, and Daniel Kahneman, "Memories of Colonoscopy: A Randomized Trial," *Pain* 104, no. 1 (July 1, 2003): 187–194, https://doi.org/10.1016/S0304-3959(03)00003-4.

53. Emily Pronin, Daniel Y. Lin, and Lee Ross, "The Bias Blind Spot: Perceptions of Bias in Self versus Others," *Personality and Social Psychology Bulletin* 28, no. 3 (March 1, 2002): 369–381, https://doi.org/10.1177/0146167202286008.

54. Gerd Gigerenzer, "On the Supposed Evidence for Libertarian Paternalism," *Review of Philosophy and Psychology* 6, no. 3 (September 1, 2015): 361–383, https://doi.org/10.1007/s13164-015-0248-1.

55. I thank a reviewer for this point and the subsequent examples.

56. Gigerenzer, "On the Supposed Evidence," 368. Gigerenzer also makes the point that the term "bias" implies that these phenomena are ingrained in human decision-making the way that visual illusions are, when in reality people can be educated out of many of these "errors." For example, we can train people to understand statistics better. While this is true for some effects, many discussed here are deeply ingrained and cannot be addressed by training people to better understand statistical reasoning.

57. Gregory Schwartz, "The Ethics of Omission," *Think* 18, no. 51 (2019): 117–121, https://doi.org/10.1017/S1477175618000404.

58. J. S. Blumenthal-Barby and Peter A. Ubel, "In Defense of 'Denial': Difficulty Knowing When Beliefs Are Unrealistic and Whether Unrealistic Beliefs Are Bad," *American Journal of Bioethics* 18, no. 9 (September 2, 2018): 4–15, https://doi.org/10.1080/15265161.2018.1498934.

59. Open Science Collaboration, "Estimating the Reproducibility of Psychological Science," *Science* 349, no. 6251 (August 28, 2015), https://doi.org/10.1126/science.aac4716.

60. Colin F. Camerer et al., "Evaluating the Replicability of Social Science Experiments in *Nature* and *Science* between 2010 and 2015," *Nature Human Behaviour* 2, no. 9 (August 27, 2019): 637–644, https://doi.org/10.1038/s41562-018-0399-z.

61. Gigerenzer, "One the Supposed Evidence for Libertarian Paternalism."

62. Daniel Kahneman and Amos Tversky, "On the Reality of Cognitive Illusions," *Psychological Review* 103, no. 3 (July 1, 1996): 582–591, https://doi.org/10.1037/0033-295X.103.3.582.

63. David Gal and Derek D. Rucker, "The Loss of Loss Aversion: Will It Loom Larger than Its Gain?," ed. Sharon Shavitt, *Journal of Consumer Psychology* 28, no. 3 (July 2018): 497–516, https://doi.org/10.1002/jcpy.1047.

## Chapter 2

1. Many philosophers have noted numerous meanings of the term "autonomy." Manuel Vargas states, "Autonomy is variously characterized as: bare agency; a species of self-governed agency; a kind of relation to the world; an ideal of self-control that may rarely be had; a kind of rule-governed activity that is frequently had; ownership-taking for what one does; interchangeable with freedom; a conception of morally

responsible agency; neither freedom nor morally responsible agency; competence for medical decision-making; authority over personal choices; self-rule; a designation for agents bound by political principles governing the basic institutions of society; freedom from external influence; freedom from external control or restriction on choice; and, the kind of thing for which external restrictions on choice are largely irrelevant." See Manuel Vargas, review of *Personal Autonomy: New Essays on Personal Autonomy and Its Role in Contemporary Moral Philosophy*, ed. James Stacey Taylor (Cambridge: Cambridge University Press, 2005), *Notre Dame Philosophical Reviews*, August 15, 2006, https://ndpr.nd.edu/news/personal-autonomy-new-essays-on-per sonal-autonomy-and-its-role-in-contemporary-moral-philosophy/.

Joel Feinberg identifies four meanings of the term: the capacity to govern oneself and make one's own decisions, the actual condition of self-government, an ideal of character, and the right to govern one's self. See Joel Feinberg, *The Moral Limits of the Criminal Law*, vol. 3, *Harm to Self* (New York: Oxford University Press, 1989), https://www.oxfordscholarship.com/view/10.1093/0195059239.001.0001/acprof -9780195059236.

And Nomy Arpaly discusses eight senses in which the term is used: agent autonomy concerns the relationship that an agent has to her motivational states, autonomy as personal efficacy concerns physical independence and not relying on others, autonomy as independence of mind concerns not blindly accepting the views of others, normative autonomy concerns one's moral right to have her decisions respected, autonomy as authenticity concerns the absence of external desires and values, heroic autonomy concerns an ideal condition that a great majority of persons do not have, and autonomy as acting rationally concerns the ability to respond to reasons. See Nomy Arpaly, *Unprincipled Virtue: An Inquiry into Moral Agency* (Oxford: Oxford University Press, 2002), https://www.oxfordscholarship.com/view/10.1093/0195152042 .001.0001/acprof-9780195152043.

2. Tom L. Beauchamp and James F. Childress, *Principles of Biomedical Ethics*, 6th ed. (New York: Oxford University Press, 2009), 101. Note that intentionality is a matter of yes/no, whereas understanding and freedom from constraint are matters of degree. Beauchamp and Childress's position is that that autonomy requires a "substantial" degree of understanding and freedom from constraint, where "substantial" is best determined by the particular context.

3. I have also developed this argument in depth elsewhere: J. S. Blumenthal-Barby, "Biases and Heuristics in Decision Making and Their Impact on Autonomy," *American Journal of Bioethics* 16, no. 5 (May 3, 2016): 5–15, https://doi.org/10.1080 /15265161.2016.1159750.

4. Michael E. Bratman, "Planning Agency, Autonomous Agency," in *Personal Autonomy: New Essays on Personal Autonomy and Its Role in Contemporary Moral Philosophy*, ed. James Stacey Taylor (New York: Cambridge University Press, 2005), 33–57.

5. Ruth R. Faden and Tom L. Beauchamp, *A History and Theory of Informed Consent* (New York: Oxford University Press, 1986), 243.

6. My thanks to Peter A. Ubel for this example.

7. There may be other factors at play in these examples that are unrelated to heuristics and biases (e.g., narratives of the "good mother" or "the cancer survivor"). While this is true, it is worth noting that these examples come from studies where researchers explicitly examined the *reasons* why certain decisions were made (e.g., to choose surgery for cancer), and rather than finding themes about identity (e.g., a "survivor"), they found themes consistent with heuristics and biases (e.g., the drive to "do something"—the commission bias).

8. Carl E. Schneider, *The Practice of Autonomy: Patients, Doctors, and Medical Decisions* (New York: Oxford University Press, 1998), 95.

9. Faden and Beauchamp, *A History and Theory of Informed Consent*, 251.

10. Beauchamp and Childress, *Principles of Biomedical Ethics*, 101; Valerie F. Reyna, "A Theory of Medical Decision Making and Health: Fuzzy Trace Theory," *Medical Decision Making* 28, no. 6 (November 1, 2008): 850–865, https://doi.org/10.1177 /0272989X08327066.

11. Moti Gorin, "Welfare First, Autonomy Second," *American Journal of Bioethics* 16, no. 5 (May 3, 2016): 18–20, https://doi.org/10.1080/15265161.2016.1159760.

12. James Stacey Taylor, *Practical Autonomy and Bioethics* (New York: Routledge, 2009), 6.

13. For a more detailed argument about the importance of true beliefs (part of understanding) for autonomy, see Suzy Killmister, "Autonomy and False Beliefs," *Philosophical Studies* 164, no. 2 (June 1, 2013): 513–531, https://doi.org/10.1007/s 11098-012-9864-0. Here, Killmister argues that an action fails to be autonomous if the agent has a particular kind of false belief about the action she is undertaking— namely, a false belief about either the nature of the act or its consequences that had that false belief not been present, the agent would have acted otherwise.

14. Thomas Grisso and Paul S. Appelbaum, *Assessing Competence to Consent to Treatment: A Guide for Physicians and Other Health Professionals* (New York: Oxford University Press, 1998), 12–13. The notion of "meaningful decisions" is instructive here, for one may make the argument that lack of understanding or false beliefs impair "decision quality" or the meaningful exercise of autonomy more so or rather than the exercise of "autonomy" per se. I do not have a stake in the game about how best to characterize the impairment, but I wish to make the normative point that poor understanding (triggered by various heuristics and biases) does indeed impair decision-making in morally concerning ways that clinicians and bioethicists should be concerned about.

15. Robert M. Veatch, *The Basics of Bioethics* (Upper Saddle River, NJ: Pearson Education, 2012), 71.

16. Alfred R. Mele, *Autonomous Agents: From Self Control to Autonomy* (New York: Oxford University Press, 1995), 181.

17. Veatch, *The Basics of Bioethics*, 71.

18. My thanks to an anonymous manuscript reviewer for this suggestion.

19. Thomas E. Hill, "The Kantian Conception of Autonomy," in *The Inner Citadel: Essays on Individual Autonomy*, ed. John Philip Christman (New York: Oxford University Press, 1989), 93; Gerald Allan Cohen, "Reason, Humanity, and the Moral Law," in *The Sources of Normativity*, by Christine M. Korsgaard, ed. Onora O'Neill (Cambridge: Cambridge University Press, 1996), 173–174.

20. Christine M. Korsgaard, *The Sources of Normativity*, ed. Onora O'Neill (Cambridge: Cambridge University Press, 1996), 97.

21. Three main normative standards for rationality employed by psychologists are the principle of dominance, the principle of invariance, and the sunk cost principle. The principle of dominance holds that a person should choose the option that is never worse than the others and may provide a better outcome. The principle of invariance holds that the same information should be understood and weighed the same regardless of how it is presented. The sunk cost principle holds that because decisions influence the future, decision-makers should weigh future consequences and not previous outcomes or behaviors. See Daniel J. Keys and Barry Schwartz, "'Leaky' Rationality: How Research on Behavioral Decision Making Challenges Normative Standards of Rationality," *Perspectives on Psychological Science* 2, no. 2 (June 1, 2007): 162–180, https://doi.org/10.1111/j.1745-6916.2007.00035.x.

22. Paul S. Appelbaum, "Clinical Practice: Assessment of Patients' Competence to Consent to Treatment," *New England Journal of Medicine* 357, no. 18 (November 1, 2007): 1834–1840, https://doi.org/10.1056/NEJMcp074045. One could even argue, provocatively, that the implications of chapter 1 are that many patients might be incapable of making their own medical decisions (lack capacity). I am not making that argument here; however, I am making the argument for bad decisions—those that are not so autonomous, are lacking in quality, and are potentially harmful.

23. There are conceptual differences between preferences, goals, and values. Typically, in the medical context, "preference" refers to the option most or least favored by the patient; "values" represent the extent to which positive or negative aspects of the health options are important to the patient, and "goals" typically refer to how the patient will satisfy their preferences (e.g., the steps they need to take). See, for example, Hilary A. Llewellyn-Thomas and R. Trafford Crump, "Decision Support for Patients: Values Clarification and Preference Elicitation," *Medical Care Research and Review* 70, no. 1 suppl. (February 2013): 50S–79S, https://doi.org/10.1177/10775587

12461182; and Angela Fagerlin et al., "Clarifying Values: An Updated Review," *BMC Medical Informatics and Decision Making* 13, no. suppl. 2 (November 29, 2013), http://dx.doi.org/10.1186/1472-6947-13-S2-S8.

24. One anonymous reviewer of this manuscript objected that choice-values concordance privileges previously stated preferences in a way that fails to account for forecasting errors. While there may indeed be some cases where forecasting errors are at play, my argument here is more general. I merely mean to make the case that there may be situations where no forecasting errors are at play—a person has a genuine established preference (not a preference formed erroneously due to a forecasting error), and a heuristic or bias leads them astray to make a decision that is not concordant with it.

25. In chapter 3 I reject this strong view and argue that at least in some cases, stable values and goals exist and are quite clear and can be used to guide and improve patients' decision-making.

26. See chapter 1 for more examples. One study I discuss there involves the effect of defaults on end-of-life decision-making. Patients who receive an advance directive with life-saving treatment (LST) framed as the default preferred it more than those who received an advance directive with no LST framed as the default.

27. Behavioral economists refer to this as "the construction of preference" or "the context dependent nature of preferences." See, for example, Sarah Lichtenstein and Paul Slovic, eds., *The Construction of Preference* (New York: Cambridge University Press, 2006).

28. Harry G. Frankfurt, "Freedom of the Will and the Concept of a Person," in *The Importance of What We Care About* (New York: Cambridge University Press, 1988), 11–25.

29. Richard Double, "Two Types of Autonomy Accounts," *Canadian Journal of Philosophy* 22 (January 1, 1992): 73, https://doi.org/10.1080/00455091.1992.10717271.

30. Double, "Two Types of Autonomy Accounts," 73.

31. Benjamin Kunkel, *Indecision* (New York: Random House, 2005), 19.

32. We need to be careful not to conflate whether a decision is autonomous with whether a decision is worthy of respect. Dwight's coin-flipping method of making decisions does not seem very *autonomous* (self-governing), and his decisions seem perhaps less *his* and more the coin's, but that does not necessarily mean that his decisions are not worthy of respect. There may be other reasons to "respect" his decisions (not in the sense of "admiring" but more in the sense of "leaving well enough alone") beyond whether his decision-making process was particularly autonomous.

33. John Christman, *The Politics of Persons: Individual Autonomy and Socio-Historical Selves* (New York: Cambridge University Press, 2011), 155. One might also wonder

whether a more "relational" model of autonomy would be more forgiving of or compatible with the realities explicated in chapter 1. I do not believe so. Relational models are many and complex, but their underlying premise is that relationships and social structures *matter* for autonomy. On some accounts, they matter because certain oppressive relations can negatively impact autonomy even if other conditions such as reflective endorsement (considered judgment) or values-choice concordance hold. On other accounts, they matter because certain relationships can assist in self-governance or even be part of constituting the autonomous self. None of these ideas fundamentally challenges or helps with the idea put forth here, which is that the way in which decisions are often made does not meet many of the core conditions of self-governance typically discussed in the ethics literature. The only way in which a relational view might change the analysis is if (1) relationships are viewed as essential or central to the exercise of a person's autonomy, and (2) those relationships serve the function of helping to fix some of the effects of decision-making phenomena such as heuristics and biases. There is no reason to think that (2) is the case. It *could* be the case if part of the intended point of such a relationship is for the other person to watch for phenomena that might impair decision-making (e.g., resulting in a decision that does not promote the patient's core values) and then counteract those, but this is not the function of normal relationships. More discussion of (2) in the physician-patient relationship and how the physician might play this role will be discussed in chapter 3. For a discussion of relational autonomy in the health care context, see, for example, the following articles: Catriona Mackenzie, "Relational Autonomy, Normative Authority and Perfectionism." *Journal of Social Philosophy* 39, no. 4 (2008): 512–533, https://doi.org/10.1111/j.1467-9833.2008 .00440.x; and Albine Moser et al., "Realizing Autonomy in Responsive Relationships," *Medicine, Health Care and Philosophy* 13, no. 3 (August 1, 2010): 215–223, https://doi .org/10.1007/s11019-010-9241-8.

34. Decision scientists are people who study the normative, descriptive, and prescriptive theories of judgments and decision-making. They come from a variety of fields, including psychology, economics, decision analysis, and other social and applied sciences. Relevant professional societies include the Society for Judgment and Decision Making, the Decision Analysis Society, and the Society for Medical Decision Making.

35. Karen R. Sepucha et al., "Establishing the Effectiveness of Patient Decision Aids: Key Constructs and Measurement Instruments," *BMC Medical Informatics and Decision Making* 13, no. 2 (November 29, 2013): S12, https://doi.org/10.1186/1472-6947 -13-S2-S12.

36. J. S. Blumenthal-Barby et al., "Assessment of Patients' and Caregivers' Informational and Decisional Needs for Left Ventricular Assist Device Placement: Implications for Informed Consent and Shared Decision-Making," *Journal of Heart and Lung Transplantation* 34, no. 9 (September 1, 2015): 1182–1189, https://doi.org/10.1016/j .healun.2015.03.026.

37. Robert G. Simmons, Susan Klein Marine, and Richard Lawrence Simmons, *Gift of Life: The Effect of Organ Transplantation on Individual, Family, and Societal Dynamics* (New Brunswick, NJ: Transaction Publishers, 1987).

38. Jamie C. Brehaut et al., "Validation of a Decision Regret Scale," *Medical Decision Making* 23, no. 4 (July 1, 2003): 281–292, https://doi.org/10.1177/0272989X03256005.

39. I acknowledge that this marriage example is typically Western (e.g., in contrast with arranged marriages).

40. For further discussion of this point, see Carolyn McLeod and Julie Ponesse, "Infertility and Moral Luck: The Politics of Women Blaming Themselves for Infertility," *International Journal of Feminist Approaches to Bioethics* 1, no. 1 (2008): 126–144, https://www.jstor.org/stable/40339215.

41. Timothy D. Wilson et al., "Introspecting about Reasons Can Reduce Post-Choice Satisfaction," *Personality and Social Psychology Bulletin* 19, no. 3 (June 1, 1993): 331–339, https://doi.org/10.1177/0146167293193010.

42. Ziv Carmon, Klaus Wertenbroch, and Marcel Zeelenberg, "Option Attachment: When Deliberating Makes Choosing Feel like Losing," *Journal of Consumer Research* 30, no. 1 (June 1, 2003): 15–29, https://doi.org/10.1086/374701.

43. Ap Dijksterhuis et al., "On Making the Right Choice: The Deliberation-Without-Attention Effect," *Science* 311, no. 5763 (February 17, 2006): 1005–1007, https://doi.org/10.1126/science.1121629.

44. R. Jay Wallace, *The View from Here: On Affirmation, Attachment, and the Limits of Regret* (New York: Oxford University Press, 2013), 3–6.

45. Wallace, *The View from Here*, 95.

46. Interestingly, validated scales have been developed to measure decisional regret in medical decision-making, and they are used all the time in studies that measure the quality of decisions. These scales ask people to rate how much they agree or disagree with the following statements: "It was the right choice," "I regret the choice that was made," "I would make the same choice if I had to do it over again," "The choice did me a lot of harm," and "The decision was a wise one." It is interesting that some of the components are more "evaluative" according to Wallace's definitions, and others are more closely linked to attitudes of affirmation. For example, we can imagine that the woman who had a child at a very young age might think it was the wrong choice and not a wise one, but she might say that she does not regret it, she would make the same choice over, and it did not do her a lot of harm (these latter three answers being driven by the fact that she now has a daughter that she loves very much). So there are some senses in which she regrets it but others in which she does not, making it difficult to come to a determination of whether she regrets it or not (based on her overall "score" on some instrument).

47. Frankfurt, "Freedom of the Will," 15.

48. Note that the most general definition of "harm," as articulated by philosopher Joel Feinberg, is simply "the thwarting, setting back, or defeating of an interest of a person." There is more to be specified here as the various accounts detailed below demonstrate. "Interests," according to Feinberg, can be of the "welfare" type and the "ulterior" type. Ulterior interests include things like "ultimate aims" (e.g., achieving fame, having a family), and welfare interests include things like life, bodily integrity, health, security, freedom (interests that serve as a foundation for satisfying the more particular ulterior type of interests). When welfare interests are set back, a person is seriously harmed, according to Feinberg. See Joel Feinberg, *The Moral Limits of the Criminal Law*, vol. 1, *Harm to Others* (New York: Oxford University Press, 1984), 33–37, https://www.oxfordscholarship.com/view/10.1093/0195046641.001.0001/acprof-978 0195046649.

49. Jason Riis et al., "Ignorance of Hedonic Adaptation to Hemodialysis: A Study Using Ecological Momentary Assessment," *Journal of Experimental Psychology: General* 134, no. 1 (2005): 3–9, https://doi.org/10.1037/0096-3445.134.1.3.

50. Hyperbolic discounting refers to discounting the value of future rewards, even more so the farther away they are.

51. Radical prostatectomy does not decrease long-term mortality in randomized trials involving patients with localized low-risk prostate cancer, but it increases patient-reported adverse effects of incontinence and sexual dysfunction (through five years). For example, at one year, ~80% of men in the surgery group experienced sexual dysfunction compared to ~40% in the observational group; at five years the difference was ~80% versus ~55%. Timothy J. Wilt et al., "Follow-Up of Prostatectomy versus Observation for Early Prostate Cancer," *New England Journal of Medicine* 377, no. 2 (July 13, 2017): 132–142, https://doi.org/10.1056/NEJMoa1615869.

52. I thank an anonymous reviewer of the manuscript for putting the point this way.

53. Both of these examples of how heuristics and biases might crowd out core values or beliefs in the decision-making process are similar to the role that what Jodi Halpern has called "concretized emotions" might play. According to Halpern, emotionally grounded beliefs (concretized emotions) can interfere with patient decision-making. She gives the example of a patient whose father died of a heart attack, and now, whenever the patient has a pain, he believes that it is an instance of him having a heart attack. Here, the patient's affective state related to his father's death shapes the reality of the patient's situation and how he deals with it in ways that are problematic and stubbornly resist correction. See Jodi Halpern, *From Detached Concern to Empathy: Humanizing Medical Practice* (New York: Oxford University Press, 2001), 7–8.

54. In *Protagoras*, Plato takes the view that we must be ignorant, because if we had knowledge of what was best for us, then certainly we would act accordingly. Plato,

*Protagoras*, trans. Stanley Lombardo and Karen Bell, in *Plato: Complete Works*, ed. John M. Cooper and D. S. Hutchinson (Indianapolis, IN: Hackett, 1997), 746–790.

55. Aristotle argues that the view that *akrasia* (weakness of will) does not exist contradicts that which appears manifestly. Sometimes, man's action conflicts with what seems better to him. Aristotle, *Nicomachean Ethics*, in *Aristotle: Selections*, trans. Terence Irwin and Gail Fine (Indianapolis, IN: Hackett, 1995), 347–449.

56. Jeffrey W. Clark and Jean A. Young, "Automatic Enrollment: The Power of the Default," Vanguard Research, February 2018, https://institutional.vanguard.com/iam /pdf/CIRAE.pdf?cbdForceDomain=true.

57. Amartya Sen, *Commodities and Capabilities* (Amsterdam: North-Holland, 1985).

58. George Sher, *Beyond Neutrality: Perfectionism and Politics* (Cambridge: Cambridge University Press, 1997). It is worth noting that Sher is a perfectionist and intends this list to be a list of the perfections.

59. Roger Crisp, "Hedonism Reconsidered," *Philosophy and Phenomenological Research* 73, no. 3 (2006): 619–645, https://doi.org/10.1111/j.1933-1592.2006.tb00551.x.

60. Elizabeth Barnes, *The Minority Body: A Theory of Disability* (New York: Oxford University Press, 2016).

61. Ben Bradley, "Doing Away with Harm," *Philosophy and Phenomenological Research* 85, no. 2 (2012): 392, https://doi.org/10.1111/j.1933-1592.2012.00615.x.

62. Bradley, "Doing Away with Harm," 396.

63. Bradley, "Doing Away with Harm," 398. And here Bradley is quoting Elizabeth Harman. Elizabeth Harman, "Harming as Causing Harm," in *Harming Future Persons: Ethics, Genetics and the Nonidentity Problem*, ed. Melinda A. Roberts and David T. Wasserman (Dordrecht: Springer, 2009), 137–154.

64. Barnes, *The Minority Body*.

65. By "real examples" I simply mean ones from actual empirical studies. All these studies are reviewed in this chapter and in chapter 1.

66. The argument that decisional heuristics and biases *may* cause harm in the above-described ways is to say that they put patients at *risk* for harm (they increase, in a nontrivial sense, the probability that harm will come about). But, some might object, is risk of harm itself a harm, and are we all harmed whenever we engage in risky things? In response, it is worth pausing to examine *why* risk of harm is harmful. In her article "When the Risk of Harm Harms," Adriana Placani argues that a risk of harm is a harm when/if it sets back individuals' legitimate interests. Thus, heuristics and biases are harmful to the extent that they set back individuals' legitimate interests. The patients in the harm examples above would not have died from a ruptured appendix, received a less effective surgery, etc.—thus, they were harmed. This relates

closely to comparative views about harm. At the same time, if one is unconvinced by the argument that an increase in risk of harm is itself a harm, we can simply reframe the argument to say that an increase in risk of harm is a bad thing; we do not need to call it a "harm." To a certain extent this becomes a semantic debate. The main normative point is that decisional heuristics and biases may cause patients to make decisions that make things worse for them or that thwart their interests as conceived in a wide variety of ways. For a more detailed discussion on this point, see Adriana Placani, "When the Risk of Harm Harms," *Law and Philosophy* 36, no. 1 (February 1, 2017): 78, https://doi.org/10.1007/s10982-016-9277-x. To be clear, Placani's argument about risk of harm as a harm is narrowly directed toward the intentional imposition of risk of harm from one person to another person, and her main claim about the nature of that harm is that it is a setting back of one's dignity and respect interests (in other words, when one person imposes risk of harm on another, the harm is that doing so disrespects the person and her dignity). Here, I am simply extracting some of her argument's key elements and applying them to risk of harm to self.

67. Peter Menzies, "Counterfactual Theories of Causation," *Stanford Encyclopedia of Philosophy*, Winter 2017 edition, ed. Edward N. Zalta, https://stanford.library.sydney .edu.au/entries/causation-counterfactual/.

68. J. S. Swindell, Amy L. McGuire, and Scott D. Halpern, "Beneficent Persuasion: Techniques and Ethical Guidelines to Improve Patients' Decisions," *Annals of Family Medicine* 8, no. 3 (May 1, 2010): 260–264, https://doi.org/10.1370/afm.1118.

69. Katrina F. Brown et al., "Omission Bias and Vaccine Rejection by Parents of Healthy Children: Implications for the Influenza A/H1N1 Vaccination Programme," *Vaccine* 28, no. 25 (June 7, 2010): 4181–4185, https://doi.org/10.1016/j.vaccine.2010 .04.012; Ilana Ritov and Jonathan Baron, "Reluctance to Vaccinate: Omission Bias and Ambiguity," *Journal of Behavioral Decision Making* 3, no. 4 (1990): 263–277, https://doi .org/10.1002/bdm.3960030404.

70. Angela Fagerlin, Brian J. Zikmund-Fisher, and Peter A. Ubel, "Cure Me Even If It Kills Me: Preferences for Invasive Cancer Treatment," *Medical Decision Making* 25, no. 6 (November 1, 2005): 614–619, https://doi.org/10.1177/0272989X05282639.

71. Amy J. Keenum et al., "Generic Medications for You, but Brand-Name Medications for Me," *Research in Social and Administrative Pharmacy* 8, no. 6 (November 1, 2012): 574–578, https://doi.org/10.1016/j.sapharm.2011.12.004.

72. Brian J. Zikmund-Fisher et al., "'I'll Do What They Did': Social Norm Information and Cancer Treatment Decisions," *Patient Education and Counseling* 85, no. 2 (November 1, 2011): 225–229, https://doi.org/10.1016/j.pec.2011.01.031.

73. Richard J. Eiser, "The Influence of Question Framing on Symptom Report and Perceived Health Status," *Psychology & Health* 15, no. 1 (February 1, 2000): 13–20, https://doi.org/10.1080/08870440008400285.

74. Eric J. Johnson and Daniel Goldstein, "Do Defaults Save Lives?," *Science* 302, no. 5649 (November 21, 2003): 1338–1339, https://doi.org/10.1126/science.1091721.

75. Val Morrison et al., "The Impact of Information Order on Intentions to Undergo Predictive Genetic Testing: An Experimental Study," *Journal of Health Psychology* 15, no. 7 (October 1, 2010): 1082–1092, https://doi.org/10.1177/1359105310364171.

76. Enrico Rubaltelli et al., "Strengthening Acceptance for Xenotransplantation: The Case of Attraction Effect," *Xenotransplantation* 15, no. 3 (2008): 159–163, https://doi.org/10.1111/j.1399-3089.2008.00474.x.

77. Bernie J. O'Brien et al., "Assessing the Value of a New Pharmaceutical: A Feasibility Study of Contingent Valuation in Managed Care," *Medical Care* 36, no. 3 (1998): 370–384, https://www.jstor.org/stable/3767330.

78. Hitinder Singh Gurm and David G. Litaker, "Framing Procedural Risks to Patients: Is 99% Safe the Same as a Risk of 1 in 100?," *Academic Medicine* 75, no. 8 (August 2000): 840, doi: 10.1097/00001888-200008000-00018.

79. One might wonder where emotions (e.g., fear, love, anger, grief, shame) fit into the analysis. Might they also impair autonomous decision-making, contribute to poor-quality decision-making (both process and outcome), and cause harm to patients and their interests? It is important to note that emotions, on average, can help decision-making and are an important part of guiding decisions and behaviors (think of the impaired decision-making of those with lesions on parts of the brain responsible for emotion). But they can sometimes lead decision-makers astray. Similar to heuristics, they are not necessarily inherently good or inherently bad, and much depends on context and degree (this point is discussed more at the end of this chapter and in chapter 1). Emotions and heuristics are similar in that they are rapid and intuitive in contrast to more cognitive and deliberative decision-making. In that sense, they are "decisional shortcuts." As I discussed in chapter 1, both are part of "System 1" decision-making. Many heuristics and biases have a strong affective component; there is even a heuristic labeled the *affect heuristic*, whereby a person's decision is heavily influenced by his emotions in the moment. The point of this chapter and of the next is not to simply label System 1 processes as "bad" or "disruptive" of good decision-making; it is rather to make the point that these phenomena can sometimes, especially if left unnoticed, unchecked, and undirected, lead to bad decisions.

80. Amartya K. Sen, "Rational Fools: A Critique of the Behavioral Foundations of Economic Theory," *Philosophy & Public Affairs* 6, no. 4 (1977): 322, https://www.jstor.org/stable/2264946.

81. Gerald Dworkin, "Against Autonomy Response," *Journal of Medical Ethics* 40, no. 5 (May 1, 2014): 352, https://doi.org/10.1136/medethics-2013-101552.

82. Thaler and Sunstein say that the evidence from psychology supports the conclusion that people aren't rational. See section I of "Libertarian Paternalism" (2003), which is called "Are Choices Rational?" Their answer is no. They write, "People do not exhibit rational expectations, fail to make forecasts that are consistent with Bayes' rule, use heuristics that lead them to make systematic blunders, exhibit preference reversals (that is, they prefer A to B and B to A) and make different choices depending on the wording of the problem." Richard H. Thaler and Cass R. Sunstein, "Libertarian Paternalism," *American Economic Review* 93, no. 2 (May 2003): 176, https://doi.org/10.1257/000282803321947001. Also see Dan Ariely's *Predictably Irrational*, in which he writes, "We are not only irrational but predictably irrational ... our irrationality happens the same way, again and again." Dan Ariely, *Predictably Irrational* (New York: HarperCollins, 2008), xviii.

83. Theories of rationality typically explain some subset of rationality, such as decision-making and belief formation, rather than rationality *simpliciter*. Two exceptions that attempt to give a fuller account are Nozick (1993) and Audi (2001) (Audi argues against some of the central points of Nozick). Other theories include one from David Hume, who argues that rationality means beliefs that are properly calibrated to experience (1738). The American pragmatists, Peirce (1955) and Dewey (1960), focused on when beliefs should change. Decision theory typically emphasizes coherence, according to which goals and beliefs cannot be self-defeating. A less-demanding approach comes from Daniel Dennett (1971), who argues that we should ascribe to others consistent beliefs and interpret their acts as satisfying their desires. Other views focus more broadly on the aims of inquiry: Max Weber's (1905) theory of substantive rationality holds that rationality depends on the worthiness of the goal and not just on the efficiency of the pursuit of the goal. These are but a few examples of the breadth of philosophical views. Full references: Robert Audi, *The Architecture of Reason: The Structure and Substance of Rationality* (Oxford: Oxford University Press, 2001); Daniel C. Dennett, "Intentional Systems," *Journal of Philosophy* 68, no. 4 (February 1971): 87–106, https://doi.org/10.2307/2025382; John Dewey, *The Quest for Certainty* (New York: Capricorn Books, 1960); David Hume, *A Treatise of Human Nature*, ed. John P. Wright, Robert Stecker, and Gary Fuller (London: Everyman, 2003 [1738]); Robert Nozick, *The Nature of Rationality* (Princeton, NJ: Princeton University Press, 1993); Charles S. Peirce, *Philosophical Writings of Peirce*, ed. Justus Buchler (New York: Dover Publications, 1955); Max Weber, *The Protestant Ethic and the Spirit of Capitalism* (London: George Allen & Unwin, 1905), http://archive.org/details /protestantethics00webe. My thanks to Eric Mathison for assistance with this note.

## Chapter 3

1. Richard H. Thaler and Cass R. Sunstein, *Nudge: Improving Decisions about Health, Wealth, and Happiness* (New Haven, CT: Yale University Press, 2008), 6.

2. Yashar Saghai, "Salvaging the Concept of Nudge," *Journal of Medical Ethics* 39, no. 8 (August 1, 2013): 491, https://doi.org/10.1136/medethics-2012-100727.

3. Saghai notes that this requires that the person have the capacity to become aware of the nudger's attempt to get her to make a certain decision/perform a certain action and to inhibit the triggered propensity to make that decision/perform that action. Saghai, "Salvaging the Concept of Nudge," 489.

4. Paul Dolan et al., "Mindspace: Influencing Behaviour through Public Policy," Institute for Government, March 2, 2010, https://www.instituteforgovernment.org .uk/publications/mindspace. I have identified and analyzed examples of the application of these techniques to health behaviors and decisions in other published work. See J. S. Blumenthal-Barby and Hadley Burroughs, "Seeking Better Health Care Outcomes: The Ethics of Using the 'Nudge,'" *American Journal of Bioethics* 12, no. 2 (2012): 1–10, https://doi.org/10.1080/15265161.2011.634481.

5. Thaler and Sunstein, *Nudge*, 6.

6. Note that soft paternalism and the other two types of paternalism discussed here (hard, libertarian) build off of Gerald Dworkin's general definition of paternalism. According to Dworkin, X acts paternalistically toward Y by doing (omitting) Z if: (1) Z (or its omission) interferes with the liberty or autonomy of Y; (2) X does so without the consent of Y; (3) X does so just because Z will improve the welfare of Y (where this includes preventing her welfare from diminishing) or, in some way, will promote the interests, values, or goods of Y. See Gerald Dworkin, "Paternalism," *Stanford Encyclopedia of Philosophy*, Winter 2017 edition, ed. Edward N. Zalta, https:// plato.stanford.edu/archives/win2017/entries/paternalism/.

7. See, for example, Cass R. Sunstein, *Why Nudge? The Politics of Libertarian Paternalism* (New Haven, CT: Yale University Press, 2014).

8. John Stuart Mill, "Chapter V," in *On Liberty* (London: John W. Parker and Son, West Strand, 1859), 168–207.

9. Thaler and Sunstein, *Nudge*, 5.

10. Thaler and Sunstein, *Nudge*, 4.

11. Thaler and Sunstein, *Nudge*, 11.

12. Scott D. Halpern, "Judging Nudges," *American Journal of Bioethics* 16, no. 5 (May 3, 2016): 16–18, https://doi.org/10.1080/15265161.2016.1159766.

13. Charles Douglas and Emily Proudfoot, "Nudging and the Complicated Real Life of 'Informed Consent,'" *American Journal of Bioethics* 13, no. 6 (2013): 16, https:// doi.org/10.1080/15265161.2013.781716. Excision achieves 100% certainty about whether the lesion is cancer, percutaneous biopsy over 99%.

14. Thom Brooks, "Should We Nudge Informed Consent?," *American Journal of Bioethics* 13, no. 6 (2013): 23, https://doi.org/10.1080/15265161.2013.781710.

15. Someone might object that she did not *intend* to influence choice in direction A by her choice architecture; she merely foresaw it. Yet, if Doctor X knows that if she presents choice architecture A, the patient will likely do A, and if she presents choice architecture B, the patient will likely do B, it is difficult to say that she did not intend to influence choice in the direction of A *more* than she intended to influence choice in the direction of B. She may have preferred to not have to make a choice between A and B, or to not influence the patient's decision-making at all, but still, in choosing the choice architecture that she did (between A and B), she intended to influence choice more in the direction of A than B—a narrow scope of intention, at least.

16. Scott D. Gelfand, "The Meta-Nudge: A Response to the Claim That the Use of Nudges during the Informed Consent Process Is Unavoidable," *Bioethics* 30, no. 8 (2016): 601–608, https://doi.org/10.1111/bioe.12266.

17. George Loewenstein et al., "Warning: You Are about to Be Nudged," *Behavioral Science & Policy* 1, no. 1 (2015): 35–42, https://doi.org/10.1353/bsp.2015.0000.

18. Thomas M. Scanlon, *What We Owe to Each Other* (Cambridge, MA: Harvard University Press, 1998), 224.

19. Peter Singer, "Famine, Affluence, and Morality," *Philosophy & Public Affairs* 1, no. 3 (1972): 229–243, http://personal.lse.ac.uk/robert49/teaching/mm/articles/Singer_1972 Famine.pdf.

20. This study is discussed in detail in chapter 5.

21. Does the view that outcomes are the most important aspect of decision-making license a move to paternalism and coercion? No. As I explain in the sentences that follow (as well as in the previous chapter and later in this chapter), part of what is meant by a "good outcome" is a decision that is concordant with a patient's underlying goals, values, and interests; there is nothing necessarily objectivist or paternalist about this view. Nor does it license coercion (e.g., threatening or forcing a person to do what is in her interest). Whether coercion (as opposed to "mere" nudging) is more or less justified is discussed further toward the end of this chapter.

22. Areej El-Jawahri et al., "A Randomized Controlled Trial of a CPR and Intubation Video Decision Support Tool for Hospitalized Patients," *Journal of General Internal Medicine* 30, no. 8 (August 2015): 1071–1080, https://doi.org/10.1007/s11606-015-3200-2.

23. Some have argued that this claim is simply paternalism in disguise. As Gregory Mitchell puts it, if choice is "so sticky" (i.e., we have trouble determining "true preferences"), then "libertarian paternalism is just paternalism." See p. 12 of Gregory

Mitchell, "Libertarian Paternalism Is an Oxymoron," *Northwestern University Law Review* 99, no. 3 (2005), https://papers.ssrn.com/abstract=615562.

24. There is a large philosophical literature on what the "fully informed" or "idealized" decision-maker means or looks like (hypothetically or theoretically, since in practice we can't know). One suggestion by Sobel is that it is what the person would prefer when her preferences or decisions are "responsive to their object as it *really is* rather than as it is falsely imagined to be." David Sobel, *From Valuing to Value: A Defense of Subjectivism* (Oxford: Oxford University Press, 2016), 6. This construct is not particularly helpful in guiding us to concrete answers. See Sobel, *From Valuing to Value*, and this review of Sobel's book: Ben Bramble, review of *From Valuing to Value: A Defense of Subjectivism*, by David Sobel, *Notre Dame Philosophical Reviews*, May 11, 2017, https://ndpr.nd.edu/news/from-valuing-to-value-a-defense-of-subjectivism/.

25. There is also a large philosophical literature on the question of adaptive preferences. See, for example, Martha C. Nussbaum, "Symposium on Amartya Sen's Philosophy: 5 Adaptive Preferences and Women's Options," *Economics & Philosophy* 17, no. 1 (April 2001): 67–88, https://doi.org/10.1017/S0266267101000153; John C. Harsanyi, "Morality and the Theory of Rational Behavior," in *Utilitarianism and Beyond*, ed. Amartya Sen and Bernard Williams (Cambridge: Cambridge University Press, 1982), 39–62; Jon Elster, *Sour Grapes: Studies in the Subversion of Rationality*, (Cambridge: Cambridge University Press, 1983); Amartya Sen, *Commodities and Capabilities* (Amsterdam: North-Holland, 1985). Going into depth here would take us too far from the main point. But it is worth noting that my strategy in this section is to argue that regardless of one's theoretical position on welfare (e.g., subjectivist—where adaptive preferences are a problem—among others, or objectivist—where there are also problems), there are clear-cut, concrete cases where we can agree about what makes a patient better or worse off, and there are also cases where the various theories converge on an answer. I address an additional way that the phenomenon of adaptive preferences might pose challenges for the decisional-improvement argument later in this section.

26. Sobel discusses this issue, arguing that we should endorse a "temporally neutral" type of subjectivism in which the reasons a person has for a certain decision or course of action "are responsive to the [informed] concerns of *all* one's [time-slices]" (e.g., current self, past self, future self—maybe we can cut out the past self since that is over and so results in counterintuitive results). Sobel, *From Valuing to Value*, 292. Thus, for example, we have a reason to avoid our future pain and suffering even if we do not care about it at the present moment. But again, it is not clear how this construct is helpful in concrete cases in providing an answer about what the choice architect should nudge toward. A related problem involves what Laurie Ann Paul refers to as "transformative experiences," which are experiences that give a person new information and perspective that they cannot get outside the experience itself. For example, someone must actually see red to know what seeing red is like. Transformative choices, then, "ask you to make a decision where you must manage different

selves at different times, with different sets of preferences. Which set of preferences should you be most concerned with? Your preferences now, or your preferences after the experience?" Laurie Ann Paul, *Transformative Experience* (Oxford: Oxford University Press, 2014), 48.

27. Sobel, *From Valuing to Value*, 67.

28. Moti Gorin et al., "Justifying Clinical Nudges," *Hastings Center Report* 47, no. 2 (March 2017): 32–38, https://doi.org/10.1002/hast.688.

29. To be more precise in the formulation of both of these examples (refusing an easy but life-saving surgery and refusing recommended screening), I am assuming the persons do not have some specific, preformed, considered preference for low levels of health intervention or some specific considered judgment or religious belief against these particular interventions (i.e., I am assuming a straightforward, garden-variety case). I am *not* taking the position that considered decisions that involve risk of harm are objectively bad. In fact, the other examples in this section involve cases where it is fairly easy and clear (we can all agree on) what would be a good outcome *because of* knowledge of the patient's particular goals, preferences, or values (a subjectivist account of the good).

30. Parfit's view was that three very different major ethical theories (consequentialism, Kantianism, contractualism) converge on the following principle: an act is wrong just when such acts are disallowed by some principle that is optimific, uniquely universally willable, and not reasonably rejectable. This was called Parfit's Triple Theory. Following this principle would supposedly lead to the best results (thus, consequentialist), condone things not universally willable (so, Kantian), and focus on things that people could not reasonably reject (so, contractual). See Derek Parfit, *On What Matters*, vol. 1 (New York: Oxford University Press, 2011), 411–417. Also relevant here is John Rawls's theory of overlapping consensus and Cass Sunstein's theory of incompletely theorized agreement. Overlapping consensus occurs when citizens all end up endorsing a core set of laws, though for different reasons. See Leif Wenar, "John Rawls," *Stanford Encyclopedia of Philosophy*, Spring 2017 edition, ed. Edward N. Zalta, https://plato.stanford.edu/archives/spr2017/entries/rawls/.

Incompletely theorized agreement occurs when people agree on an abstract guiding principle, but do not agree on its application to particular cases or issues. For example, two people might agree that murder is wrong, but not agree on the morality of abortion. See Cass R. Sunstein, "Incompletely Theorized Agreements Commentary," *Harvard Law Review* 108 (1994): 1739.

31. Essentially, this response and the one before it embrace a sort of pluralism and/or pragmatism about the good.

32. In chapter 5 I discuss the use of choice architecture in prostate cancer decision-making in more depth, using it as one of the longer case studies of nudging and choice architecture in medical decision-making.

33. See Nussbaum, "Symposium on Amartya Sen's Philosophy"; Harsanyi, "Moral-ity and the Theory of Rational Behavior"; Elster, *Sour Grapes*; Sen, *Commodities and Capabilities*. I also talk more about the related paradox of "the impossibility of regret" in chapter 2 when I discuss how decisional biases might lead to regret, a component of bad decisions.

34. Andrea Abbott et al., "Perceptions of Contralateral Breast Cancer: An Overestima-tion of Risk," *Annals of Surgical Oncology* 18, no. 11 (September 27, 2011): 3129–3136, https://doi.org/10.1245/s10434-011-1914-x; Pamela R. Portschy, Karen M. Kuntz, and Todd M. Tuttle, "Survival Outcomes after Contralateral Prophylactic Mastectomy: A Decision Analysis," *JNCI: Journal of the National Cancer Institute* 106, no. 8 (August 1, 2014), https://doi.org/10.1093/jnci/dju160; Abenaa M. Brewster et al., "Prospective Assessment of Psychosocial Outcomes of Contralateral Prophylactic Mastectomy," *Journal of Clinical Oncology* 35, no. 15, suppl. (May 20, 2017): 6569, https://doi.org/10.1200/JCO.2017.35.15_suppl.6569.

35. See William Glod, "How Nudges Often Fail to Treat People According to Their Own Preferences," *Social Theory and Practice* 41, no. 4 (2015): 599–617, https://www.jstor.org/stable/24575751. Glod calls this the informational constraints argument against nudging.

36. Peter A. Ubel, Karen A. Scherr, and Angela Fagerlin, "Empowerment Failure: How Shortcomings in Physician Communication Unwittingly Undermine Patient Auton-omy," *American Journal of Bioethics* 17, no. 11 (November 2017): 31–39, https://doi.org/10.1080/15265161.2017.1378753.

37. Grüne-Yanoff makes this criticism against libertarian paternalism more gener-ally. See Till Grüne-Yanoff, "Old Wine in New Casks: Libertarian Paternalism Still Violates Liberal Principles," *Social Choice and Welfare* 38, no. 4 (April 1, 2012): 635–645, https://doi.org/10.1007/s00355-011-0636-0.

38. J. S. Blumenthal-Barby and Heather Krieger, "Cognitive Biases and Heuristics in Medical Decision Making: A Critical Review Using a Systematic Search Strategy," *Medical Decision Making* 35, no. 4 (May 1, 2015): 539–557, https://doi.org/10.1177/0272989X14547740. Though it is worth noting that these were mostly studies with hypothetical decision-making vignettes, rather than actual decision-making.

39. I thank an anonymous reviewer for raising these issues.

40. Gerd Gigerenzer, "On the Supposed Evidence for Libertarian Paternalism," *Review of Philosophy and Psychology* 6, no. 3 (2015): 361–383, https://doi.org/10.1007/s13164-015-0248-1.

41. Laura Kray and Richard Gonzalez, "Differential Weighting in Choice versus Advice: I'll Do This, You Do That," *Journal of Behavioral Decision Making* 12, no. 3 (1999): 207–217, https://doi.org/10.1002/(SICI)1099-0771(199909)12:3<207::AID-B DM322>3.0.CO;2-P.

42. See the decision aid inventory at Ottawa Hospital Research Institute, "A to Z Inventory of Decision Aids," accessed July 14, 2020, https://decisionaid.ohri.ca /AZinvent.php; Angela Fagerlin et al., "Clarifying Values: An Updated Review," *BMC Medical Informatics and Decision Making* 13, no. 2 (November 29, 2013): S8, https:// doi.org/10.1186/1472-6947-13-S2-S8.

43. Robert M. Veatch, "Abandoning Informed Consent," *Hastings Center Report* 25, no. 2 (April 1995): 5–12, https://www.jstor.org/stable/3562859.

44. Paul Hamilton, "A Republican Argument against Nudging and Informed Consent," *HEC Forum: An Interdisciplinary Journal on Hospitals' Ethical and Legal Issues* 30, no. 3 (September 2018): 280–281, https://doi.org/10.1007/s10730-017-9343-2.

45. D. Moller, "Abortion and Moral Risk," *Philosophy* 86, no. 337 (2011): 425–443.

46. The moral risk objection could also apply to nudging by way of the autonomy argument discussed later in this chapter. Run that way, this time the deep moral wrong would be infringement on autonomy rather than making a patient worse off in terms of decisional outcomes. I do not think the analogy holds there either, for similar reasons. If we *thought* that nudging did not necessarily or typically constitute an autonomy violation but were *wrong*, then we will have ended up failing to foster the exercise of agency and rational deliberation *in a particular instance*—this is perhaps a moral wrong, but not a *serious or deep* moral wrong.

47. House of Lords, Science and Technology Selection Committee, *Behaviour Change*, Second Report, July 2011, https://publications.parliament.uk/pa/ld201012/ldselect /ldsctech/179/17902.htm; Theresa M. Marteau et al., "Judging Nudging: Can Nudging Improve Population Health?," *BMJ (Clinical Research Ed.)* 342 (January 25, 2011): d228, https://doi.org/10.1136/bmj.d228; Geof Rayner and Tim Lang, "Is Nudge an Effective Public Health Strategy to Tackle Obesity? No," *BMJ* 342 (April 14, 2011): d2177, https://doi.org/10.1136/bmj.d2177; Jacqui Wise, "Nudge or Fudge? Doctors Debate Best Approach to Improve Public Health," *BMJ* 342 (January 27, 2011): d580, https://doi.org/10.1136/bmj.d580. Relatedly, Grüne-Yanoff has argued that there is a lack of evidence about the causal mechanisms underlying nudge techniques, and that this lack undermines the ethical justification for their implementation. See Till Grüne-Yanoff, "Why Behavioral Policy Needs Mechanistic Evidence," *Economics & Philosophy* 32, no. 3 (November 2016): 463–483, https://doi.org/10.1017 /S0266267115000425.

48. Sarah Conly, *Against Autonomy: Justifying Coercive Paternalism* (Cambridge: Cambridge University Press, 2012).

49. Wise, "Nudge or Fudge?," d580.

50. Gretchen B. Chapman et al., "Opting In vs Opting Out of Influenza Vaccination," *JAMA* 304, no. 1 (July 7, 2010): 43–44, https://doi.org/10.1001/jama.2010.892; Katherine L. Milkman et al., "Using Implementation Intentions Prompts to Enhance

Influenza Vaccination Rates," *Proceedings of the National Academy of Sciences* 108, no. 26 (June 28, 2011): 10415–10420, https://doi.org/10.1073/pnas.1103170108.

51. Daniella Meeker et al., "Nudging Guideline-Concordant Antibiotic Prescribing: A Randomized Clinical Trial," *JAMA Internal Medicine* 174, no. 3 (March 1, 2014): 425–431, https://doi.org/10.1001/jamainternmed.2013.14191; David Tannenbaum et al., "Nudging Physician Prescription Decisions by Partitioning the Order Set: Results of a Vignette-Based Study," *Journal of General Internal Medicine* 30, no. 3 (March 1, 2015): 298–304, https://doi.org/10.1007/s11606-014-3051-2.

52. Loewenstein et al., "Warning," 35–42; Angelo Volandes et al., "Video Decision Support Tool for Advance Care Planning in Dementia: Randomised Controlled Trial," *BMJ* 338 (May 28, 2009): b2159, https://doi.org/10.1136/bmj.b2159.

53. Angelo E. Volandes and Elmer D. Abbo, "Flipping the Default: A Novel Approach to Cardiopulmonary Resuscitation in End-Stage Dementia," *Journal of Clinical Ethics* 18, no. 2 (2007): 122–139, https://pubmed.ncbi.nlm.nih.gov/17682620/.

54. Eric J. Johnson and Daniel Goldstein, "Do Defaults Save Lives?," *Science* 302, no. 5649 (November 21, 2003): 1338–1339, https://doi.org/10.1126/science.1091721.

55. Catherine Hanssens, "Legal and Ethical Implications of Opt-Out HIV Testing," *Clinical Infectious Diseases* 45, suppl. 4 (December 15, 2007): S232–239, https://doi .org/10.1086/522543.

56. Issac M. Lipkus et al., "Breast Cancer Risk Perceptions and Breast Cancer Worry: What Predicts What?," *Journal of Risk Research* 8, no. 5 (July 1, 2005): 439–452, https://doi.org/10.1080/1366987042000311018.

57. Gretchen A. Brenes and Electra D Paskett, "Predictors of Stage of Adoption for Colorectal Cancer Screening," *Preventive Medicine* 31, no. 4 (October 1, 2000): 410–416, https://doi.org/10.1006/pmed.2000.0729.

58. Blumenthal-Barby and Burroughs, "Seeking Better Health Care Outcomes," 1–10.

59. Shlomo Benartzi et al., "Should Governments Invest More in Nudging?," *Psychological Science* 28, no. 8 (August 1, 2017): 1041–1055, https://doi.org/10.1177/0956797 617702501.

60. Thaler and Sunstein, *Nudge*, 220, 109, 205, 202.

61. J. S. Blumenthal-Barby, "Between Reason and Coercion: Ethically Permissible Influence in Health Care and Health Policy Contexts," *Kennedy Institute of Ethics Journal* 22, no. 4 (January 3, 2012): 345–366, https://kiej.georgetown.edu/home_files/22.4 .blumenthal-barby.pdf.

62. I am not making the argument that governmental nudging is unjustified. Indeed, democratic government is expected to act in citizens' interests. As I say, this

topic is debatable and not my focus here. I mean only to draw the contrast and say that there *may* be *more* convincing reasons why nudging and choice architecture are acceptable in the physician-patient relationship (because of special fiduciary duties) compared to other contexts.

63. In the case of other care providers who might not be assumed to have a fiduciary-type relationship with the patient, professional and ethical norms and principles guide providers to protect and promote patients' interests, as discussed further in the subsequent section.

64. The principles of beneficence and nonmaleficence are two of the "four principles of medical ethics" expressed in Beauchamp and Childress's *Principles of Biomedical Ethics*. (See Tom L. Beauchamp and James F. Childress, *Principles of Biomedical Ethics*, 6th ed. [New York: Oxford University Press, 2009].) The other two are autonomy and justice. I discuss autonomy in the next section. I do not discuss justice because it is not especially relevant to the defense or critique of nudging and choice architecture in patient decision-making. Justice has us generally concerned with fair, equitable, and appropriate treatment in light of what is due or owed to persons, but in this context, that boils down to protection and promotion of patient interests and respect for autonomy since there are no issues of distributive justice at stake. There are other ethical principles beyond these four that could be considered. For example, in the nursing literature, in addition to the four principles just named, there is also an appeal to accountability, veracity, and fidelity. Veracity may be relevant in that it could be an argument against certain types of nudges. This will be discussed in chapter 4 in the section on transparent and nontransparent nudges.

65. Beauchamp and Childress, *Principles of Biomedical Ethics*, 152–153. See chapter 2 for a more detailed discussion of the definition of harm.

66. Robert J. Volk et al., "Designing Normative Messages about Active Surveillance for Men with Localized Prostate Cancer," *Journal of Health Communication* 20, no. 9 (September 2, 2015): 1014–1020, https://doi.org/10.1080/10810730.2015.1018618.

67. For a more detailed discussion about harm, welfare, and risk of harm as a harm, see chapter 2.

68. James Rachels, "Active and Passive Euthanasia," *New England Journal of Medicine* 292, no. 2 (January 9, 1975): 78–80, https://doi.org/10.1056/NEJM197501092920206.

69. Adriana Placani, "When the Risk of Harm Harms," *Law and Philosophy* 36, no. 1 (February 1, 2017): 77–100, https://doi.org/10.1007/s10982-016-9277-x. Note that "non-trivial" is, according to Placani, determined by the probability of (and increase in) a harm occurring, the expected severity of the harm, and the importance or significance of the result. There are objective and subjective (value-based) elements to this account.

70. See John Oberdiek, "Towards a Right against Risking," *Law and Philosophy* 28, no. 4 (July 1, 2009): 376, https://doi.org/10.1007/s10982-008-9039-5. Oberdiek does clarify that risk won't always diminish autonomy, because sometimes the risk is valuable (e.g., in climbing a mountain I choose to take on risk, the elimination of which would alter the intrinsic nature of the activity). Oberdiek, "Towards a Right against Risking," 378.

71. Shelly Kagan, *The Limits of Morality* (Oxford: Clarendon Press, 1989), 88.

72. Douglas MacKay and Alexandra Robinson, "The Ethics of Organ Donor Registration Policies: Nudges and Respect for Autonomy," *American Journal of Bioethics* 16, no. 11 (November 1, 2016): 3–12, https://doi.org/10.1080/15265161.2016.1222007.

73. More specifically, Grüne-Yanoff poses the autonomy violation in terms of the attempt to "deliberately circumvent people's rational reasoning and deliberating faculties, and instead seek to influence their choices through knowledge of the biases to which they are susceptible." See Grüne-Yanoff, "Old Wine in New Casks," 636. And Hausman and Welch write, "One should be concerned about the risk that exploiting decision-making foibles will ultimately diminish people's autonomous decision-making capacities." See Daniel Hausman and Brynn Welch, "Debate: To Nudge or Not to Nudge," *Journal of Political Philosophy* 18, no. 1 (2010): 135, https://doi.org/10.1111/j.1467-9760.2009.00351.x.

74. Hausman and Welch, "Debate," 128.

75. Geoff Keeling, "Autonomy, Nudging and Post-Truth Politics," *Journal of Medical Ethics* 44, no. 10 (October 1, 2018): 722, https://doi.org/10.1136/medethics-2017-104616.

76. Luc Bovens, "The Ethics of Nudge," in *Preference Change: Approaches from Philosophy, Economics and Psychology*, ed. Till Grüne-Yanoff and Sven Ove Hansson (Dordrecht: Springer, 2009), 207–219.

77. Thomas Ploug and Søren Holm, "Doctors, Patients, and Nudging in the Clinical Context: Four Views on Nudging and Informed Consent," *American Journal of Bioethics* 15, no. 10 (October 3, 2015): 28–38, https://doi.org/10.1080/15265161.2015.1074303.

78. Keeling, "Autonomy, Nudging and Post-Truth Politics," 721; William Simkulet, "Nudging, Informed Consent and Bullshit," *Journal of Medical Ethics* 44, no. 8 (August 1, 2018): 536–542, https://doi.org/10.1136/medethics-2017-104480.

79. Shane Ryan makes a similar point and argues that for this reason, libertarian paternalism is not soft paternalism but hard paternalism. See Shane Ryan, "Libertarian Paternalism Is Hard Paternalism," *Analysis* 78, no. 1 (January 1, 2018): 65–73, https://doi.org/10.1093/analys/anx150.

80. It is fair to point out that this also poses a difficulty for nudges. Several techniques may need to be tried before finding one that is effective; however, it is

easier to find one that works than to have to strip away a dozen. And nudgers have the option of employing several techniques at once to increase the chance that one sticks. This is in fact what many do—see, for example, the work of the Penn Medicine Nudge Unit. Penn Medicine, "The Nudge Unit," accessed June 19, 2019, https://nudgeunit.upenn.edu/.

81. Shlomo Cohen, "A Philosophical Misunderstanding at the Basis of Opposition to Nudging," *American Journal of Bioethics* 15, no. 10 (October 3, 2015): 39, https://doi.org/10.1080/15265161.2015.1074313.f.

82. George Sher, *Beyond Neutrality: Perfectionism and Politics* (Cambridge: Cambridge University Press, 1997), 63–64. Sher does admit, however, that "there is a grain of truth" in the idea that nonrationally influencing people's preferences undermines autonomy (when defining autonomous choices as choices that are made in response to good, or sufficiently strong, reasons).

83. Sher, *Beyond Neutrality*, 101.

84. Carl Schneider, *The Practice of Autonomy: Patients, Doctors, and Medical Decisions* (New York: Oxford University Press, 1998).

85. Jack Ende et al., "Measuring Patients' Desire for Autonomy: Decision Making and Information-Seeking Preferences among Medical Patients," *Journal of General Internal Medicine* 4, no. 1 (January 1, 1989): 23–30, https://doi.org/10.1007/BF02596485.

86. Lesley F. Degner and Jeff A. Sloan, "Decision Making during Serious Illness: What Role Do Patients Really Want to Play?," *Journal of Clinical Epidemiology* 45, no. 9 (1992): 941–950, https://doi.org/10.1016/0895-4356(92)90110-9; H. J. Sutherland et al., "Cancer Patients: Their Desire for Information and Participation in Treatment Decisions," *Journal of the Royal Society of Medicine* 82, no. 5 (May 1989): 260–263, https://www.ncbi.nlm.nih.gov/pmc/articles/PMC1292127/pdf/jrsocmed00150-0016.pdf.

87. Here I use language from MacKay and Robinson, "The Ethics of Organ Donor Registration Policies."

88. Both are equivalent autonomy violations, however. Some have failed to recognize this, conflating the value of autonomy and autonomy per se in the context of discussing the ethics of nudging. See J. S. Blumenthal-Barby and Peter A. Ubel, "Gunmen and Ice Cream Cones: Harm to Autonomy and Harm to Persons," *American Journal of Bioethics* 16, no. 11 (2016): 13–14, https://doi.org/10.1080/15265161.2016.1222021, in response to MacKay and Robinson, "The Ethics of Organ Donor Registration Policies," in the same issue.

89. Madison Powers, Ruth Faden, and Yashar Saghai, "Liberty, Mill and the Framework of Public Health Ethics," *Public Health Ethics* 5, no. 1 (April 1, 2012): 6–15, https://doi.org/10.1093/phe/phs002.

90. For example, Ploug and Holm have discussed the theoretical ambiguity in the notion of "high stakes." For example, is it a reference to contexts where an individual has strong preferences or values? Or a reference to high risks? See Thomas Ploug and Søren Holm, "Informed Consent, Libertarian Paternalism, and Nudging: A Response," *American Journal of Bioethics* 15, no. 12 (December 2, 2015): W10–13, https://doi.org/10.1080/15265161.2015.1096081.

91. Let us set aside where there might be an independent ethical justification, such as the good outcomes that could be produced. I take up the ethics of nudging for medical or public health welfarism in chapter 4.

92. James Delaney and David B. Hershenov, "Why Consent May Not Be Needed for Organ Procurement," *American Journal of Bioethics* 9, no. 8 (August 3, 2009): 3–10, https://doi.org/10.1080/15265160902985019.

93. Here it is helpful to introduce a distinction between two aspects of autonomy. As Enoch (2017) argues, there are two concerns implicated in the value of autonomy: concern for sovereignty and concern for nonalienation. Concern for sovereignty involves respecting that decisions are a person's own to make, and concern for nonalienation involves ensuring that a person's life goes in a way that is consistent with her deeper values and commitments. My response in this section is admittedly only defending the aspect of autonomy that has to do with nonalienation. However, my other responses in this section defend concerns about sovereignty (the person having a say in the process by which decisions are made). See David Enoch, "Hypothetical Consent and the Value(s) of Autonomy," *Ethics* 128, no. 1 (September 22, 2017): 6–36, https://doi.org/10.1086/692939.

A related distinction has been made by Danny Scoccia, who points out that there are Kantian and non-Kantian objections to nudges. Kantian objections claim that nudges diminish autonomy because they involve nonrational persuasion that poses a threat to sovereignty. Non-Kantian objections claim that nudges diminish autonomy because they do not accord with the target's own evaluation of the alternatives (an alienation concern). See Danny Scoccia, "Paternalisms and Nudges," *Economics & Philosophy* 35, no. 1 (March 2019): 79–102, https://doi.org/10.1017/S02662 67118000093.

94. Nudges could also be neutral with respect to autonomy, neither bolstering it nor threatening it.

95. Sher, *Beyond Neutrality*, 60n25.

96. Someone might object that the problem with nudges is that they fail to respect or recognize a pro tanto reason to prefer rational persuasion, avoiding autonomy concerns altogether. This person may be willing to concede that autonomy need not prevail at all costs (e.g., if rational persuasion fails), but the point is that rational persuasion is preferable from an autonomy perspective. I have two points in response. The first is that this argument makes the dubious assumption that there

is such a thing as "pure argument" or "pure reason" that is unaffected by framing effects, emotion, etc. I discuss this topic in depth later in the chapter. The second is that this raises the issue of prophylactic nudging (nudging done from the get-go) versus nudging only after bad decision-making occurs and/or persists. I defend some degree of prophylactic nudging, where we have reason to assume that patients are inclined to make decisions that are not highly autonomous or that negatively impact their well-being.

97. Hamilton, "A Republican Argument against Nudging." Andreas Schmidt acknowledges a similar worry though goes on to argue that democratically controlled and transparent nudging can be a mechanism to counter and control opaque nudging by powerful private companies. See Andreas T. Schmidt, "The Power to Nudge," *American Political Science Review* 111, no. 2 (May 2017): 404–417, https://doi.org/10.1017/S0003055417000028.

98. That is not to say that there might be consequentialist-based arguments to differentiate the two. For example, intentional manipulation may lead to worse outcomes or to the manipulated parties feeling more upset. I address those concerns elsewhere in the chapter. Here I am focusing on autonomy-based concerns.

99. Harry G. Frankfurt, "Frankfurt-Style Compatibilism: Reply to John Martin Fischer," in *Contours of Agency: Essays on Themes from Harry Frankfurt*, ed. Sarah Buss and Lee Overton (Cambridge, MA: MIT Press, 2002), 28. There is, however, a way in which the "other" as intentional cause versus environment as cause may be relevant for autonomy, and that is that an agent may be more likely to repudiate a desire/decision formation that is directed by the will of another than they are a random one. It is also worth clarifying that this particular quote by Frankfurt was concerned with character formation more broadly rather than specific choices/decisions/actions, but the general point still stands.

100. Muireann Quigley, "Nudging for Health: On Public Policy and Designing Choice Architecture," *Medical Law Review* 21, no. 4 (December 1, 2013): 588–621, https://doi.org/10.1093/medlaw/fwt022. Quigley also discusses the difference between intentional and random choice architecture in the context of the government nudging toward health. She is generally supportive of intentional choice architecture, writing that "if nudge-type interventions are shown to be genuinely effective in the applied setting, this would give us reason to think that deliberately designed nudges could promote our interests as autonomous persons more effectively than a random assortment of influences." Quigley, "Nudging for Health," 614. She does, however, recognize one concern that warrants attention: in the long-term, intentional choice architecture might lead to infantilization and a decrease in individual responsibility. Quigley argues that on the contrary, nudges can bolster decision-making capacities by reducing overall cognitive load. To this, I would add that it is unlikely that a physician intentionally "puppeteering" choice through the design of choice architecture for a particular decision is going to decrease individual responsibility in

the long run. Nor need this feel infantilizing, as I point out in this paragraph and develop further in the subsequent section.

101. Evan Riley, "The Beneficent Nudge Program and Epistemic Injustice," *Ethical Theory and Moral Practice* 20, no. 3 (June 1, 2017): 597–616, https://doi.org/10.1007/s10677-017-9805-2.

102. Cass R. Sunstein, "The Ethics of Nudging," *Yale Journal on Regulation* 32, no. 2 (2015): 413–450, https://digitalcommons.law.yale.edu/cgi/viewcontent.cgi?article=1415&context=yjreg.

103. Gerald Dworkin, "Against Autonomy Response," *Journal of Medical Ethics* 40, no. 5 (2014): 352, https://doi.org/10.1136/medethics-2013-101552.

104. Others have invoked the notion of preauthorization here. For example, Niker and colleagues argue that preauthorized nudging can promote autonomy, especially on more relational views of autonomy. They define preauthorization as follows: "We understand pre-authorization as a process by which an individual gives a certain agent preferential access to influencing her decision-making processes." The principle of endorsement gives more latitude than the notion of preauthorization, however, since, "commonly, pre-authorization occurs before a specific decision is made, and usually for decisions about which certain values, convictions, or viewpoints of the pre-authorized agent are relevant, although it can also occur contemporaneously." See Fay Niker, Peter B. Reiner, and Gidon Felsen, "Pre-Authorization: A Novel Decision-Making Heuristic That May Promote Autonomy," *American Journal of Bioethics* 16, no. 5 (May 3, 2016): 27–28, https://doi.org/10.1080/15265161.2016.1159761.

105. For example, Harry Frankfurt and David Velleman. For an overview, see Francois Schroeter, "Endorsement and Autonomous Agency," *Philosophy and Phenomenological Research* 69, no. 3 (2004): 633–659, https://www.jstor.org/stable/40040770?seq=1.

106. Sarah Buss, "Valuing Autonomy and Respecting Persons: Manipulation, Seduction, and the Basis of Moral Constraints," *Ethics* 115, no. 2 (January 1, 2005): 218, 220, https://doi.org/10.1086/426304. For a nice discussion of these issues, also see Robert Noggle, "Autonomy and the Paradox of Self-Creation: Infinite Regresses, Finite Selves, and the Limits of Authenticity," in *Personal Autonomy: New Essays on Personal Autonomy and Its Role in Contemporary Moral Philosophy*, ed. James Stacey Taylor (Cambridge: Cambridge University Press, 2005), 87–108.

107. Cass R. Sunstein, *The Ethics of Influence: Government in the Age of Behavioral Science* (New York: Cambridge University Press, 2016), 118. A caveat to this is that Sunstein and colleagues did find that people tend to prefer System 2 nudges (those that target or work from deliberative processes) more than System 1 nudges (those that target unconscious or subconscious processes), *but* they shift more in favor of

System 1–type nudges when they learn that they are more effective. This does not mean they disapprove of System 1–type nudges, just that they prefer System 2–type in pair-wise comparisons.

108. Blumenthal-Barby, "Between Reason and Coercion."

109. Scott D. Halpern et al., "Default Options in Advance Directives Influence How Patients Set Goals for End-of-Life Care," *Health Affairs (Project Hope)* 32, no. 2 (February 2013): 408–417, https://doi.org/10.1377/hlthaff.2012.0895.

110. Lucke also recognizes this point. See Jayne Lucke, "Context Is All Important in Investigating Attitudes: Acceptability Depends on the Nature of the Nudge, Who Nudges, and Who Is Nudged," *American Journal of Bioethics* 13, no. 6 (2013): 24–25, https://doi.org/10.1080/15265161.2013.781709. Context is all important in investigating attitudes: acceptability depends on the nature of the nudge, who nudges, and who is nudged. A related point is why patients' objections to nonargumentative influence or nudging should matter at all if *the objections too* are likely the result of certain heuristics and biases (including framing effects, as eluded to here). One reason is that it may be possible to ask questions about endorsement in ways that do not trigger certain heuristics and biases and get closer to patients' true views on whether or not they have fundamental objections to (versus whether they endorse or don't mind) well-intentioned and responsible nudging and choice architecture from their physicians. That having been said, the fact that objections or endorsement may themselves be subject to heuristics and biases may mean that this should not be the main normative argument that proponents or opponents of nudging and choice architecture hang their hats on. There may be more reason to focus on arguments about decisional improvement, unavoidability (to some extent), justified soft paternalism, and possibly autonomy promotion (from a theoretical point of view).

111. This could go either way. We may think such a description would make a patient more inclined to endorse the nudge: since everyone else is nudging them, their physician might as well, too, especially since the physician is likely more inclined to try to understand and nudge toward good rather than bad. On the other hand, we might think the description would make a patient less inclined to endorse it: since everyone else is nudging them, they do not want their physician to do so because the doctor's office is the one sacrosanct place where they will not be nudged. I thank an audience member at the University of Utah philosophy department colloquium series for this point.

112. As Ploug and Holm object, "All of the exceptional cases just described of autonomous agents that would render nudging bypassing reflection legitimate rest on the assumption that the doctor is able to tell that the patient is 'a man of action' or 'managing by unreflectiveness' or 'indifferent to manipulation.' But unless the patient offers this information, the doctor is not in a good position to make this judgment. Informed consent requirements must therefore embrace the diversity

in second-order views about the quality of reasons for action by securing adequate information, understanding and the absence of undue influence, and so on." Ploug and Holm, "Informed Consent, Libertarian Paternalism, and Nudging," W10–12.

113. Ruth R. Faden and Tom L. Beauchamp, *A History and Theory of Informed Consent* (New York: Oxford University Press, 1986), 261.

114. Douglas J. Opel et al., "The Influence of Provider Communication Behaviors on Parental Vaccine Acceptance and Visit Experience," *American Journal of Public Health* 105, no. 10 (October 2015): 1998–2004, https://doi.org/10.2105/AJPH.2014.302425; Texas Children's Hospital, "Facing Meningitis," November 14, 2011, video, 3:43, https://www.youtube.com/watch?v=h2-U1S74OH0&hl=en_US&version=3https %3A%2F%2Fwww.texaschildrens.org%2Fdepartments%2Fimmunization-project.

115. Plato, *Republic*, trans. G. M. A. Grube and C. D. C. Reeve, in *Plato: Complete Works*, ed. John M. Cooper and D. S. Hutchinson (Indianapolis, IN: Hackett, 1997), 971–1223; Charles L. Griswold, "Plato on Rhetoric and Poetry," *Stanford Encyclopedia of Philosophy*, Fall 2016 edition, ed. Edward N. Zalta, https://stanford.library.sydney .edu.au/entries/plato-rhetoric/.

116. Plato, *Gorgias*, trans. Donald J. Zeyl, in Cooper and Hutchinson, *Plato: Complete Works*, 791–870; Griswold, "Plato on Rhetoric and Poetry."

117. Aristotle, *Rhetoric*, in *Aristotle: Selections*, trans. Terence Irwin and Gail Fine (Indianapolis, IN: Hackett, 1995), 517–542; Griswold, "Plato on Rhetoric and Poetry."

118. Plato, *Phaedrus*, trans. Alexander Nehamas and Paul Woodruff, in Cooper and Hutchinson, *Plato: Complete Works*, 506–556; Griswold, "Plato on Rhetoric and Poetry."

119. Nudging does not necessarily pose a threat, and the autonomy-nudging analysis is very complicated. See chapter 2, the section "Are Patients Generally Autonomous? Lessons from Behavioral Economics," and in this chapter, the sections "Argument 3: The Argument from Justified Soft Paternalism and Respect for Autonomy" and "Argument 4: Patients Don't Mind and the Principle of Endorsement."

120. In the next chapter I go into more detail about conceptual distinctions between coercion, manipulation, rational persuasion, and where choice architecture and nudging fit in this schema.

121. This relates to a point made by Luc Bovens that nudges are morally problematic to the extent that they induce preference changes that disturb the coherence of the all-things-considered preferences of an agent. See Bovens, "The Ethics of Nudge."

122. Victor Kumar, "Nudges and Bumps," *Georgetown Journal of Law & Public Policy* 14 (2016): 872–873, http://www.victorkumar.org/uploads/6/1/5/2/61526489/kumar _-_nudges_and_bumps__final_.pdf.

123. Till Grüne-Yanoff, Caterina Marchionni, and Markus A. Feufel. "Toward a Framework for Selecting Behavioural Policies: How to Choose between Boosts and Nudges," *Economics & Philosophy* 34, no. 2 (July 2018): 246, https://doi.org/10.1017 /S0266267118000032. See also Till Grüne-Yanoff and Ralph Hertwig, "Nudge versus Boost: How Coherent Are Policy and Theory?," *Minds and Machines* 26, no. 1 (March 1, 2016): 149–183, https://doi.org/10.1007/s11023-015-9367-9.

124. Balazs Aczel et al., "Is It Time for Studying Real-Life Debiasing? Evaluation of the Effectiveness of an Analogical Intervention Technique," *Frontiers in Psychology* 6 (2015): 1120, https://doi.org/10.3389/fpsyg.2015.01120.

125. See Guillaume Beaulac and Tim Kenyon, "Critical Thinking Education and Debiasing (AILACT Essay Prize Winner 2013)," *Informal Logic* 34, no. 4 (December 10, 2014): 341–363, https://doi.org/10.22329/il.v34i4.4203. Here, researchers point out that teaching subjects about various biases does not make them less susceptible to them, in part because of bias blind spot (people think they are personally immune to them). Note, however, that there *may* be more promise for debiasing strategies when it comes to physician decision-making. This is because it makes sense for physicians to go through meta-cognition training programs (where they learn and think about biases) since they make these decisions (diagnosing, prescribing) day after day over their career. Such programs are less relevant for patients who are making one-time decisions or unique decisions over time. See Pat Croskerry, "Cognitive Forcing Strategies in Clinical Decision-Making," *Annals of Emergency Medicine* 41, no. 1 (January 1, 2003): 110–120, https://doi.org/10.1067/mem.2003.22.

126. Pat Croskerry, Geeta Singhal, and Sílvia Mamede, "Cognitive Debiasing 2: Impediments to and Strategies for Change," *BMJ Quality & Safety* 22, suppl. 2 (October 1, 2013): ii65, https://doi.org/10.1136/bmjqs-2012-001713.

127. Ramona Ludolph and Peter J. Schulz, "Debiasing Health-Related Judgments and Decision Making: A Systematic Review," *Medical Decision Making* 38, no. 1 (January 1, 2018): 3–13, https://doi.org/10.1177/0272989X17716672.

128. At the same time, opposite effects have been found. For example, one study found that none of four separate manipulations worked against the optimism bias in 222 New Jersey residents' perception of risk factors for several health problems. In fact, some manipulations actually *strengthened* the bias. Neil D. Weinstein and William M. Klein, "Resistance of Personal Risk Perceptions to Debiasing Interventions," *Health Psychology* 14, no. 2 (1995): 132–140, https://doi.org/10.1037/0278-6133.14.2.132.

129. Kumar, "Nudges and Bumps," 861–876.

130. Grüne-Yanoff, Marchionni, and Feufel, "Toward a Framework for Selecting Behavioural Policies."

131. Grüne-Yanoff, Marchionni, and Feufel, "Toward a Framework for Selecting Behavioural Policies," 257.

132. Grüne-Yanoff, Marchionni, and Feufel, "Toward a Framework for Selecting Behavioural Policies," 257.

133. Grüne-Yanoff and Hertwig, "Nudge versus Boost."

**Chapter 4**

1. J. S. Blumenthal-Barby, "Between Reason and Coercion: Ethically Permissible Influence in Health Care and Health Policy Contexts," *Kennedy Institute of Ethics Journal* 22, no. 4 (January 3, 2012): 345–366, https://kiej.georgetown.edu/home_files /22.4.blumenthal-barby.pdf.

2. Richard H. Thaler and Cass R. Sunstein, *Nudge: Improving Decisions about Health, Wealth, and Happiness* (New Haven, CT: Yale University Press, 2008), 6.

3. Yashar Saghai draws the distinction as between nudges that totally bypass deliberation (similar to what I am calling "nontransparent") and ones that trigger "incompletely deliberative" processes or that "channel deliberation into one pre-determined path without entirely bypassing it" (similar to what I am calling "transparent"). But he then lumps both into the category of nudges (with the characteristic that they "are relying on shallow cognitive processes") and treats them as normatively equivalent. Yashar Saghai, "Salvaging the Concept of Nudge," *Journal of Medical Ethics* 39, no. 8 (August 1, 2013): 489, https://doi.org/10.1136/medethics-2012-100727. Hansen and Jespersen draw a similar distinction to my nontransparent vs. transparent nudges with their Type 1 versus Type 2 nudges. Type 1 nudges, such as defaults, work without engaging with reflective deliberation or conscious choice at all. Type 2 nudges, such as framing, work by affecting reflective choices (more attention is placed on loss frame). They also distinguish between transparent and nontransparent nudges, where they mean nudges in which the intent and mechanism *behind* the nudge is clear (transparent), as opposed to ones where it is not (nontransparent). See Pelle Hansen and Andreas Jespersen, "Nudge and the Manipulation of Choice: A Framework for the Responsible Use of the Nudge Approach to Behaviour Change in Public Policy," *European Journal of Risk Regulation* 1 (March 1, 2013): 3–28, https://doi .org/10.1017/S1867299X00002762.

There are also what Luc Bovens calls "type" and "token" transparency in nudging. In type transparency, the nudger is transparent about the fact that nudges will be/are being used, and in token transparency the nudger is transparent about a particular nudge at a particular time. See Luc Bovens, "The Ethics of Nudge," in *Preference Change: Approaches from Philosophy, Economics and Psychology*, ed. Till Grüne-Yanoff and Sven Ove Hansson (Dordrecht: Springer, 2009), 207–219.

4. See Saghai, "Salvaging the Concept of Nudge." Saghai calls nudges that preserve choice set but are hard to resist because of impact on inhibitory capacities "prods."

5. Thaler and Sunstein, *Nudge*, 244.

6. Cass R. Sunstein, "The Ethics of Nudging," *Yale Journal on Regulation* 32, no. 2 (2015): 415–450, at 416n8, https://digitalcommons.law.yale.edu/cgi/viewcontent .cgi?article=1415&context=yjreg.

7. Sunstein, "The Ethics of Nudging," 415, 448.

8. Sunstein, "The Ethics of Nudging," 427.

9. Victor Kumar, "Nudges and Bumps," *Georgetown Journal of Law & Public Policy* 14 (2016): 861–876.

10. Till Grüne-Yanoff, Caterina Marchionni, and Markus A. Feufel, "Toward a Framework for Selecting Behavioural Policies: How to Choose between Boosts and Nudges," *Economics & Philosophy* 34, no. 2 (July 2018): 243–266, https://doi.org/10 .1017/S0266267118000032. See also Till Grüne-Yanoff and Ralph Hertwig, "Nudge Versus Boost: How Coherent Are Policy and Theory?," *Minds and Machines* 26, no. 1 (March 1, 2016): 149–183, https://doi.org/10.1007/s11023-015-9367-9.

11. Sunstein, "The Ethics of Nudging," 427.

12. Neil Levy, "Nudges in a Post-Truth World," *Journal of Medical Ethics* 43, no. 8 (2017): 495–500, https://doi.org/10.1136/medethics-2017-104153.

13. Andres Moles, "Nudging for Liberals," *Social Theory and Practice* 41, no. 4 (2015): 644–667.

14. Robert Noggle, "Manipulation, Salience, and Nudges," *Bioethics* 32, no. 3 (2018): 164–170, https://doi.org/10.1111/bioe.12421.

15. Noggle, "Manipulation, Salience, and Nudges," 169.

16. William Simkulet, "Informed Consent and Nudging," *Bioethics* 33, no. 1 (2019): 178, https://doi.org/10.1111/bioe.12449.

17. Simkulet, "Informed Consent and Nudging," 173, in which he paraphrases Harry Frankfurt, "On Bullshit," *Raritan* 6, no. 2 (1986): 81–100.

18. Simkulet, "Informed Consent and Nudging," 173.

19. J. S. Blumenthal-Barby and Peter A. Ubel, "Truth Be Told: Not All Nudging Is Bullshit," *Journal of Medical Ethics* 44, no. 8 (August 2018): 547, https://doi.org/10 .1136/medethics-2017-104317. Here I respond to Simkulet's charge that nudging is "bullshit" because it aims only at persuading agents to do or choose certain things at the expense of aiming at truth and understanding. I argue that persuasion and understanding are not mutually exclusive aims, and I give examples of nudges that aim at both. For more on Simkulet's charge of bullshitting, see William Simkulet, "Nudging, Informed Consent and Bullshit," *Journal of Medical Ethics* 44, no. 8 (August 1, 2018): 536–542, https://doi.org/10.1136/medethics-2017-104480.

20. Chris Mills, "The Choice Architect's Trilemma," *Res Publica* 24, no. 3 (2018): 412, https://doi.org/10.1007/s11158-017-9363-4.

21. This example may be part rational persuasion and part nudge, in the sense that it uses both appeal to reason and established values but also triggers shallow cognitive processes such as emotions and the desire to adhere to social norms for the sake of norms.

22. While this is the only section of the book where I use the term "manipulation," the entire book (especially chapters 3 and 4) addresses concerns about person A shaping the choice of person B by way of nonrational, noncoercive influence (i.e., about "manipulation" as some define it). I just happen to think the term is conceptually unclear and normatively unhelpful (at best) or misleading (at worst), so I try largely to avoid it. See Blumenthal-Barby, "Between Reason and Coercion."

23. Robert Noggle, "Manipulative Actions: A Conceptual and Moral Analysis," *American Philosophical Quarterly* 33, no. 1 (1996): 43–55, https://www.jstor.org/stable /20009846.

24. Anne Barnhill, "What Is Manipulation?," in *Manipulation: Theory and Practice*, ed. Christian Coons and Michael Weber (New York: Oxford University Press, 2014), 54.

25. Claudia Mills, "Politics and Manipulation," *Social Theory and Practice* 21, no. 1 (1995): 100, https://www.jstor.org/stable/23560376.

26. Ruth R. Faden and Tom L. Beauchamp, *A History and Theory of Informed Consent* (New York: Oxford University Press 1986), 354.

27. Faden and Beauchamp, *A History and Theory of Informed Consent*.

28. Blumenthal-Barby, "Between Reason and Coercion."

29. Another framework for influence commonly appealed to is the Nuffield intervention ladder, although it is for the public health context. The categories outlined there are: do nothing or monitor the situation; provide information and educate people, enable choice (e.g., make the preferred choice easy or free); guide choice through changing the default; guide choice through incentives; guide choice through disincentives; restrict choice; and eliminate choice. One weakness of this framework is that it does not account for the full range of behavioral economics insights, focusing primarily on defaults. See Nuffield Council on Bioethics, "Policy Process and Practice," in *Public Health: Ethical Issues* (London: Nuffield Council on Bioethics, 2007), 29–48, accessed July 15, 2020, https://www.nuffieldbioethics.org/publications/public -health.

30. One finds these when reviewing several definitions of shared decision-making. See, for example, Cathy Charles, Amiram Gafni, and Tim Whelan, "Shared Decision-Making in the Medical Encounter: What Does It Mean? (or It Takes at Least Two to Tango)," *Social Science & Medicine* 44, no. 5 (March 1, 1997): 681–692, https://doi .org/10.1016/S0277-9536(96)00221-3; Michael J. Barry and Susan Edgman-Levitan, "Shared Decision Making: The Pinnacle of Patient-Centered Care," *New England*

*Journal of Medicine* 366, no. 9 (March 1, 2012): 780–781, https://doi.org/10.1056 /NEJMp1109283l; Stacey L. Sheridan, Russell P. Harris, and Steven H. Woolf, "Shared Decision Making about Screening and Chemoprevention: A Suggested Approach from the U.S. Preventive Services Task Force," *American Journal of Preventive Medicine* 26, no. 1 (January 1, 2004): 56–66, https://doi.org/10.1016/j.amepre.2003.09.011; Patricia E. Deegan and Robert E. Drake, "Shared Decision Making and Medication Management in the Recovery Process," *Psychiatric Services* 57, no. 11 (November 1, 2006): 1636–1639, https://doi.org/10.1176/ps.2006.57.11.1636.

31. See the beginning of chapter 3 for a more extensive discussion of nudging and related definitions.

32. I discuss this point extensively in the beginning of the previous chapter under the heading "Preface to the Arguments: Nudging Is Unavoidable, Neutrality Is Impossible."

33. Simon N. Whitney, "A New Model of Medical Decisions: Exploring the Limits of Shared Decision Making," *Medical Decision Making* 23, no. 4 (July 1, 2003): 279, https://doi.org/10.1177/0272989X03256006.

34. All discussed in chapter 1.

35. Paul Dolan et al., "Mindspace: Influencing Behaviour through Public Policy," Institute for Government, March 2, 2010, 26 https://www.instituteforgovernment .org.uk/publications/mindspace.

36. Ottawa Hospital Research Institute, "Decision Aid Summary," accessed July 2, 2019, https://decisionaid.ohri.ca/Azsumm.php?ID=1149. Note that this decision aid received almost perfect scores on quality according to criteria set forth by the International Patient Decision Aids Standards Collaboration. Decision aids are tools that physicians can use to facilitate a shared decision-making approach; policy initiatives are increasingly linking them with SDM.

37. Michel E. Bratman, "Shared Cooperative Activity," *Philosophical Review* 101, no. 2 (1992): 327–341, https://doi.org/10.2307/2185537.

38. Shared decision-making is a type of shared agency.

39. Emily Oshima Lee and Ezekiel J. Emanuel, "Shared Decision Making to Improve Care and Reduce Costs," *New England Journal of Medicine* 368, no. 1 (January 3, 2013): 6–8, https://doi.org/10.1056/NEJMp1209500; Victor M. Montori, Marleen Kunneman, and Juan P. Brito, "Shared Decision Making and Improving Health Care: The Answer Is Not In," *JAMA* 318, no. 7 (August 15, 2017): 617, https://doi.org/10.1001/jama.2017 .10168.

40. Dawn Stacey et al., "Decision Aids for People Facing Health Treatment or Screening Decisions," *Cochrane Database of Systematic Reviews*, no. 4 (2017): CD001431, https://doi.org/10.1002/14651858.CD001431.pub5; Annette M. O'Connor et al.,

"Decision Aids for People Facing Health Treatment or Screening Decisions," *Cochrane Database of Systematic Reviews*, no. 3 (2009): CD001431, https://doi.org/10.1002/14651 858.CD001431.pub2.

41. Peter A. Ubel et al., "Testing whether Decision Aids Introduce Cognitive Biases: Results of a Randomized Trial," *Patient Education and Counseling* 80, no. 2 (August 1, 2010): 158–163, https://doi.org/10.1016/j.pec.2009.10.021.

42. If one wants to draw a dichotomy between the two, which I resist.

43. Again, that is if one insists on drawing a dichotomy between the two approaches or painting them as opposite or in tension.

44. J. S. Blumenthal-Barby et al., "Decision Aids: When 'Nudging' Patients to Make a Particular Choice Is More Ethical than Balanced, Nondirective Content," *Health Affairs* 32, no. 2 (February 1, 2013): 303–310, https://doi.org/10.1377/hlthaff.2012 .0761.

45. Russell Korobkin, "Libertarian Welfarism," *California Law Review* 97, no. 6 (2009): 1651–1685, https://www.jstor.org/stable/20677921.

46. For a discussion of nudges in the public health context, see J. S. Blumenthal-Barby, Zainab Shipchandler, and Julika Kaplan, "An Ethical Framework for Public Health Nudges: A Case Study of Incentives as Nudges for Vaccination in Rural India," in *Nudging Health: Health Law and Behavioral Economics*, ed. I. Glenn Cohen, Holly Fernandez Lynch, and Christopher T. Robertson (Baltimore: Johns Hopkins University Press, 2016), 112–123. Other essays in that volume that also address the ethics of social nudges and the limits of legitimate intervention include Russell Korobkin's "Three Choice Architecture Paradigms for Healthcare Policy," 15–26, Sarah Conly's "Better Off Dead: Paternalism and Persistent Unconsciousness," 287–296, and David Orentlicher's "Presumed Consent to Organ Donation," 339–350.

47. Philip M. Rosoff, Who Should Ration?," *AMA Journal of Ethics* 19, no. 2 (2017): 164–173, https://doi.org/10.1001/journalofethics.2017.19.2.ecas4-1702.

48. Mark C. Navin, "The Ethics of Vaccination Nudges in Pediatric Practice," *HEC Forum* 29, no. 1 (March 1, 2017): 43–57, https://doi.org/10.1007/s10730-016-9311-2.

49. William Hagman et al., "Public Views on Policies Involving Nudges," *Review of Philosophy and Psychology* 6, no. 3 (September 1, 2015): 439–453, https://doi.org/10 .1007/s13164-015-0263-2.

## Chapter 5

1. This chapter presents findings of actual nudging in four contexts. The data from the psychiatry context is not new; it has been presented in a published manuscript, which is cited. The data from the pediatric context is largely presented for the

first time here with the exception of a commentary on the general ethical issue of nudging in pediatric critical care, which is cited. All of the direct quotes from the qualitative interviews with pediatric intensivists are presented here for the first time. That study was approved by an institutional review board (IRB). Much of the data from the fetal surgery context is also presented here for the first time. The published manuscript that is cited presents findings around general trends of surgeons discussing risk in qualitative more than quantitative terms when the odds are bad, but all the nudge examples and quotes presented in this chapter are new. The study was IRB approved. Finally, the data from the prostate cancer context are partly new. Namely, the data presented on incentives and framing effects from the survey study are presented here for the first time; the data about the impact of normative messaging have been presented already in the cited published manuscript, though the ethical analysis occurs for the first time here. The study was IRB approved.

2. Recall, Thaler and Sunstein's definition says that a nudge is "any aspect of the choice architecture that alters people's behavior in a predictable way without forbidding any options or significantly changing their economic incentives." Richard H. Thaler and Cass R. Sunstein, *Nudge: Improving Decisions about Health, Wealth, and Happiness* (New Haven, CT: Yale University Press, 2008), 6.

And Saghai's is that "A nudges B when A makes it more likely that B will φ, primarily triggered by B's shallow cognitive processes, while A's influence preserves B's choice-set and is substantially noncontrolling (i.e., preserves B's freedom of choice)." Yashar Saghai, "Salvaging the Concept of Nudge," *Journal of Medical Ethics* 39, no. 8 (August 1, 2013): 491, https://doi.org/10.1136/medethics-2012-100727.

"Shallow cognitive processes" include System 1 processes such as biases, heuristics, emotions, and fast, intuitive decision-making.

3. This chart is adapted from a previously published paper: J. S. Blumenthal-Barby et al., "Methods of Influencing the Decisions of Psychiatric Patients: An Ethical Analysis," *Harvard Review of Psychiatry* 21, no. 5 (October 2013): 275–279, https://doi.org/10.1097/HRP.0b013e3182a75d4f.

4. Blumenthal-Barby et al., "Methods of Influencing the Decisions of Psychiatric Patients."

5. Contrast this with a case where the medication might cause side effects that would put aspects of the patient's health at risk (e.g., result in significant weight gain that would stress his heart) or that would negatively impact other important goals (e.g., he is an artist who draws on his malaise for part of his inspiration). These cases would be less clear cut.

6. Much of this ethical analysis overlaps with the ethical analysis in my and my colleague's previous work: J. S. Blumenthal-Barby et al., "Should Neonatologists Give Opinions Withdrawing Life-Sustaining Treatment?," *Pediatrics* 138, no. 6 (December 1, 2016): 1–7, https://doi.org/10.1542/peds.2016-2585.

7. R. Ruano et al., "A Randomized Controlled Trial of Fetal Endoscopic Tracheal Occlusion versus Postnatal Management of Severe Isolated Congenital Diaphragmatic Hernia," *Ultrasound in Obstetrics & Gynecology: The Official Journal of the International Society of Ultrasound in Obstetrics and Gynecology* 39, no. 1 (January 2012): 20–27, https://doi.org/10.1002/uog.10142; J. C. Jani et al., "Severe Diaphragmatic Hernia Treated by Fetal Endoscopic Tracheal Occlusion," *Ultrasound in Obstetrics & Gynecology: The Official Journal of the International Society of Ultrasound in Obstetrics and Gynecology* 34, no. 3 (September 2009): 304–310, https://doi.org/10.1002/uog .6450; J. Deprest, E. Gratacos, and K. H. Nicolaides, "Fetoscopic Tracheal Occlusion (FETO) for Severe Congenital Diaphragmatic Hernia: Evolution of a Technique and Preliminary Results," *Ultrasound in Obstetrics & Gynecology* 24, no. 2 (2004): 121–126, https://doi.org/10.1002/uog.1711.

8. Michael R. Harrison et al., "A Prospective Study of the Outcome for Fetuses with Diaphragmatic Hernia," *JAMA* 271, no. 5 (February 2, 1994): 382–384, https://doi .org/10.1001/jama.1994.03510290064038; Gerben Stege, Alan Fenton, and Bruce Jaffray, "Nihilism in the 1990s: The True Mortality of Congenital Diaphragmatic Hernia," *Pediatrics* 112, no. 3 (September 1, 2003): 532–535, https://doi.org/10.1542 /peds.112.3.532.

9. N. Scott Adzick et al., "A Randomized Trial of Prenatal versus Postnatal Repair of Myelomeningocele," *Obstetrical & Gynecological Survey* 66, no. 6 (June 2011): 340–341, https://doi.org/10.1097/OGX.0b013e31822c180a; Ruano et al., "A Randomized Controlled Trial of Fetal Endoscopic Tracheal Occlusion"; Jani et al., "Severe Diaphragmatic Hernia Treated by Fetal Endoscopic Tracheal Occlusion"; Deprest, Gratacos, and Nicolaides, "Fetoscopic Tracheal Occlusion."

10. J. S. Blumenthal-Barby et al., "Communication about Maternal-Fetal Surgery for Myelomeningocele and Congenital Diaphragmatic Hernia: Preliminary Findings with Implications for Informed Consent and Shared Decision-Making," *Journal of Perinatal Medicine* 44, no. 6 (2015): 645–653, https://doi.org/10.1515/jpm-2015-0039.

11. Laurence B. McCullough and Frank A. Chervenak, "A Critical Analysis of the Concept and Discourse of 'Unborn Child,'" *American Journal of Bioethics* 8, no. 7 (September 4, 2008): 34–39, https://doi.org/10.1080/15265160802248161.

12. H. Ballentine Carter, "Active Surveillance for Prostate Cancer: An Underutilized Opportunity for Reducing Harm," *JNCI Monographs* 2012, no. 45 (December 1, 2012): 175–183, https://doi.org/10.1093/jncimonographs/lgs036.

13. Peter Branney et al., "Choosing Health, Choosing Treatment: Patient Choice after Diagnosis of Localized Prostate Cancer," *Urology* 74, no. 5 (November 1, 2009): 968–971, https://doi.org/10.1016/j.urology.2009.03.015.

14. Adam B. Weiner et al., "National Trends in the Management of Low and Intermediate Risk Prostate Cancer in the United States," *Journal of Urology* 193, no. 1 (January 1, 2015): 95–102, https://doi.org/10.1016/j.juro.2014.07.111.

15. Incentives do not technically count as a nudge, but we considered this a nudge case because we tested two different framings of the incentive: a direct payment per active surveillance visit versus coverage of copayment per active surveillance visit.

16. Robert J. Volk et al., "Designing Normative Messages about Active Surveillance for Men with Localized Prostate Cancer," *Journal of Health Communication* 20, no. 9 (September 2, 2015): 1014–1020, https://doi.org/10.1080/10810730.2015.1018618.

17. J. S. Blumenthal-Barby, Denise Lee, and Robert J. Volk, "Toward Ethically Responsible Choice Architecture in Prostate Cancer Treatment Decision-Making," *CA: A Cancer Journal for Clinicians* 65, no. 4 (2015): 257–260, https://doi.org/10.3322/caac.21283.

18. Peter A. Ubel, Karen A. Scherr, and Angela Fagerlin, "Empowerment Failure: How Shortcomings in Physician Communication Unwittingly Undermine Patient Autonomy," *American Journal of Bioethics* 17, no. 11 (November 2, 2017): 31–39, https://doi.org/10.1080/15265161.2017.1378753.

19. Jonathan Bergman and Mark S. Litwin, "Quality of Life in Men Undergoing Active Surveillance for Localized Prostate Cancer," *JNCI Monographs* 2012, no. 45 (December 1, 2012): 242–249, https://doi.org/10.1093/jncimonographs/lgs026.

20. Lara Bellardita et al., "How Does Active Surveillance for Prostate Cancer Affect Quality of Life? A Systematic Review," *European Urology* 67, no. 4 (April 1, 2015): 637–645, https://doi.org/10.1016/j.eururo.2014.10.028; Anna Bill-Axelson et al., "Long-Term Distress after Radical Prostatectomy versus Watchful Waiting in Prostate Cancer: A Longitudinal Study from the Scandinavian Prostate Cancer Group-4 Randomized Clinical Trial," *European Urology* 64, no. 6 (December 1, 2013): 920–928, https://doi.org/10.1016/j.eururo.2013.02.025.

## Conclusion

1. Richard H. Thaler and Cass R. Sunstein, *Nudge: Improving Decisions about Health, Wealth, and Happiness* (New Haven, CT: Yale University Press, 2008), 3.

# Bibliography

Abbott, Andrea, Natasha Rueth, Susan Pappas-Varco, Karen Kuntz, Elizabeth Kerr, and Todd Tuttle. "Perceptions of Contralateral Breast Cancer: An Overestimation of Risk." *Annals of Surgical Oncology* 18, no. 11 (September 27, 2011): 3129–3136. https://doi.org/10.1245/s10434-011-1914-x.

Aczel, Balazs, Bence Bago, Aba Szollosi, Andrei Foldes, and Bence Lukacs. "Is It Time for Studying Real-Life Debiasing? Evaluation of the Effectiveness of an Analogical Intervention Technique." *Frontiers in Psychology* 6 (2015): 1120. https://www.frontiersin.org/articles/10.3389/fpsyg.2015.01120/full.

Adzick, N. Scott, Elizabeth A. Thom, Catherine Y. Spong, John W. Brock III, Pamela K. Burrows, Mark P. Johnson, Lori J. Howell, et al. "A Randomized Trial of Prenatal versus Postnatal Repair of Myelomeningocele." *Obstetrical & Gynecological Survey* 66, no. 6 (June 2011): 340–341. https://doi.org/10.1097/OGX.0b013e31822c180a.

Allen, Jennifer D., Anshu P. Mohllajee, Rachel C. Shelton, Megan K. D. Othus, Holly B. Fontenot, and Richard Hanna. "Stage of Adoption of the Human Papillomavirus Vaccine among College Women." *Preventive Medicine* 48, no. 5 (May 1, 2009): 420–425. https://doi.org/10.1016/j.ypmed.2008.12.005.

Allen, Larry A., Jonathan E. Yager, Michele Jonsson Funk, Wayne C. Levy, James A. Tulsky, Margaret T. Bowers, Gwen C. Dodson, Christopher M. O'Connor, and G. Michael Felker. "Discordance between Patient-Predicted and Model-Predicted Life Expectancy among Ambulatory Patients with Heart Failure." *JAMA* 299, no. 21 (June 4, 2008): 2533–2542. https://doi.org/10.1001/jama.299.21.2533.

Amsterlaw, Jennifer, Brian Zikmund-Fisher, Angela Fagerlin, and Peter A. Ubel. "Can Avoidance of Complications Lead to Biased Healthcare Decisions?" *Judgment and Decision Making* 1 (2006): 64–75. http://journal.sjdm.org/06008/jdm06008.htm.

Appelbaum, Paul S. "Clinical Practice: Assessment of Patients' Competence to Consent to Treatment." *New England Journal of Medicine* 357, no. 18 (November 1, 2007): 1834–1840. https://doi.org/10.1056/NEJMcp074045.

Ariely, Dan. *Predictably Irrational*. New York: HarperCollins, 2008.

Aristotle. *Nicomachean Ethics*. In *Aristotle: Selections*, translated by Terence Irwin and Gail Fine, 347–449. Indianapolis, IN: Hackett, 1995.

Aristotle. *Rhetoric*. In *Aristotle: Selections*, translated by Terence Irwin and Gail Fine. Indianapolis, IN: Hackett, 1995.

Arpaly, Nomy. *Unprincipled Virtue: An Inquiry into Moral Agency*. Oxford: Oxford University Press, 2002. https://www.oxfordscholarship.com/view/10.1093/0195152042 .001.0001/acprof-9780195152043.

Audi, Robert. *The Architecture of Reason: The Structure and Substance of Rationality*. Oxford: Oxford University Press, 2001.

Banks, Sara M., Peter Salovey, Susan Greener, Alexander J. Rothman, Anne Moyer, John Beauvais, and Elissa Epel. "The Effects of Message Framing on Mammography Utilization." *Health Psychology* 14, no. 2 (1995): 178–184. https://doi.org/10.1037 /0278-6133.14.2.178.

Barnes, Elizabeth. *The Minority Body: A Theory of Disability*. New York: Oxford University Press, 2016.

Barnhill, Anne. "What Is Manipulation?" In *Manipulation: Theory and Practice*, edited by Christian Coons and Michael Weber, 51–72. New York: Oxford University Press, 2014.

Barry, Michael J., and Susan Edgman-Levitan. "Shared Decision Making—The Pinnacle of Patient-Centered Care." *New England Journal of Medicine* 366, no. 9 (March 1, 2012): 780–781. https://doi.org/10.1056/NEJMp1109283.

Beauchamp, Tom L., and James F. Childress. *Principles of Biomedical Ethics*. 6th ed. New York: Oxford University Press, 2009.

Beaulac, Guillaume, and Tim Kenyon. "Critical Thinking Education and Debiasing (AILACT Essay Prize Winner 2013)." *Informal Logic* 34, no. 4 (December 10, 2014): 341–363. https://doi.org/10.22329/il.v34i4.4203.

Bellardita, Lara, Riccardo Valdagni, Roderick van den Bergh, Hans Randsdorp, Claudia Repetto, Lionne D. F. Venderbos, J. Athene Lane, and Ida J. Korfage. "How Does Active Surveillance for Prostate Cancer Affect Quality of Life? A Systematic Review." *European Urology* 67, no. 4 (April 1, 2015): 637–645. https://doi.org/10.1016/j.eururo .2014.10.028.

Benartzi, Shlomo, John Beshears, Katherine L. Milkman, Cass R. Sunstein, Richard H. Thaler, Maya Shankar, Will Tucker-Ray, William J. Congdon, and Steven Galing. "Should Governments Invest More in Nudging?" *Psychological Science* 28, no. 8 (August 1, 2017): 1041–1055. https://doi.org/10.1177/0956797617702501.

Benson, Buster. "Cognitive Bias Cheat Sheet." Medium: Better Humans, September 1, 2016. https://medium.com/better-humans/cognitive-bias-cheat-sheet-55a472476b18.

Bergman, Jonathan, and Mark S. Litwin. "Quality of Life in Men Undergoing Active Surveillance for Localized Prostate Cancer." *JNCI Monographs* 2012, no. 45 (December 1, 2012): 242–249. https://doi.org/10.1093/jncimonographs/lgs026.

Bill-Axelson, Anna, Hans Garmo, Lars Holmberg, Jan-Erik Johansson, Hans-Olov Adami, Gunnar Steineck, Eva Johansson, and Jennifer R. Rider. "Long-Term Distress after Radical Prostatectomy versus Watchful Waiting in Prostate Cancer: A Longitudinal Study from the Scandinavian Prostate Cancer Group-4 Randomized Clinical Trial." *European Urology* 64, no. 6 (December 1, 2013): 920–928. https://doi.org/10.1016/j.eururo.2013.02.025.

Blumenthal-Barby, J. S. "Between Reason and Coercion: Ethically Permissible Influence in Health Care and Health Policy Contexts." *Kennedy Institute of Ethics Journal* 22, no. 4 (January 3, 2012): 345–366. https://kiej.georgetown.edu/home_files/22.4.blumenthal-barby.pdf.

Blumenthal-Barby, J. S. "Biases and Heuristics in Decision Making and Their Impact on Autonomy." *American Journal of Bioethics* 16, no. 5 (May 3, 2016): 5–15. https://doi.org/10.1080/15265161.2016.1159750.

Blumenthal-Barby, J. S., and Hadley Burroughs. "Seeking Better Health Care Outcomes: The Ethics of Using the 'Nudge.'" *American Journal of Bioethics* 12, no. 2 (2012): 1–10. https://doi.org/10.1080/15265161.2011.634481.

Blumenthal-Barby, J. S., Scott B. Cantor, Heidi Voelker Russell, Aanand D. Naik, and Robert J. Volk. "Decision Aids: When 'Nudging' Patients to Make a Particular Choice Is More Ethical than Balanced, Nondirective Content." *Health Affairs* 32, no. 2 (February 1, 2013): 303–310. https://doi.org/10.1377/hlthaff.2012.0761.

Blumenthal-Barby, J. S., Kristin M. Kostick, Estevan D. Delgado, Robert J. Volk, Holland M. Kaplan, L. A. Wilhelms, Sheryl A. McCurdy, Jerry D. Estep, Matthias Loebe, and Courtenay R. Bruce. "Assessment of Patients' and Caregivers' Informational and Decisional Needs for Left Ventricular Assist Device Placement: Implications for Informed Consent and Shared Decision-Making." *Journal of Heart and Lung Transplantation* 34, no. 9 (September 1, 2015): 1182–1189. https://doi.org/10.1016/j.healun.2015.03.026.

Blumenthal-Barby, J. S., and Heather Krieger. "Cognitive Biases and Heuristics in Medical Decision Making: A Critical Review Using a Systematic Search Strategy." *Medical Decision Making* 35, no. 4 (May 1, 2015): 539–557. https://doi.org/10.1177/0272989X14547740.

Blumenthal-Barby, J. S., Heather Krieger, Anne Wei, David Kim, Oluyinka O. Olutoye, and Darrell L. Cass. "Communication about Maternal-Fetal Surgery for

Myelomeningocele and Congenital Diaphragmatic Hernia: Preliminary Findings with Implications for Informed Consent and Shared Decision-Making." *Journal of Perinatal Medicine* 44, no. 6 (2015): 645–653. https://doi.org/10.1515/jpm-2015-0039.

Blumenthal-Barby, J. S., Denise Lee, and Robert J. Volk. "Toward Ethically Responsible Choice Architecture in Prostate Cancer Treatment Decision-Making." *CA: A Cancer Journal for Clinicians* 65, no. 4 (2015): 257–260. https://doi.org/10.3322/caac .21283.

Blumenthal-Barby, J. S., Laura Loftis, Christy L. Cummings, William Meadow, Monica Lemmon, Peter A. Ubel, Laurence McCullough, Emily Rao, and John D. Lantos. "Should Neonatologists Give Opinions Withdrawing Life-Sustaining Treatment?" *Pediatrics* 138, no. 6 (December 1, 2016): 1–7. https://doi.org/10.1542/peds.2016-2585.

Blumenthal-Barby, J. S., Laurence B. McCullough, Heather Krieger, and John Coverdale. "Methods of Influencing the Decisions of Psychiatric Patients: An Ethical Analysis." *Harvard Review of Psychiatry* 21, no. 5 (October 2013): 275–279. https://doi.org/10 .1097/HRP.0b013e3182a75d4f.

Blumenthal-Barby, J. S., Zainab Shipchandler, and Julika Kaplan. "An Ethical Framework for Public Health Nudges: A Case Study of Incentives as Nudges for Vaccination in Rural India." In *Nudging Health: Health Law and Behavioral Economics*, edited by I. Glenn Cohen, Holly Fernandez Lynch, and Christopher T. Robertson, 112–123. Baltimore: Johns Hopkins University Press, 2016.

Blumenthal-Barby, J. S., and Peter A. Ubel. "Gunmen and Ice Cream Cones: Harm to Autonomy and Harm to Persons." *American Journal of Bioethics* 16, no. 11 (2016): 13–14. https://doi.org/10.1080/15265161.2016.1222021.

Blumenthal-Barby, J. S., and Peter A. Ubel. "In Defense of 'Denial': Difficulty Knowing When Beliefs Are Unrealistic and Whether Unrealistic Beliefs Are Bad." *American Journal of Bioethics* 18, no. 9 (September 2, 2018): 4–15. https://doi.org/10.1080/15265161 .2018.1498934.

Blumenthal-Barby, J. S., and Peter A. Ubel. "Truth Be Told: Not All Nudging Is Bullshit." *Journal of Medical Ethics* 44, no. 8 (August 2018): 547. https://doi.org/10.1136 /medethics-2017-104317.

Bovens, Luc. "The Ethics of Nudge." In *Preference Change: Approaches from Philosophy, Economics and Psychology*, edited by Till Grüne-Yanoff and Sven Ove Hansson, 207–219. Dordrecht: Springer, 2009.

Bradley, Ben. "Doing Away with Harm." *Philosophy and Phenomenological Research* 85, no. 2 (2012): 390–412. https://doi.org/10.1111/j.1933-1592.2012.00615.x.

Bramble, Ben. Review of *From Valuing to Value: A Defense of Subjectivism*, by David Sobel. *Notre Dame Philosophical Reviews*, May 11, 2017. https://ndpr.nd.edu/news/from -valuing-to-value-a-defense-of-subjectivism/.

Branney, Peter, Alan White, Sunjay Jain, Chris Hiley, and Paul Flowers. "Choosing Health, Choosing Treatment: Patient Choice after Diagnosis of Localized Prostate Cancer." *Urology* 74, no. 5 (November 1, 2009): 968–971. https://doi.org/10.1016/j.urology.2009.03.015.

Bratman, Michael E. "Planning Agency, Autonomous Agency." In *Personal Autonomy: New Essays on Personal Autonomy and Its Role in Contemporary Moral Philosophy*, edited by James Stacey Taylor, 33–57. New York: Cambridge University Press, 2005.

Bratman, Michael E. "Shared Cooperative Activity." *Philosophical Review* 101, no. 2 (1992): 327–341. https://doi.org/10.2307/2185537.

Braxton, Carla C., Celia N. Robinson, and Samir S. Awad. "Escalation of Commitment in the Surgical ICU." *Critical Care Medicine* 45, no. 4 (April 2017): e433–436. https://doi.org/10.1097/CCM.0000000000002261.

Brehaut, Jamie C., Annette M. O'Connor, Timothy J. Wood, Thomas F. Hack, Laura Siminoff, Elisa Gordon, and Deb Feldman-Stewart. "Validation of a Decision Regret Scale." *Medical Decision Making* 23, no. 4 (July 1, 2003): 281–292. https://doi.org/10.1177/0272989X03256005.

Brenes, Gretchen A., and Electra D. Paskett. "Predictors of Stage of Adoption for Colorectal Cancer Screening." *Preventive Medicine* 31, no. 4 (October 1, 2000): 410–416. https://doi.org/10.1006/pmed.2000.0729.

Brewster, Abenaa M., Susan K. Peterson, Isabelle Bedrosian, Alastair Mark Thompson, Dalliah MaShon Black, Jonathan Nelson, Robert Cook, et al. "Prospective Assessment of Psychosocial Outcomes of Contralateral Prophylactic Mastectomy." *Journal of Clinical Oncology* 35, no. 15, suppl. (May 20, 2017): 6569. https://doi.org/10.1200/JCO.2017.35.15_suppl.6569.

Brooks, Thom. "Should We Nudge Informed Consent?" *American Journal of Bioethics* 13, no. 6 (2013): 22–23. https://doi.org/10.1080/15265161.2013.781710.

Brown, Katrina F., J. Simon Kroll, Michael J. Hudson, Mary Ramsay, John Green, Charles A. Vincent, Graham Fraser, and Nick Sevdalis. "Omission Bias and Vaccine Rejection by Parents of Healthy Children: Implications for the Influenza A/H1N1 Vaccination Programme." *Vaccine* 28, no. 25 (June 7, 2010): 4181–4185. https://doi.org/10.1016/j.vaccine.2010.04.012.

Buss, Sarah. "Valuing Autonomy and Respecting Persons: Manipulation, Seduction, and the Basis of Moral Constraints." *Ethics* 115, no. 2 (January 1, 2005): 195–235. https://doi.org/10.1086/426304.

Camerer, Colin F., Anna Dreber, Felix Holzmeister, Teck-Hua Ho, Jürgen Huber, Magnus Johannesson, Michael Kirchler, et al. "Evaluating the Replicability of Social Science Experiments in *Nature* and *Science* between 2010 and 2015." *Nature Human*

*Behaviour* 2, no. 9 (August 27, 2019): 637–644. https://doi.org/10.1038/s41562-018 -0399-z.

Camerer, Colin F., George Loewenstein, and Matthew Rabin, eds. *Advances in Behavioral Economics*. Princeton, NJ: Princeton University Press, 2004.

Carmon, Ziv, Klaus Wertenbroch, and Marcel Zeelenberg. "Option Attachment: When Deliberating Makes Choosing Feel like Losing." *Journal of Consumer Research* 30, no. 1 (June 1, 2003): 15–29. https://doi.org/10.1086/374701.

Carter, H. Ballentine. "Active Surveillance for Prostate Cancer: An Underutilized Opportunity for Reducing Harm." *JNCI Monographs* 2012, no. 45 (December 1, 2012): 175–183. https://doi.org/10.1093/jncimonographs/lgs036.

Chajut, Eran, Avner Caspi, Rony Chen, Moshe Hod, and Dan Ariely. "In Pain Thou Shalt Bring Forth Children: The Peak-and-End Rule in Recall of Labor Pain." *Psychological Science* 25, no. 12 (December 2014): 2266–2271. https://doi.org/10.1177 /0956797614551004.

Chapman, Gretchen B., Meng Li, Helen Colby, and Haewon Yoon. "Opting In vs. Opting Out of Influenza Vaccination." *JAMA* 304, no. 1 (July 7, 2010): 43–44. https://doi.org/10.1001/jama.2010.892.

Charles, Cathy, Amiram Gafni, and Tim Whelan. "Shared Decision-Making in the Medical Encounter: What Does It Mean? (or It Takes at Least Two to Tango)." *Social Science & Medicine* 44, no. 5 (March 1, 1997): 681–692. https://doi.org/10.1016/S0277 -9536(96)00221-3.

Chen, Jennifer C., Richelle J. Cooper, Ana Lopez-O'Sullivan, and David L. Schriger. "Measuring Patient Tolerance for Future Adverse Events in Low-Risk Emergency Department Chest Pain Patients." *Annals of Emergency Medicine* 64, no. 2 (August 1, 2014): 127–136. https://doi.org/10.1016/j.annemergmed.2013.12.025.

Christman, John. *The Politics of Persons: Individual Autonomy and Socio-Historical Selves*. New York: Cambridge University Press, 2011.

Clark, Jeffrey W., and Jean A. Young. "Automatic Enrollment: The Power of the Default." Vanguard Research, February 2018. https://institutional.vanguard.com/iam /pdf/CIRAE.pdf?cbdForceDomain=true.

Cohen, Gerald Allan. "Reason, Humanity, and the Moral Law." In *The Sources of Normativity*, by Christine M. Korsgaard, 167–188. Edited by Onora O'Neill. Cambridge: Cambridge University Press, 1996.

Cohen, Shlomo. "A Philosophical Misunderstanding at the Basis of Opposition to Nudging." *American Journal of Bioethics* 15, no. 10 (October 3, 2015): 39–41. https:// doi.org/10.1080/15265161.2015.1074313.

Coleman, Martin D. "Sunk Cost and Commitment to Medical Treatment." *Current Psychology* 29, no. 2 (June 1, 2010): 121–134. https://doi.org/10.1007/s12144-010-9077-7.

Conly, Sarah. *Against Autonomy: Justifying Coercive Paternalism.* Cambridge: Cambridge University Press, 2012.

Conly, Sarah. "Better Off Dead: Paternalism and Persistent Unconsciousness." In *Nudging Health: Health Law and Behavioral Economics*, edited by I. Glenn Cohen, Holly Fernandez Lynch, and Christopher T. Robertson, 287–296. Baltimore: Johns Hopkins University Press, 2016.

Crisp, Roger. "Hedonism Reconsidered." *Philosophy and Phenomenological Research* 73, no. 3 (2006): 619–645. https://doi.org/10.1111/j.1933-1592.2006.tb00551.x.

Croskerry, Pat. "Cognitive Forcing Strategies in Clinical Decisionmaking." *Annals of Emergency Medicine* 41, no. 1 (January 1, 2003): 110–120. https://doi.org/10.1067/mem.2003.22.

Croskerry, Pat, Geeta Singhal, and Sílvia Mamede. "Cognitive Debiasing 2: Impediments to and Strategies for Change." *BMJ Quality & Safety* 22, suppl. 2 (October 1, 2013): ii65–72. https://doi.org/10.1136/bmjqs-2012-001713.

Croyle, Robert T., Yi-chun Sun, and Douglas H. Louie. "Psychological Minimization of Cholesterol Test Results: Moderators of Appraisal in College Students and Community Residents." *Health Psychology* 12, no. 6 (1993): 503–507. https://doi.org/10.1037/0278-6133.12.6.503.

Deegan, Patricia E., and Robert E. Drake. "Shared Decision Making and Medication Management in the Recovery Process." *Psychiatric Services* 57, no. 11 (November 1, 2006): 1636–1639. https://doi.org/10.1176/ps.2006.57.11.1636.

Degner, Lesley F., and Jeff A. Sloan. "Decision Making during Serious Illness: What Role Do Patients Really Want to Play?" *Journal of Clinical Epidemiology* 45, no. 9 (1992): 941–950. https://doi.org/10.1016/0895-4356(92)90110-9.

Delaney, James, and David B. Hershenov. "Why Consent May Not Be Needed for Organ Procurement." *American Journal of Bioethics* 9, no. 8 (August 3, 2009): 3–10. https://doi.org/10.1080/15265160902985019.

Dennett, Daniel C. "Intentional Systems." *Journal of Philosophy* 68, no. 4 (February 1971): 87–106. https://doi.org/10.2307/2025382.

Deprest, J., E. Gratacos, and K. H. Nicolaides. "Fetoscopic Tracheal Occlusion (FETO) for Severe Congenital Diaphragmatic Hernia: Evolution of a Technique and Preliminary Results." *Ultrasound in Obstetrics & Gynecology* 24, no. 2 (2004): 121–126. https://doi.org/10.1002/uog.1711.

Dewey, John. *The Quest for Certainty.* New York: Capricorn Books, 1960.

Dijksterhuis, Ap, Maarten W. Bos, Loran F. Nordgren, and Rick B. van Baaren. "On Making the Right Choice: The Deliberation-without-Attention Effect." *Science* 311, no. 5763 (February 17, 2006): 1005–1007. https://doi.org/10.1126/science.1121629.

Dolan, Paul, Dominic King, David Halpern, Michael Hallsworth, and Ivo Vlaev. "Mindspace: Influencing Behaviour through Public Policy," Institute for Government, March 2, 2010. https://www.instituteforgovernment.org.uk/publications/mindspace.

Double, Richard. "Two Types of Autonomy Accounts." *Canadian Journal of Philosophy* 22 (January 1, 1992): 65–80. https://doi.org/10.1080/00455091.1992.10717271.

Douglas, Charles, and Emily Proudfoot. "Nudging and the Complicated Real Life of 'Informed Consent.'" *American Journal of Bioethics* 13, no. 6 (2013): 16–17. https://doi.org/10.1080/15265161.2013.781716.

Dworkin, Gerald. "Against Autonomy Response." *Journal of Medical Ethics* 40, no. 5 (May 1, 2014): 352–353. https://doi.org/10.1136/medethics-2013-101552.

Dworkin, Gerald. "Paternalism." *Stanford Encyclopedia of Philosophy*, Winter 2017 edition, edited by Edward N. Zalta. https://plato.stanford.edu/archives/win2017/entries/paternalism/.

Eiser, J. Richard. "The Influence of Question Framing on Symptom Report and Perceived Health Status." *Psychology & Health* 15, no. 1 (February 1, 2000): 13–20. https://doi.org/10.1080/08870440008400285.

El-Jawahri, Areej, Susan L. Mitchell, Michael K. Paasche-Orlow, Jennifer S. Temel, Vicki A. Jackson, Renee R. Rutledge, Mihir Parikh, et al. "A Randomized Controlled Trial of a CPR and Intubation Video Decision Support Tool for Hospitalized Patients." *Journal of General Internal Medicine* 30, no. 8 (August 2015): 1071–1080. https://doi.org/10.1007/s11606-015-3200-2.

Elster, Jon. *Sour Grapes: Studies in the Subversion of Rationality*. Cambridge: Cambridge University Press, 1983.

Ende, Jack, Lewis Kazis, Arlene Ash, and Mark A. Moskowitz. "Measuring Patients' Desire for Autonomy: Decision Making and Information-Seeking Preferences among Medical Patients." *Journal of General Internal Medicine* 4, no. 1 (January 1, 1989): 23–30. https://doi.org/10.1007/BF02596485.

Enoch, David. "Hypothetical Consent and the Value(s) of Autonomy." *Ethics* 128, no. 1 (September 22, 2017): 6–36. https://doi.org/10.1086/692939.

Facione, Noreen C., and Peter A. Facione. "The Cognitive Structuring of Patient Delay in Breast Cancer." *Social Science & Medicine* 63, no. 12 (December 1, 2006): 3137–3149. https://doi.org/10.1016/j.socscimed.2006.08.014.

Faden, Ruth R., and Tom L. Beauchamp. *A History and Theory of Informed Consent*. New York: Oxford University Press, 1986.

Fagerlin, Angela, Michael Pignone, Purva Abhyankar, Nananda Col, Deb Feldman-Stewart, Teresa Gavaruzzi, Jennifer Kryworuchko, et al. "Clarifying Values: An Updated Review." *BMC Medical Informatics and Decision Making* 13, no. suppl. 2 (November 29, 2013). https://doi.org/10.1186/1472-6947-13-S2-S8.

Fagerlin, Angela, Brian J. Zikmund-Fisher, and Peter A. Ubel. "Cure Me Even If It Kills Me: Preferences for Invasive Cancer Treatment." *Medical Decision Making* 25, no. 6 (November 1, 2005): 614–619. https://doi.org/10.1177/0272989X05282639.

Feinberg, Joel. *The Moral Limits of the Criminal Law.* Vol. 1, *Harm to Others.* New York: Oxford University Press, 1984. https://www.oxfordscholarship.com/view/10.1093/0195046641.001.0001/acprof-9780195046649.

Feinberg, Joel. *The Moral Limits of the Criminal Law.* Vol. 3, *Harm to Self.* New York: Oxford University Press, 1989. https://www.oxfordscholarship.com/view/10.1093/0195059239.001.0001/acprof-9780195059236.

Frankfurt, Harry G. "Frankfurt-Style Compatibilism: Reply to John Martin Fischer." In *Contours of Agency: Essays on Themes from Harry Frankfurt*, edited by Sarah Buss and Lee Overton, 27–31. Cambridge, MA: MIT Press, 2002.

Frankfurt, Harry G. "Freedom of the Will and the Concept of a Person." In *The Importance of What We Care About: Philosophical Essays*, 11–25. New York: Cambridge University Press, 1988.

Frankfurt, Harry. "On Bullshit." *Raritan* 6, no. 2 (1986): 81–100.

Gal, David, and Derek D. Rucker. "The Loss of Loss Aversion: Will It Loom Larger than Its Gain?" Edited by Sharon Shavitt. *Journal of Consumer Psychology* 28, no. 3 (July 2018): 497–516. https://doi.org/10.1002/jcpy.1047.

Gelfand, Scott D. "The Meta-Nudge—A Response to the Claim That the Use of Nudges during the Informed Consent Process Is Unavoidable." *Bioethics* 30, no. 8 (2016): 601–608. https://doi.org/10.1111/bioe.12266.

Gigerenzer, Gerd. "On the Supposed Evidence for Libertarian Paternalism." *Review of Philosophy and Psychology* 6, no. 3 (September 1, 2015): 361–383. https://doi.org/10.1007/s13164-015-0248-1.

Glod, William. "How Nudges Often Fail to Treat People According to Their Own Preferences." *Social Theory and Practice* 41, no. 4 (2015): 599–617. https://www.jstor.org/stable/24575751.

Gorin, Moti. "Welfare First, Autonomy Second." *American Journal of Bioethics* 16, no. 5 (May 3, 2016): 18–20. https://doi.org/10.1080/15265161.2016.1159760.

Gorin, Moti, Steven Joffe, Neal Dickert, and Scott Halpern. "Justifying Clinical Nudges." *Hastings Center Report* 47, no. 2 (2017): 32–38. https://doi.org/10.1002/hast.688.

Grisso, Thomas, and Paul S. Appelbaum. *Assessing Competence to Consent to Treatment: A Guide for Physicians and Other Health Professionals.* New York: Oxford University Press, 1998.

Griswold, Charles L. "Plato on Rhetoric and Poetry." *Stanford Encyclopedia of Philosophy*, Fall 2016 edition, edited by Edward N. Zalta. https://stanford.library.sydney.edu.au/entries/plato-rhetoric/.

Grüne-Yanoff, Till. "Old Wine in New Casks: Libertarian Paternalism Still Violates Liberal Principles." *Social Choice and Welfare* 38, no. 4 (April 1, 2012): 635–645. https://doi.org/10.1007/s00355-011-0636-0.

Grüne-Yanoff, Till. "Why Behavioral Policy Needs Mechanistic Evidence." *Economics & Philosophy* 32, no. 3 (November 2016): 463–483. https://doi.org/10.1017/S0266267115000425.

Grüne-Yanoff, Till, and Ralph Hertwig. "Nudge versus Boost: How Coherent Are Policy and Theory?" *Minds and Machines* 26, no. 1 (March 1, 2016): 149–183. https://doi.org/10.1007/s11023-015-9367-9.

Grüne-Yanoff, Till, Caterina Marchionni, and Markus A. Feufel. "Toward a Framework for Selecting Behavioural Policies: How to Choose between Boosts and Nudges." *Economics & Philosophy* 34, no. 2 (July 2018): 243–266. https://doi.org/10.1017/S0266267118000032.

Gurm, Hitinder Singh, and David G. Litaker. "Framing Procedural Risks to Patients: Is 99% Safe the Same as a Risk of 1 in 100?" *Academic Medicine* 75, no. 8 (August 2000): 840–842. doi: 10.1097/00001888-200008000-00018.

Hagman, William, David Andersson, Daniel Västfjäll, and Gustav Tinghög. "Public Views on Policies Involving Nudges." *Review of Philosophy and Psychology* 6, no. 3 (September 1, 2015): 439–453. https://doi.org/10.1007/s13164-015-0263-2.

Halpern, Jodi. *From Detached Concern to Empathy: Humanizing Medical Practice.* New York: Oxford University Press, 2001.

Halpern, Scott D. "Judging Nudges." *American Journal of Bioethics* 16, no. 5 (May 3, 2016): 16–18. https://doi.org/10.1080/15265161.2016.1159766.

Halpern, Scott D., George Loewenstein, Kevin G. Volpp, Elizabeth Cooney, Kelly Vranas, Caroline M. Quill, Mary S. Mckenzie, et al. "Default Options in Advance Directives Influence How Patients Set Goals for End-of-Life Care." *Health Affairs (Project Hope)* 32, no. 2 (February 2013): 408–417. https://doi.org/10.1377/hlthaff.2012.0895.

Hamilton, Paul. "A Republican Argument against Nudging and Informed Consent." *HEC Forum: An Interdisciplinary Journal on Hospitals' Ethical and Legal Issues* 30, no. 3 (September 2018): 267–282. https://doi.org/10.1007/s10730-017-9343-2.

Hansen, Pelle, and Andreas Jespersen. "Nudge and the Manipulation of Choice: A Framework for the Responsible Use of the Nudge Approach to Behaviour Change in Public Policy." *European Journal of Risk Regulation* 1 (March 1, 2013): 3–28. https://doi.org/10.1017/S1867299X00002762.

Hanssens, Catherine. "Legal and Ethical Implications of Opt-Out HIV Testing." *Clinical Infectious Diseases* 45, no. suppl. 4 (December 15, 2007): S232–239. https://doi.org/10.1086/522543.

Harman, Elizabeth. "Harming as Causing Harm." In *Harming Future Persons: Ethics, Genetics and the Nonidentity Problem*, edited by Melinda A. Roberts and David T. Wasserman, 137–154. Dordrecht: Springer, 2009.

Harrison, Michael R., N. Scott Adzick, James M. Estes, and Lori J. Howell. "A Prospective Study of the Outcome for Fetuses with Diaphragmatic Hernia." *JAMA* 271, no. 5 (February 2, 1994): 382–384. https://doi.org/10.1001/jama.1994.03510290064038.

Harsanyi, John C. "Morality and the Theory of Rational Behavior." In *Utilitarianism and Beyond*, edited by Amartya Sen and Bernard Williams, 39–62. Cambridge: Cambridge University Press, 1982.

Hausman, Daniel M., and Brynn Welch. "Debate: To Nudge or Not to Nudge." *Journal of Political Philosophy* 18, no. 1 (2010): 123–136. https://doi.org/10.1111/j.1467-9760.2009.00351.x.

Hill, Thomas E. "The Kantian Conception of Autonomy." In *The Inner Citadel: Essays on Individual Autonomy*, edited by John Philip Christman, 91–105. New York: Oxford University Press, 1989.

House of Lords, Science and Technology Selection Committee. *Behaviour Change.* Second Report, July 2011. https://publications.parliament.uk/pa/ld201012/ldselect/ldsctech/179/17902.htm.

Hume, David. *A Treatise of Human Nature.* Edited by John P. Wright, Robert Stecker, and Gary Fuller. London; Everyman, 2003 [1738].

Jani, J. C., K. H. Nicolaides, E. Gratacós, C. M. Valencia, E. Doné, J.-M. Martinez, L. Gucciardo, R. Cruz, and J. A. Deprest. "Severe Diaphragmatic Hernia Treated by Fetal Endoscopic Tracheal Occlusion." *Ultrasound in Obstetrics & Gynecology: The Official Journal of the International Society of Ultrasound in Obstetrics and Gynecology* 34, no. 3 (September 2009): 304–310. https://doi.org/10.1002/uog.6450.

Johnson, Eric J., and Daniel Goldstein. "Do Defaults Save Lives?" *Science* 302, no. 5649 (November 21, 2003): 1338–1339. https://doi.org/10.1126/science.1091721.

Kagan, Shelly. *The Limits of Morality.* Oxford: Clarendon Press, 1989.

Kahneman, Daniel. *Thinking, Fast and Slow.* New York: Farrar, Straus and Giroux, 2011.

Kahneman, Daniel, and Amos Tversky. "On the Reality of Cognitive Illusions." *Psychological Review* 103, no. 3 (July 1, 1996): 582–591. https://doi.org/10.1037/0033-295X .103.3.582.

Keeling, Geoff. "Autonomy, Nudging and Post-Truth Politics." *Journal of Medical Ethics* 44, no. 10 (October 1, 2018): 721–722. https://doi.org/10.1136/medethics-2017 -104616.

Keenum, Amy J., Jennifer E. DeVoe, Deena J. Chisolm, and Lorraine S. Wallace. "Generic Medications for You, but Brand-Name Medications for Me." *Research in Social and Administrative Pharmacy* 8, no. 6 (November 1, 2012): 574–578. https://doi .org/10.1016/j.sapharm.2011.12.004.

Keys, Daniel J., and Barry Schwartz. "'Leaky' Rationality: How Research on Behavioral Decision Making Challenges Normative Standards of Rationality." *Perspectives on Psychological Science* 2, no. 2 (June 1, 2007): 162–180. https://doi.org/10.1111/j.1745 -6916.2007.00035.x.

Killmister, Suzy. "Autonomy and False Beliefs." *Philosophical Studies* 164, no. 2 (June 1, 2013): 513–531. https://doi.org/10.1007/s11098-012-9864-0.

Korobkin, Russell. "Libertarian Welfarism." *California Law Review* 97, no. 6 (2009): 1651–1685. https://www.jstor.org/stable/20677921.

Korsgaard, Christine M. *The Sources of Normativity.* Edited by Onora O'Neill. Cambridge: Cambridge University Press, 1996.

Kray, Laura, and Richard Gonzalez. "Differential Weighting in Choice versus Advice: I'll Do This, You Do That." *Journal of Behavioral Decision Making* 12, no. 3 (1999): 207–217. https://doi.org/10.1002/(SICI)1099-0771(199909)12:3<207::AID-BDM322>3 .0.CO;2-P.

Kressel, Laura M., and Gretchen B. Chapman. "The Default Effect in End-of-Life Medical Treatment Preferences." *Medical Decision Making* 27, no. 3 (May 1, 2007): 299–310. https://doi.org/10.1177/0272989X07300608.

Kumar, Victor. "Nudges and Bumps." *Georgetown Journal of Law & Public Policy* 14 (2016): 861–876. http://www.victorkumar.org/uploads/6/1/5/2/61526489/kumar _-_nudges_and_bumps__final_.pdf.

Kunkel, Benjamin. *Indecision.* New York: Random House, 2005.

Lee, Stephanie J., Diane Fairclough, Joseph H. Antin, and Jane C. Weeks. "Discrepancies between Patient and Physician Estimates for the Success of Stem Cell Transplantation." *JAMA* 285, no. 8 (February 28, 2001): 1034–1038. https://doi.org/10.1001 /jama.285.8.1034.

Levy, Neil. "Nudges in a Post-Truth World." *Journal of Medical Ethics* 43, no. 8 (2017): 495–500. https://doi.org/10.1136/medethics-2017-104153.

Liberman, Akiva, and Shelly Chaiken. "Defensive Processing of Personally Relevant Health Messages." *Personality and Social Psychology Bulletin* 18, no. 6 (December 1, 1992): 669–679. https://doi.org/10.1177/0146167292186002.

Lichtenstein, Sarah, and Paul Slovic, eds. *The Construction of Preference*. New York: Cambridge University Press, 2006.

Lipkus, Isaac M., William M. P. Klein, Celette Sugg Skinner, and Barbara K. Rimer. "Breast Cancer Risk Perceptions and Breast Cancer Worry: What Predicts What?" *Journal of Risk Research* 8, no. 5 (July 1, 2005): 439–452. https://doi.org/10.1080/136698 7042000311018.

Llewellyn-Thomas, Hilary A., and R. Trafford Crump. "Decision Support for Patients: Values Clarification and Preference Elicitation." *Medical Care Research and Review* 70, no. 1, suppl. (February 2013): 50S–79S. https://doi.org/10.1177/1077558712461182.

Loewenstein, George, Cindy Bryce, David Hagmann, and Sachin Rajpal. "Warning: You Are about to Be Nudged." *Behavioral Science & Policy* 1, no. 1 (2015): 35–42. https://doi.org/10.1353/bsp.2015.0000.

Lucke, Jayne. "Context Is All Important in Investigating Attitudes: Acceptability Depends on the Nature of the Nudge, Who Nudges, and Who Is Nudged." *American Journal of Bioethics* 13, no. 6 (2013): 24–25. https://doi.org/10.1080/15265161.2013 .781709.

Ludolph, Ramona, and Peter J. Schulz. "Debiasing Health-Related Judgments and Decision Making: A Systematic Review." *Medical Decision Making* 38, no. 1 (January 1, 2018): 3–13. https://doi.org/10.1177/0272989X17716672.

MacKay, Douglas, and Alexandra Robinson. "The Ethics of Organ Donor Registration Policies: Nudges and Respect for Autonomy." *American Journal of Bioethics* 16, no. 11 (November 1, 2016): 3–12. https://doi.org/10.1080/15265161.2016.1222007.

Mackenzie, Catriona. "Relational Autonomy, Normative Authority and Perfectionism." *Journal of Social Philosophy* 39, no. 4 (2008): 512–533. https://doi.org/10.1111/j .1467-9833.2008.00440.x.

Malenka, David J., John A. Baron, Sarah Johansen, Jon W. Wahrenberger, and Jonathan M. Ross. "The Framing Effect of Relative and Absolute Risk." *Journal of General Internal Medicine* 8, no. 10 (October 1, 1993): 543–548. https://doi.org/10.1007/BF02599636.

Marteau, Theresa M., David Ogilvie, Martin Roland, Marc Suhrcke, and Michael P. Kelly. "Judging Nudging: Can Nudging Improve Population Health?" *BMJ (Clinical Research Ed.)* 342 (January 25, 2011): d228. https://doi.org/10.1136/bmj.d228.

Matlock, Daniel D., Jacqueline Jones, Carolyn T. Nowels, Amy Jenkins, Larry A. Allen, and Jean S. Kutner. "Evidence of Cognitive Bias in Decision Making around Implantable-Cardioverter Defibrillators: A Qualitative Framework Analysis." *Journal*

*of Cardiac Failure* 23, no. 11 (November 1, 2017): 794–799. https://doi.org/10.1016/j
.cardfail.2017.03.008.

McClelland, Gary H., and Beverly H. Hackenberg. "Subjective Probabilities for Sex of
Next Child: U.S. College Students and Philippine Villagers." *Journal of Population* 1,
no. 2 (June 1, 1978): 132–147. https://doi.org/10.1007/BF01277598.

McCullough, Laurence B., and Frank A. Chervenak. "A Critical Analysis of the
Concept and Discourse of 'Unborn Child.'" *American Journal of Bioethics* 8, no. 7
(September 4, 2008): 34–39. https://doi.org/10.1080/15265160802248161.

McLeod, Carolyn, and Julie Ponesse. "Infertility and Moral Luck: The Politics of
Women Blaming Themselves for Infertility." *International Journal of Feminist Approaches
to Bioethics* 1, no. 1 (2008): 126–144. https://www.jstor.org/stable/40339215.

Meeker, Daniella, Tara K. Knight, Mark W. Friedberg, Jeffrey A. Linder, Noah J. Goldstein, Craig R. Fox, Alan Rothfeld, Guillermo Diaz, and Jason N. Doctor. "Nudging
Guideline-Concordant Antibiotic Prescribing: A Randomized Clinical Trial." *JAMA
Internal Medicine* 174, no. 3 (March 1, 2014): 425–431. https://doi.org/10.1001/jamain
ternmed.2013.14191.

Mendel, R., E. Traut-Mattausch, E. Jonas, S. Leucht, J. M. Kane, K. Maino, W. Kissling,
and J. Hamann. "Confirmation Bias: Why Psychiatrists Stick to Wrong Preliminary
Diagnoses." *Psychological Medicine* 41, no. 12 (December 2011): 2651–2659. https://
doi.org/10.1017/S0033291711000808.

Menzies, Peter. "Counterfactual Theories of Causation." *Stanford Encyclopedia of
Philosophy*, Winter 2017 edition, edited by Edward N. Zalta. https://stanford.library
.sydney.edu.au/entries/causation-counterfactual/.

Milkman, Katherine L., John Beshears, James J. Choi, David Laibson, and Brigitte
C. Madrian. "Using Implementation Intentions Prompts to Enhance Influenza Vaccination Rates." *Proceedings of the National Academy of Sciences* 108, no. 26 (June 28,
2011): 10415–10420. https://doi.org/10.1073/pnas.1103170108.

Mill, John Stuart. "Chapter V." In *On Liberty*, 168–207. London: John W. Parker and
Son, West Strand, 1859.

Mills, Chris. "The Choice Architect's Trilemma." *Res Publica* 24, no. 3 (2018): 395–
414. https://doi.org/10.1007/s11158-017-9363-4.

Mills, Claudia. "Politics and Manipulation." *Social Theory and Practice* 21, no. 1 (1995):
97–112. https://www.jstor.org/stable/23560376.

Mitchell, Gregory. "Libertarian Paternalism Is an Oxymoron." *Northwestern University Law Review* 99, no. 3 (2005). https://papers.ssrn.com/abstract=615562.

Moles, Andres. "Nudging for Liberals." *Social Theory and Practice* 41, no. 4 (2015):
644–667. https://www.jstor.org/stable/24575753.

Moller, D. "Abortion and Moral Risk." *Philosophy* 86, no. 337 (2011): 425–443. https://www.jstor.org/stable/23014824.

Montori, Victor M., Marleen Kunneman, and Juan P. Brito. "Shared Decision Making and Improving Health Care: The Answer Is Not In." *JAMA* 318, no. 7 (August 15, 2017): 617–618. https://doi.org/10.1001/jama.2017.10168.

Morrison, Val, Bethan J. Henderson, Caroline Taylor, Nonn A'Ch Dafydd, and Abbie Unwin. "The Impact of Information Order on Intentions to Undergo Predictive Genetic Testing: An Experimental Study." *Journal of Health Psychology* 15, no. 7 (October 1, 2010): 1082–1092. https://doi.org/10.1177/1359105310364171.

Moser, Albine, Rob Houtepen, Cor Spreeuwenberg, and Guy Widdershoven. "Realizing Autonomy in Responsive Relationships." *Medicine, Health Care and Philosophy* 13, no. 3 (August 1, 2010): 215–223. https://doi.org/10.1007/s11019-010-9241-8.

Navin, Mark C. "The Ethics of Vaccination Nudges in Pediatric Practice." *HEC Forum* 29, no. 1 (March 1, 2017): 43–57. https://doi.org/10.1007/s10730-016-9311-2.

Niker, Fay, Peter B. Reiner, and Gidon Felsen. "Pre-Authorization: A Novel Decision-Making Heuristic That May Promote Autonomy." *American Journal of Bioethics* 16, no. 5 (May 3, 2016): 27–29. https://doi.org/10.1080/15265161.2016.1159761.

Noggle, Robert. "Autonomy and the Paradox of Self-Creation: Infinite Regresses, Finite Selves, and the Limits of Authenticity." In *Personal Autonomy: New Essays on Personal Autonomy and Its Role in Contemporary Moral Philosophy*, edited by James Stacey Taylor, 87–108. Cambridge: Cambridge University Press, 2005.

Noggle, Robert. "Manipulation, Salience, and Nudges." *Bioethics* 32, no. 3 (2018): 164–170. https://doi.org/10.1111/bioe.12421.

Noggle, Robert. "Manipulative Actions: A Conceptual and Moral Analysis." *American Philosophical Quarterly* 33, no. 1 (1996): 43–55. https://www.jstor.org/stable/20009846.

Nozick, Robert. *The Nature of Rationality*. Princeton, NJ: Princeton University Press, 1993.

Nussbaum, Martha C. "Symposium on Amartya Sen's Philosophy: 5 Adaptive Preferences and Women's Options." *Economics & Philosophy* 17, no. 1 (April 2001): 67–88. https://doi.org/10.1017/S0266267101000153.

Oberdiek, John. "Towards a Right against Risking." *Law and Philosophy* 28, no. 4 (July 1, 2009): 367–392. https://doi.org/10.1007/s10982-008-9039-5.

O'Brien, Bernie J., Ron Goeree, Amiram Gafni, George W. Torrance, Mark V. Pauly, Haim Erder, Jim Rusthoven, Jane Weeks, Melissa Cahill, and Bruce LaMont. "Assessing the Value of a New Pharmaceutical: A Feasibility Study of Contingent Valuation in Managed Care." *Medical Care* 36, no. 3 (1998): 370–384. https://www.jstor.org/stable/3767330.

O'Connor, Annette M., Carol L. Bennett, Dawn Stacey, Michael Barry, Nananda F. Col, Karen B. Eden, Vikki A. Entwistle, et al. "Decision Aids for People Facing Health Treatment or Screening Decisions." *Cochrane Database of Systematic Reviews*, no. 3 (2009): CD001431. https://doi.org/10.1002/14651858.CD001431.pub2.

Opel, Douglas J., Rita Mangione-Smith, Jeffrey D. Robinson, John Heritage, Victoria DeVere, Halle S. Salas, Chuan Zhou, and James A. Taylor. "The Influence of Provider Communication Behaviors on Parental Vaccine Acceptance and Visit Experience." *American Journal of Public Health* 105, no. 10 (October 2015): 1998–2004. https://doi .org/10.2105/AJPH.2014.302425.

Open Science Collaboration. "Estimating the Reproducibility of Psychological Science." *Science* 349, no. 6251 (August 28, 2015). https://doi.org/10.1126/science.aac4716.

Oshima Lee, Emily, and Ezekiel J. Emanuel. "Shared Decision Making to Improve Care and Reduce Costs." *New England Journal of Medicine* 368, no. 1 (January 3, 2013): 6–8. https://doi.org/10.1056/NEJMp1209500.

Ottawa Hospital Research Institute. "A to Z Inventory of Decision Aids." Accessed July 14, 2020. https://decisionaid.ohri.ca/AZinvent.php.

Ottawa Hospital Research Institute. "Decision Aid Summary." Accessed July 2, 2019. https://decisionaid.ohri.ca/Azsumm.php?ID=1149.

Parfit, Derek. *On What Matters*. Vol. 1. New York: Oxford University Press, 2011.

Paul, Laurie Ann. *Transformative Experience*. Oxford: Oxford University Press, 2014.

Peirce, Charles S. *Philosophical Writings of Peirce*. Edited by Justus Buchler. New York: Dover Publications, 1955.

Penn Medicine. "The Nudge Unit." Accessed June 19, 2019. https://nudgeunit.upenn .edu/.

Placani, Adriana. "When the Risk of Harm Harms." *Law and Philosophy* 36, no. 1 (February 1, 2017): 77–100. https://doi.org/10.1007/s10982-016-9277-x.

Plato. *Gorgias*. Translated by Donald J. Zeyl. In *Plato: Complete Works*, edited by John M. Cooper and D. S. Hutchinson, 791–870. Indianapolis, IN: Hackett, 1997.

Plato. *Phaedrus*. Translated by Alexander Nehamas and Paul Woodruff. In *Plato: Complete Works*, edited by John M. Cooper and D. S. Hutchinson, 506–556. Indianapolis, IN: Hackett, 1997.

Plato. *Protagoras*. Translated by Stanley Lombardo and Karen Bell. In *Plato: Complete Works*, edited by John M. Cooper and D. S. Hutchinson, 746–790. Indianapolis, IN: Hackett, 1997.

Plato. *Republic*. Translated by G. M. A. Grube and C. D. C. Reeve. In *Plato: Complete Works*, edited by John M. Cooper and D. S. Hutchinson, 971–1223. Indianapolis, IN: Hackett, 1997.

Ploug, Thomas, and Søren Holm. "Doctors, Patients, and Nudging in the Clinical Context: Four Views on Nudging and Informed Consent." *American Journal of Bioethics* 15, no. 10 (October 3, 2015): 28–38. https://doi.org/10.1080/15265161.2015.1074303.

Ploug, Thomas, and Søren Holm. "Informed Consent, Libertarian Paternalism, and Nudging: A Response." *American Journal of Bioethics* 15, no. 12 (December 2, 2015): W10–13. https://doi.org/10.1080/15265161.2015.1096081.

"Policy Process and Practice." In *Public Health: Ethical Issues*, 29–48. London: Nuffield Council on Bioethics. Accessed July 15, 2020. https://www.nuffieldbioethics.org/publications/public-health.

Portschy, Pamela R., Karen M. Kuntz, and Todd M. Tuttle. "Survival Outcomes after Contralateral Prophylactic Mastectomy: A Decision Analysis." *JNCI: Journal of the National Cancer Institute* 106, no. 8 (August 1, 2014). https://doi.org/10.1093/jnci/dju160.

Powers, Madison, Ruth Faden, and Yashar Saghai. "Liberty, Mill and the Framework of Public Health Ethics." *Public Health Ethics* 5, no. 1 (April 1, 2012): 6–15. https://doi.org/10.1093/phe/phs002.

Pronin, Emily, Daniel Y. Lin, and Lee Ross. "The Bias Blind Spot: Perceptions of Bias in Self versus Others." *Personality and Social Psychology Bulletin* 28, no. 3 (March 1, 2002): 369–381. https://doi.org/10.1177/0146167202286008.

Quigley, Muireann. "Nudging for Health: On Public Policy and Designing Choice Architecture." *Medical Law Review* 21, no. 4 (December 1, 2013): 588–621. https://doi.org/10.1093/medlaw/fwt022.

Rachels, James. "Active and Passive Euthanasia." *New England Journal of Medicine* 292, no. 2 (January 9, 1975): 78–80. https://doi.org/10.1056/NEJM197501092920206.

Rayner, Geof, and Tim Lang. "Is Nudge an Effective Public Health Strategy to Tackle Obesity? No." *BMJ* 342 (April 14, 2011): d2177. https://doi.org/10.1136/bmj.d2177.

Redelmeier, Donald A., Joel Katz, and Daniel Kahneman. "Memories of Colonoscopy: A Randomized Trial." *Pain* 104, no. 1 (July 1, 2003): 187–194. https://doi.org/10.1016/S0304-3959(03)00003-4.

Reyna, Valerie F. "A Theory of Medical Decision Making and Health: Fuzzy Trace Theory." *Medical Decision Making* 28, no. 6 (November 1, 2008): 850–865. https://doi.org/10.1177/0272989X08327066.

Riis, Jason, George Loewenstein, Jonathan Baron, Christopher Jepson, Angela Fagerlin, and Peter A. Ubel. "Ignorance of Hedonic Adaptation to Hemodialysis: A Study Using Ecological Momentary Assessment." *Journal of Experimental Psychology: General* 134, no. 1 (2005): 3–9. https://doi.org/10.1037/0096-3445.134.1.3.

Riley, Evan. "The Beneficent Nudge Program and Epistemic Injustice." *Ethical Theory and Moral Practice* 20, no. 3 (June 1, 2017): 597–616. https://doi.org/10.1007/s10677 -017-9805-2.

Ritov, Ilana, and Jonathan Baron. "Reluctance to Vaccinate: Omission Bias and Ambiguity." *Journal of Behavioral Decision Making* 3, no. 4 (1990): 263–277. https:// doi.org/10.1002/bdm.3960030404.

Rosoff, Philip M. "Who Should Ration?" *AMA Journal of Ethics* 19, no. 2 (2017): 164– 173. https://doi.org/10.1001/journalofethics.2017.19.2.ecas4-1702.

Ruano, R., C. T. Yoshisaki, M. M. da Silva, M. E. J. Ceccon, M. S. Grasi, U. Tannuri, and M. Zugaib. "A Randomized Controlled Trial of Fetal Endoscopic Tracheal Occlusion versus Postnatal Management of Severe Isolated Congenital Diaphragmatic Hernia." *Ultrasound in Obstetrics & Gynecology: The Official Journal of the International Society of Ultrasound in Obstetrics and Gynecology* 39, no. 1 (January 2012): 20–27. https://doi.org/10.1002/uog.10142.

Rubaltelli, Enrico, Patrizia Burra, Valentina Sartorato, Daniele Canova, Giacomo Germani, Silvia Tomat, Ermanno Ancona, Emanuele Cozzi, and Rino Rumiati. "Strengthening Acceptance for Xenotransplantation: The Case of Attraction Effect." *Xenotransplantation* 15, no. 3 (2008): 159–163. https://doi.org/10.1111/j.1399-3089 .2008.00474.x.

Ryan, Shane. "Libertarian Paternalism Is Hard Paternalism." *Analysis* 78, no. 1 (January 1, 2018): 65–73. https://doi.org/10.1093/analys/anx150.

Saghai, Yashar. "Salvaging the Concept of Nudge." *Journal of Medical Ethics* 39, no. 8 (August 1, 2013): 487–493. https://doi.org/10.1136/medethics-2012-100727.

Scanlon, Thomas M. *What We Owe to Each Other.* Cambridge, MA: Harvard University Press, 1998.

Schmidt, Andreas T. "The Power to Nudge." *American Political Science Review* 111, no. 2 (May 2017): 404–417. https://doi.org/10.1017/S0003055417000028.

Schneider, Carl. *The Practice of Autonomy: Patients, Doctors, and Medical Decisions.* New York: Oxford University Press, 1998.

Schroeter, François. "Endorsement and Autonomous Agency." *Philosophy and Phenomenological Research* 69, no. 3 (2004): 633–659. https://www.jstor.org/stable/40040770 ?seq=1.

Schwartz, Gregory. "The Ethics of Omission." *Think* 18, no. 51 (2019): 117–121. https://doi.org/10.1017/S1477175618000404.

Schwartz, Janet A., and Gretchen B. Chapman. "Are More Options Always Better? The Attraction Effect in Physicians' Decisions about Medications." *Medical Decision Making* 19, no. 3 (August 1, 1999): 315–323. https://doi.org/10.1177/0272989X9901900310.

Scoccia, Danny. "Paternalisms and Nudges." *Economics & Philosophy* 35, no. 1 (March 2019): 79–102. https://doi.org/10.1017/S0266267118000093.

Sen, Amartya. *Commodities and Capabilities*. Amsterdam: North-Holland, 1985.

Sen, Amartya K. "Rational Fools: A Critique of the Behavioral Foundations of Economic Theory." *Philosophy & Public Affairs* 6, no. 4 (1977): 317–344. https://www.jstor.org/stable/2264946.

Sepucha, Karen R., Cornelia M. Borkhoff, Joanne Lally, Carrie A. Levin, Daniel D. Matlock, Chirk Jenn Ng, Mary E. Ropka, et al. "Establishing the Effectiveness of Patient Decision Aids: Key Constructs and Measurement Instruments." *BMC Medical Informatics and Decision Making* 13, no. 2 (November 29, 2013): S12. https://doi.org/10.1186/1472-6947-13-S2-S12.

Sher, George. *Beyond Neutrality: Perfectionism and Politics*. Cambridge: Cambridge University Press, 1997.

Sheridan, Stacey L., Russell P. Harris, and Steven H. Woolf. "Shared Decision Making about Screening and Chemoprevention: A Suggested Approach from the U.S. Preventive Services Task Force." *American Journal of Preventive Medicine* 26, no. 1 (January 1, 2004): 56–66. https://doi.org/10.1016/j.amepre.2003.09.011.

Simkulet, William. "Informed Consent and Nudging." *Bioethics* 33, no. 1 (2019): 169–184. https://doi.org/10.1111/bioe.12449.

Simkulet, William. "Nudging, Informed Consent and Bullshit." *Journal of Medical Ethics* 44, no. 8 (August 1, 2018): 536–542. https://doi.org/10.1136/medethics-2017-104480.

Simmons, Roberta G., Susan Klein Marine, and Richard Lawrence Simmons. *Gift of Life: The Effect of Organ Transplantation on Individual, Family, and Societal Dynamics*. New Brunswick, NJ: Transaction Publishers, 1987.

Simonson, Itamar. "Choice Based on Reasons: The Case of Attraction and Compromise Effects." *Journal of Consumer Research* 16, no. 2 (1989): 158–174. https://doi.org/10.1086/209205.

Singer, Peter. "Famine, Affluence, and Morality." *Philosophy & Public Affairs* 1, no. 3 (1972): 229–243. http://personal.lse.ac.uk/robert49/teaching/mm/articles/Singer_1972 Famine.pdf.

Smith, Dylan, George Loewenstein, Christopher Jepson, Aleksandra Jankovich, Harold Feldman, and Peter Ubel. "Mispredicting and Misremembering: Patients with Renal Failure Overestimate Improvements in Quality of Life after a Kidney Transplant." *Health Psychology: Official Journal of the Division of Health Psychology, American Psychological Association* 27, no. 5 (September 2008): 653–658. https://doi.org/10.1037/a0012647.

Smith, Dylan M., Ryan L. Sherriff, Laura Damschroder, George Loewenstein, and Peter A. Ubel. "Misremembering Colostomies? Former Patients Give Lower Utility Ratings than Do Current Patients." *Health Psychology: Official Journal of the Division of Health Psychology, American Psychological Association* 25, no. 6 (November 2006): 688–695. https://doi.org/10.1037/0278-6133.25.6.688.

Sobel, David. *From Valuing to Value: A Defense of Subjectivism.* Oxford: Oxford University Press, 2016.

Stacey, Dawn, France Légaré, Krystina Lewis, Michael J. Barry, Carol L. Bennett, Karen B. Eden, Margaret Holmes-Rovner, et al. "Decision Aids for People Facing Health Treatment or Screening Decisions." *Cochrane Database of Systematic Reviews,* no. 4 (2017): CD001431. https://doi.org/10.1002/14651858.CD001431.pub5.

Stege, Gerben, Alan Fenton, and Bruce Jaffray. "Nihilism in the 1990s: The True Mortality of Congenital Diaphragmatic Hernia." *Pediatrics* 112, no. 3 (September 1, 2003): 532–535. https://doi.org/10.1542/peds.112.3.532.

Sunstein, Cass R. *The Ethics of Influence: Government in the Age of Behavioral Science.* New York: Cambridge University Press, 2016.

Sunstein, Cass R. "The Ethics of Nudging." *Yale Journal on Regulation* 32, no. 2 (2015): 413–450. https://digitalcommons.law.yale.edu/cgi/viewcontent.cgi?article=1415&context=yjreg.

Sunstein, Cass R. "Incompletely Theorized Agreements Commentary." *Harvard Law Review* 108 (1994): 1733–1772.

Sunstein, Cass R. *Why Nudge? The Politics of Libertarian Paternalism.* New Haven, CT: Yale University Press, 2014.

Sutherland, H. J., H. A. Llewellyn-Thomas, G. A. Lockwood, D. L. Tritchler, and J. E. Till. "Cancer Patients: Their Desire for Information and Participation in Treatment Decisions." *Journal of the Royal Society of Medicine* 82, no. 5 (May 1989): 260–263. https://www.ncbi.nlm.nih.gov/pmc/articles/PMC1292127/pdf/jrsocmed00150-0016.pdf.

Swindell, J. S., Amy L. McGuire, and Scott D. Halpern. "Beneficent Persuasion: Techniques and Ethical Guidelines to Improve Patients' Decisions." *Annals of Family Medicine* 8, no. 3 (May 1, 2010): 260–264. https://doi.org/10.1370/afm.1118.

Tannenbaum, David, Jason N. Doctor, Stephen D. Persell, Mark W. Friedberg, Daniella Meeker, Elisha M. Friesema, Noah J. Goldstein, Jeffrey A. Linder, and Craig R. Fox. "Nudging Physician Prescription Decisions by Partitioning the Order Set: Results of a Vignette-Based Study." *Journal of General Internal Medicine* 30, no. 3 (March 1, 2015): 298–304. https://doi.org/10.1007/s11606-014-3051-2.

Taylor, James Stacey. *Practical Autonomy and Bioethics.* New York: Routledge, 2009.

Texas Children's Hospital. *Facing Meningitis*. November 14, 2011. Video, 3:43. https://www.youtube.com/watch?v=h2-U1S74OH0&hl=en_US&version=3https%3A%2F%2Fwww.texaschildrens.org%2Fdepartments%2Fimmunization-project.

Thaler, Richard. "Toward a Positive Theory of Consumer Choice." *Journal of Economic Behavior & Organization* 1, no. 1 (March 1, 1980): 39–60. https://doi.org/10.1016/0167 -2681(80)90051-7.

Thaler, Richard H., and Cass R. Sunstein. "Libertarian Paternalism." *American Economic Review* 93, no. 2 (May 2003): 175–179. https://doi.org/10.1257/000282803321947001.

Thaler, Richard H., and Cass R. Sunstein. *Nudge: Improving Decisions about Health, Wealth, and Happiness*. New Haven, CT: Yale University Press, 2008.

Ubel, Peter A., Christopher Jepson, and Jonathan Baron. "The Inclusion of Patient Testimonials in Decision Aids: Effects on Treatment Choices." *Medical Decision Making* 21, no. 1 (2001): 60–68. https://doi.org/10.1177/0272989X0102100108.

Ubel, Peter A., Karen A. Scherr, and Angela Fagerlin. "Empowerment Failure: How Shortcomings in Physician Communication Unwittingly Undermine Patient Autonomy." *American Journal of Bioethics* 17, no. 11 (November 2017): 31–39. https://doi .org/10.1080/15265161.2017.1378753.

Ubel, Peter A., Dylan M. Smith, Brian J. Zikmund-Fisher, Holly A. Derry, Jennifer McClure, Azadeh Stark, Cheryl Wiese, Sarah Greene, Aleksandra Jankovic, and Angela Fagerlin. "Testing whether Decision Aids Introduce Cognitive Biases: Results of a Randomized Trial." *Patient Education and Counseling* 80, no. 2 (August 1, 2010): 158–163. https://doi.org/10.1016/j.pec.2009.10.021.

Vargas, Manuel. Review of *Personal Autonomy: New Essays on Personal Autonomy and Its Role in Contemporary Moral Philosophy*, edited by James Stacey Taylor. *Notre Dame Philosophical Reviews*, August 15, 2006. https://ndpr.nd.edu/news/personal-au tonomy-new-essays-on-personal-autonomy-and-its-role-in-contemporary-moral-phi losophy/.

Veatch, Robert M. "Abandoning Informed Consent." *Hastings Center Report* 25, no. 2 (April 1995): 5–12. https://www.jstor.org/stable/3562859.

Veatch, Robert M. *The Basics of Bioethics*. Upper Saddle River, NJ: Pearson Education, 2012.

Volandes, Angelo E., and Elmer D. Abbo. "Flipping the Default: A Novel Approach to Cardiopulmonary Resuscitation in End-Stage Dementia." *Journal of Clinical Ethics* 18, no. 2 (2007): 122–139. https://pubmed.ncbi.nlm.nih.gov/17682620/.

Volandes, Angelo E., Michael K. Paasche-Orlow, Michael J. Barry, Muriel R. Gillick, Kenneth L. Minaker, Yuchiao Chang, E. Francis Cook, Elmer D. Abbo, Areej El-Jawahri, and Susan L. Mitchell. "Video Decision Support Tool for Advance Care

Planning in Dementia: Randomised Controlled Trial." *BMJ* 338 (May 28, 2009): b2159. https://doi.org/10.1136/bmj.b2159.

Volk, Robert J., Gianna T. Kinsman, Yen-Chi L. Le, Paul Swank, Jennifer Blumenthal-Barby, Stephanie L. McFall, Theresa L. Byrd, Patricia Dolan Mullen, and Scott B. Cantor. "Designing Normative Messages about Active Surveillance for Men with Localized Prostate Cancer." *Journal of Health Communication* 20, no. 9 (September 2, 2015): 1014–1020. https://doi.org/10.1080/10810730.2015.1018618.

Wallace, R. Jay. *The View from Here: On Affirmation, Attachment, and the Limits of Regret.* New York: Oxford University Press, 2013.

Wansink, Brian, Robert J. Kent, and Stephen J. Hoch. "An Anchoring and Adjustment Model of Purchase Quantity Decisions." *Journal of Marketing Research* 35, no. 1 (February 1, 1998): 71–81. https://doi.org/10.1177/002224379803500108.

Weber, Max. *The Protestant Ethic and the Spirit of Capitalism.* London: George Allen & Unwin, 1905. http://archive.org/details/protestantethics00webe.

Weiner, Adam B., Sanjay G. Patel, Ruth Etzioni, and Scott E. Eggener. "National Trends in the Management of Low and Intermediate Risk Prostate Cancer in the United States." *Journal of Urology* 193, no. 1 (January 1, 2015): 95–102. https://doi.org/10.1016/j.juro.2014.07.111.

Weinstein, Neil. "Unrealistic Optimism about Future Life Events." *Journal of Personality and Social Psychology* 39, no. 5 (November 1, 1980): 806–820. https://doi.org/10.1037/0022-3514.39.5.806.

Weinstein, Neil D., and William M. Klein. "Resistance of Personal Risk Perceptions to Debiasing Interventions." *Health Psychology* 14, no. 2 (1995): 132–140. https://doi.org/10.1037/0278-6133.14.2.132.

Wenar, Leif. "John Rawls." *Stanford Encyclopedia of Philosophy.* Spring 2017 edition, edited by Edward N. Zalta. https://plato.stanford.edu/archives/spr2017/entries/rawls/.

White, Douglas B., Natalie Ernecoff, Praewpannarai Buddadhumaruk, Seoyeon Hong, Lisa Weissfeld, J. Randall Curtis, John M. Luce, and Bernard Lo. "Prevalence of and Factors Related to Discordance about Prognosis between Physicians and Surrogate Decision Makers of Critically Ill Patients." *JAMA* 315, no. 19 (May 17, 2016): 2086–2094. https://doi.org/10.1001/jama.2016.5351.

Whitney, Simon N. "A New Model of Medical Decisions: Exploring the Limits of Shared Decision Making." *Medical Decision Making* 23, no. 4 (July 1, 2003): 275–280. https://doi.org/10.1177/0272989X03256006.

Wilson, Timothy D., Douglas J. Lisle, Jonathan W. Schooler, Sara D. Hodges, Kristen J. Klaaren, and Suzanne J. LaFleur. "Introspecting about Reasons Can Reduce Post-Choice Satisfaction." *Personality and Social Psychology Bulletin* 19, no. 3 (June 1, 1993): 331–339. https://doi.org/10.1177/0146167293193010.

Wilt, Timothy J., Karen M. Jones, Michael J. Barry, Gerald L. Andriole, Daniel Culkin, Thomas Wheeler, William J. Aronson, and Michael K. Brawer. "Follow-Up of Prostatectomy versus Observation for Early Prostate Cancer." *New England Journal of Medicine* 377, no. 2 (July 13, 2017): 132–142. https://doi.org/10.1056/NEJMoa1615869.

Wise, Jacqui. "Nudge or Fudge? Doctors Debate Best Approach to Improve Public Health." *BMJ* 342 (January 27, 2011): d580. https://doi.org/10.1136/bmj.d580.

Zikmund-Fisher, Brian J., Angela Fagerlin, and Peter A. Ubel. "'Is 28% Good or Bad?' Evaluability and Preference Reversals in Health Care Decisions." *Medical Decision Making* 24, no. 2 (March 1, 2004): 142–148. https://doi.org/10.1177/0272989X04263154.

Zikmund-Fisher, Brian J., Paul D. Windschitl, Nicole Exe, and Peter A. Ubel. "'I'll Do What They Did': Social Norm Information and Cancer Treatment Decisions." *Patient Education and Counseling* 85, no. 2 (November 1, 2011): 225–229. https://doi.org/10.1016/j.pec.2011.01.031.

# Index

**Basic Bioethics**

Arthur Caplan, editor

**Books Acquired under the Editorship of Glenn McGee and Arthur Caplan**

Peter A. Ubel, *Pricing Life: Why It's Time for Health Care Rationing*

Mark G. Kuczewski and Ronald Polansky, eds., *Bioethics: Ancient Themes in Contemporary Issues*

Suzanne Holland, Karen Lebacqz, and Laurie Zoloth, eds., *The Human Embryonic Stem Cell Debate: Science, Ethics, and Public Policy*

Gita Sen, Asha George, and Piroska Östlin, eds., *Engendering International Health: The Challenge of Equity*

Carolyn McLeod, *Self-Trust and Reproductive Autonomy*

Lenny Moss, *What Genes Can't Do*

Jonathan D. Moreno, ed., *In the Wake of Terror: Medicine and Morality in a Time of Crisis*

Glenn McGee, ed., *Pragmatic Bioethics, 2d edition*

Timothy F. Murphy, *Case Studies in Biomedical Research Ethics*

Mark A. Rothstein, ed., *Genetics and Life Insurance: Medical Underwriting and Social Policy*

Kenneth A. Richman, *Ethics and the Metaphysics of Medicine: Reflections on Health and Beneficence*

David Lazer, ed., *DNA and the Criminal Justice System: The Technology of Justice*

Harold W. Baillie and Timothy K. Casey, eds., *Is Human Nature Obsolete? Genetics, Bioengineering, and the Future of the Human Condition*

Robert H. Blank and Janna C. Merrick, eds., *End-of-Life Decision Making: A Cross-National Study*

Norman L. Cantor, *Making Medical Decisions for the Profoundly Mentally Disabled*

Margrit Shildrick and Roxanne Mykitiuk, eds., *Ethics of the Body: Post-Conventional Challenges*

Alfred I. Tauber, *Patient Autonomy and the Ethics of Responsibility*

David H. Brendel, *Healing Psychiatry: Bridging the Science/Humanism Divide*

Jonathan Baron, *Against Bioethics*

Michael L. Gross, *Bioethics and Armed Conflict: Moral Dilemmas of Medicine and War*

Karen F. Greif and Jon F. Merz, *Current Controversies in the Biological Sciences: Case Studies of Policy Challenges from New Technologies*

Deborah Blizzard, *Looking Within: A Sociocultural Examination of Fetoscopy*

Ronald Cole-Turner, ed., *Design and Destiny: Jewish and Christian Perspectives on Human Germline Modification*

Holly Fernandez Lynch, *Conflicts of Conscience in Health Care: An Institutional Compromise*

Mark A. Bedau and Emily C. Parke, eds., *The Ethics of Protocells: Moral and Social Implications of Creating Life in the Laboratory*

Jonathan D. Moreno and Sam Berger, eds., *Progress in Bioethics: Science, Policy, and Politics*

Eric Racine, *Pragmatic Neuroethics: Improving Understanding and Treatment of the Mind-Brain*

Martha J. Farah, ed., *Neuroethics: An Introduction with Readings*

Jeremy R. Garrett, ed., *The Ethics of Animal Research: Exploring the Controversy*

**Books Acquired under the Editorship of Arthur Caplan**

Sheila Jasanoff, ed., *Reframing Rights: Bioconstitutionalism in the Genetic Age*

Christine Overall, *Why Have Children? The Ethical Debate*

Yechiel Michael Barilan, *Human Dignity, Human Rights, and Responsibility: The New Language of Global Bioethics and Bio-Law*

Tom Koch, *Thieves of Virtue: When Bioethics Stole Medicine*

Timothy F. Murphy, *Ethics, Sexual Orientation, and Choices about Children*

Daniel Callahan, *In Search of the Good: A Life in Bioethics*

Robert Blank, *Intervention in the Brain: Politics, Policy, and Ethics*

Gregory E. Kaebnick and Thomas H. Murray, eds., *Synthetic Biology and Morality: Artificial Life and the Bounds of Nature*

Dominic A. Sisti, Arthur L. Caplan, and Hila Rimon-Greenspan, eds., *Applied Ethics in Mental Healthcare: An Interdisciplinary Reader*

Barbara K. Redman, *Research Misconduct Policy in Biomedicine: Beyond the Bad-Apple Approach*

Russell Blackford, *Humanity Enhanced: Genetic Choice and the Challenge for Liberal Democracies*

Nicholas Agar, *Truly Human Enhancement: A Philosophical Defense of Limits*

Bruno Perreau, *The Politics of Adoption: Gender and the Making of French Citizenship*

Carl Schneider, *The Censor's Hand: The Misregulation of Human-Subject Research*

Lydia S. Dugdale, ed., *Dying in the Twenty-First Century: Towards a New Ethical Framework for the Art of Dying Well*

John D. Lantos and Diane S. Lauderdale, *Preterm Babies, Fetal Patients, and Childbearing Choices*

Harris Wiseman, *The Myth of the Moral Brain*

Arthur L. Caplan and Jason Schwartz, eds., *Vaccine Ethics and Policy: An Introduction with Readings*

Tom Koch, *Ethics in Everyday Places: Mapping Moral Stress, Distress, and Injury*

Nicole Piemonte, *Afflicted: How Vulnerability Can Heal Medical Education and Practice*

Printed in the United States
by Baker & Taylor Publisher Services